# TRANSATLANTIC RAILWAYMAN

MITCHELL DEAVER

authorHOUSE®

*AuthorHouse™*
*1663 Liberty Drive*
*Bloomington, IN 47403*
*www.authorhouse.com*
*Phone: 1 (800) 839-8640*

*Published by AuthorHouse 07/21/2015*

*ISBN: 978-1-5049-2057-5 (sc)*
*ISBN: 978-1-5049-2056-8 (e)*

*Library of Congress Control Number: 2015910570*

*Print information available on the last page.*

TO THE RAILROADERS OF AMERICA

# PREFACE

*When on Conrail during the 1990s I worked with different personnel almost every day. A problem arises of identifying them in this book. Whether I gave their real identity, which I should not because they are entitled to privacy, or whether I invented names, the result would be the same: the reader would suffer a huge number of different names constantly peppering the narrative. To overcome the difficulty, I have avoided using names whenever possible, and where needed, I have called every engineer John, every conductor Steve, every brakeman Dave and every vehicle driver Ed. Some false names have been used elsewhere.*

*Any strong language used in original conversations has been replaced by milder vocabulary.*

*MD*
*June 2015*

# CHAPTER 1

# BLUE SKIES

"We're going to see the Statue of Liberty!" exclaimed my wife. Indeed we were. A five-day Atlantic crossing aboard the QE2 ocean liner had been delayed by heavy seas resulting in our arriving on the Hudson River in New York at dawn rather than a scheduled middle-of-the-night docking time, thus affording a clear view of the famous landmark. The transatlantic voyage conveyed a forty-three year old Englishman about to start a new life in America, that removal consequent upon his having met and married a United States citizen. Soon after meeting in 1985, an amicable agreement had been reached whereby my wife and I would remain in our London home for an unspecified period, then we would relocate. Now in December 1988 that relocation was taking place.

Choice of the QE2 as vehicle of emigration came about through an aversion to flying. Though expensive, the sea journey nevertheless allowed more time to adjust between old and new. An aeroplane flight would have allowed but half a day to mentally sever connections and to prepare for a new life, whereas the Atlantic crossing not only allowed more time for the same adjustment but provided diversions should the mind become overloaded with momentousness of the occasion.

One evening's entertainment at sea featured a hypnotist. I had seen the same act in the 1970s when visiting a Liverpool night spot that was part cabaret club and part discotheque. The act had not changed! The hypnotist used the same hands-clasped-on-the-head method of identifying audience members susceptible to hypnosis. A selected band of volunteers, if that is the correct term for individuals chosen by the procedure, were plunged into a deeper level of hypnosis to execute hilarious pranks. The hypnotist attempted to induce one subject to sing an advertising jingle from the 1950s: "The Esso sign means happy motoring/The Esso sign means happy motoring/The Esso..." but since the victim was too young to know the tune he just mouthed nothing, jiggled his feet and looked happy. Exactly the same thing happened with another youthful participant in the 1970s night club.

Another evening saw a female singer do her best to perform whilst the ship heaved and lurched in heavy seas. As the piano she held onto first tipped this way then that, the woman's high-heeled shoes provided no adhesion as she slid about the stage fighting to retain balance and decorum whilst singing. She recognized the humour in her predicament and grinned between lyrics.

The same tempest that rudely interfered with the above performance amused in other ways. View through the porthole next to our breakfast table alternated between a wall of green water and a sheet of blue sky as the vessel rolled incessantly in mountainous seas. As the Atlantic Ocean's mean disposition threw the liner about like a toy boat, any stroll round the vessel was akin to fairground entertainment. The fun lasted until repeated and violent movement confined me to the cabin where I lay on my back to suppress nausea. My wife fared a little better. Only once in the crossing were seas calm enough for passengers to go on deck. We grabbed the opportunity to take fresh air, to watch dolphins escort us through their domain, to look at the wintry North Atlantic Ocean which was the same bow, stern, port and starboard: cold, choppy, homogeneous, disturbingly endless.

Along with all other holidays at sea, Cunard's QE2 provided vast amounts of food more or less round the clock so that one could spend all conscious time at the table, like the Mad Hatter's Tea Party. Only through great restraint did I not change shape during the five-day crossing.

The Statue of Liberty, still draped in dawn's tulle, stood proudly, protectively, as one more immigrant passed beneath her benign gaze. Thousands had passed before, but less stylishly. I would be spared the indignity of parading in front of officials who would record my name inaccurately. Immigration documents that had been initiated at the

American Embassy in London were reshuffled and rubber stamped on board ship so that I was free to set foot on American soil.

At the breakfast table on this final morning my wife insisted we swop places so I could enjoy the approach to New York. Relaxing in a tailored dog's-tooth-check jacket, delight radiated from her pretty face surrounded by a mass of blonde curls as she relished being back in her native country, as she smiled at the poignancy of her husband's gazing at the Statue of Liberty. It was celebration for me too, the culmination of several month's preparation and fulfillment of our long term plan to settle in the United States. We disembarked into the cold New York air, my wife in a black overcoat that fitted her beautifully, I in signalman's great coat that fitted me tolerably. My wife's mother and father welcomed us at the quayside, where we loaded all seventeen items of baggage into their vehicle. We would reside in that part of Pennsylvania State in which my wife grew up, an area best known as home of the Amish people, Lancaster County.

\* \* \*

Such is the extent to which Hollywood and television have disseminated the essence of America around the world, almost any new arrival in the country should feel quite at home! Some of my earliest British television memories are of American shows "Amos and Andy" and "I Love Lucy". I recall seeing a dubbed version of "Kojak" in Spain. Further insights into the American way of life were gained in a brief 1985 visit to meet my wife's parents – the last time I flew incidentally – and of course my wife herself was a cornucopia of information. There was a further, surprising source available in Britain that described day-to-day aspects of American culture, that spoke of such things as newspaper delivery boys, the great heat of summer, back yard barbeques and knee-length shorts that would be laughing-stock in England but which were normal in the States. Despite the publishers of *MAD* magazine boasting it to be absolute rubbish, the periodical nevertheless provided great insight into the more mundane aspects of American life.

America's prosperity is impressive, examples being the dizzying variety of brands on supermarket shelves from toothbrushes to tinned soup and the number of rival car dealerships jostling for business in one street. New businesses are seen to spring up everywhere, even if not all survive. Width of streets, height of skyscrapers and vastness of car parks – parking lots in America - all reinforce America's reputation for bigness. Even in the relatively densely populated north-east, dwellings are more widely spaced than in Britain. To look further afield, huge tracts of the United States are still sparsely populated, even in the twenty-first century. Cultural wealth and collective self-confidence are further attributes one associates with America.

No matter how dazzling these preconceived ideas of America were, all were put to shade by a string of unexpected first impressions. Above all, literally and figuratively, were blue skies. In England more often than not the sun is absent. Most days of the week in America the sun shines. The first few weeks of 1989 saw invigorating clear blue skies almost every day, even if temperatures were below freezing. To look up and see nothing but blue void was a rarity in Britain: in America it was commonplace, even if in hot weather the colour became diffused. At the height of the 1989 summer I would be outdoors to enjoy the sun at every opportunity, even in ninety degree temperatures (thirty-three degrees Celsius). I could not understand why such days were referred to as the four Hs – hazy, hot, humid and horrible. As time passed however the mad dog syndrome faded and, like everybody else, I avoided intense heat. Blue skies no longer predominate as the climate has changed, but the memory remains.

The second most striking feature that sequestered the mind from popular images of America was the proliferation of wild life. When growing up in rural Yorkshire I saw very few wild animals, but in my new home they were everywhere. Most common were woodchucks (locally called ground hogs) that inhabited every grass verge, that burrowed deep holes in fields and railway embankments. Abundance of wild life was evidenced by large amounts of road kill, not only of woodchucks but nocturnal creatures such as racoons, possums and skunks. Forty-three years in Britain had flushed out one fox and no snakes; now I would see plenty of both. New species of birds filled the skies, the brilliant red cardinal, the raucous blue jay, soaring hawks and vultures and numerous species of sparrow with intricately-coloured plumage too delicate to appreciate at distance.

Concerning the people themselves, it was the American's devotion to work that impressed me most. The work ethic drilled into me in Yorkshire, though never lost, was bettered by the American who took work even more seriously. An Englishman would not question the need to work, but would complain, even jest about it: "I'd like to spend a few minutes with the bloke who invented work". American workers tirelessly pursued their employment without dissension and without questioning its need; they seemed under-represented in popular images of the country. Another misrepresentation was that all Americans were loud in speech. In reality many speak at a pitch no greater than the average Briton, a few speak softer. Only a tiny percentage matched a stereotype of filling a room with the equivalent of a brass band every time the mouth opened. Finally on the subject of surprising first impressions was discovery that religious belief was far more important to American people than British.

* * *

First of January 1989 triggered a search for work. My wife was immediately successful in obtaining temporary employment in word processing. Circumstances surrounding this lone Englishman's seeking employment amongst Americans were peculiar.

First, right from the outset I felt the need to be on best behaviour for fear Americans may judge the whole race by performance of one example now in their midst. By nature conservative, it was unlikely I would disgrace my home country, the only peccadillo being occasional outbursts of outlandish humour. I concluded that key to being a sound ambassador was to avoid polemics. Second, my employment history was unusual. From ages sixteen to thirty-five a string of white-collar jobs stretched from native North Yorkshire to Birmingham and then to Liverpool. In 1980 I realized a boyhood dream and became a signalman, moving to London to pursue that career. Cupid's intervention in 1985 resulted in a move to America. The position of British Railways signalman, though the best job I had had in my whole life, involved working rotating shifts of nights, afternoons and mornings. I vowed never again to inflict such awkward hours on my wife, so if railway opportunities did arise in my new home, which was the hope, being an American signalman was out of the question. (Time would reveal such work would have sentenced me to permanent night shift until seniority built up.)

Before looking for railway work, I felt a need to bed in in the new culture. I followed my wife's lead in enrolling with temporary employment agencies that put me to work in Lancaster County in positions that included bookkeeping, heaving about rolls of carpet and bagging pretzels. Skills in typing decanted the newcomer into an assignment preparing export documentation for agricultural equipment. The environment of low office partitions and the (then) mellow rings of American telephones felt like being on a television set of shows I used to watch in England. My supervisor was female; the role reversal would have been inconsequential were not Secretary's Day celebrated during the time I worked for her. On the red-letter day I was summoned to the entrance lobby where, much to my discomfort, I was presented with a box of chocolates by my employer, the temporary agency. I survived the ordeal; in any case in times of equal opportunity protest would have been futile. The most entertaining moment at the shipping office occurred an hour after we had begun work. A man in a nearby cubicle, clearly unhappy in his work, declared, "Gosh, it's nine o'clock already!"

By spring of 1989 sufficient exposure to a new way of life built confidence to apply for work in the railway industry, that I should now call the railroad industry. In eastern Pennsylvania dominant employers were Conrail for freight traffic and Amtrak for passenger traffic, but I was not drawn. I cannot now remember why I felt intimidated by them, maybe I thought they would laugh at the idea of a freshly arrived Englishman applying for a position in such august American entities. So I looked elsewhere. The *Handy Railroad Atlas of the United States* published by Rand McNally revealed a small railroad in adjacent York County called the Maryland & Pennsylvania. I telephoned to ask for a job and, after passing a medical examination (called a physical in America) was given one, as brakeman.

# CHAPTER 2

# MARYLAND & PENNSYLVANIA RAILROAD

"Climb on!" said the brakeman to his trainee. The clumsy Englishman gripped handrails on locomotive number 82 and clambered untidily, nervously up precipitous steps to a platform on the front of the engine. Progress was not helped by a pair of heavy work boots lined with steel toe inserts that had to be worn at all times when on or about railroad tracks. Such footwear, along with work gloves provided by the employer, encumbered a person unaccustomed to wearing them. My tutor the brakeman, a large man with bushy hair and beard to match, gently shoulder-charged me on the front of the engine forcing me to move a few feet sideways. (An indelible memory from earliest days on the Maryland and Pennsylvania Railroad was the number of burly, bearded, long-haired men who worked there. It seemed everywhere I looked large spherical hirsute men attended to their labours.) "Hold on now!" said the brakeman. I held on.

At the time a three-man traincrew was the norm: engineer, the American term for train driver; conductor, equivalent of guard; and brakeman, whose position approximated to a shunter. The American conductor enjoyed greater status than the British guard. The brakeman glanced over his shoulder to ensure both the engineer (one of the large men previously described) and conductor (a wiry man whose sharply chiselled features would not have been out of place on a billboard advertising cigarettes) were safely seated. The brakeman then gave a hand signal to move forward.

When a British guard or shunter wanted his train to move away from him, his hand signal was a forward-rolling motion of the forearm. When an American conductor or brakeman wanted his locomotive to move in a forward direction, he slowly waved the full length of his arm at the engineer. A British guard gave a sweeping, beckoning motion for his train to move towards him. An American conductor presented to the engineer circular motion of the arm for the locomotive to move backwards. Direction of movement in Britain was relative to the guard's position. Forwards or backwards in America depended which way the locomotive was facing. American engines had a cab only at one end. Most British locomotives had a cab at both ends. Be that as it may, the brakeman's hand signal was more a dabbing action of the wrist than a slow wave, but such is the predisposition to economy of people at work.

At a few minutes after 07:00 hours on Thursday 25th May 1989, engine 82, a Class SW9 1200 horsepower switcher built by Electro-Motive Diesels, rumbled westwards on the Maryland and Pennsylvania's single track East Branch, stopping at each level crossing – grade crossing – for the brakeman to alight, walk to the centre of the highway, hold an orange flag horizontally to halt vehicular traffic, and for the engine to restart. The brakeman hopped on the locomotive as it passed at slow speed. In 1989 it was permissible to get on and off moving vehicles. After a couple of crossings, the brakeman said, "Wanna do it?" I did it, without mishap. When we had finished flagging East Branch crossings, the brakeman said, "Now, roll that flag up neatly and wedge it in *there*!" He pointed to a crevice. He instructed with such vehemence I feared for my life. The brakeman studied me for a moment. "Why are you so nervous? You're doing all right."

"Well, I don't want to make a mistake. I'm just a nervous kind of person, you know," I said honestly.

The A1 crew, as they were officially known, proceeded to carry out work in Poorhouse Yard, a five-track layout in the eastern half of central York City. The British term shunting was translated to switching, or shifting, or sometimes drilling. Points were switches. When I was a youngster in Britain, freight vehicles were called trucks. By the 1970s the term was wagon. In America it was car. The British collective term for railway vehicles was rolling stock, the American rolling equipment, or simply equipment. To propel a train became to shove a train, even though we were taught at school that shove was poor English.

Latitudinal timbers to which rails are fastened were known as sleepers in Britain, as crossties in America, or simply ties. A two-axle wheel assembly underneath each end of long railway vehicles was described as a bogie in Britain. It was referred to as a truck in America – nothing to do with a highway vehicle of the same name. Many freight wagons in Britain did not have bogies, just two rigid axles. Two-axle cars were quite rare in America.

Mercifully, some transatlantic terms were unchanged. A light engine was still a locomotive without a train, and running round still the operation of transferring an engine from one end of a train to the other. As we shifted cars in Poorhouse Yard I stayed by the brakeman's side to learn.

To explain the term brakeman, my understanding is that in days before trains were air-braked throughout, brakemen used to walk along the tops of cars to apply hand brakes located on car ends. This precarious activity has often been mimicked on film with the hero fighting the villain. One Maryland and Pennsylvania man told me brakemen as recently as the 1970s used to ride the tops of cars – not to apply hand brakes, but to convey hand-signals prior to universal use of radios. In marshalling yards (classification yards in America) before power-operated retarders were installed, brakemen would ride a car over a hump and gradually apply the hand brake to bring the vehicle to a gentle stop. Platforms were fitted for employees to stand on in order to apply the circular hand brakes, ladders were fitted on car sides to reach the platforms. By the 1990s the brakeman's duties were mainly throwing switches, so he would be better described as conductor's assistant.

The layout of the twenty-five mile Maryland and Pennsylvania Railroad was, peculiarly, star-shaped. The East, West and Central Branches converged on and terminated at Poorhouse Yard. An undemanding first day visited each branch, served local industries, exchanged cars – interchanged cars in America - with another railroad called York Rail, received inbound cars from Conrail and gave them back outbound traffic. Conrail's tracks met the Maryland and Pennsylvania's at Poorhouse Yard.

Then suddenly at 11.00 hours the day was over. As men completed paperwork and prepared to leave for home, I stood around, unable to understand the early finish. Seeing my bewilderment, the conductor walked over, shook his head, grinned reassuringly and said, "It's not always such a short day. We don't usually get a quit. It's just that we didn't have a lot to do today. Most days we'll put in an eight-hour day, and maybe even get a spot of overtime." A quit is completing in less than eight hours all work that had to be done and going home early as consequence. In America eight hour's pay is guaranteed for each turn of railroad duty, almost without exception.

The illustration on the front cover of this book is of me striking up a typical conductor's pose. Although the photograph was staged, it accurately depicts a conductor in the process of riding the hind end of a shoving move, observing the railroad ahead, and telling the engineer over the radio the distance to be covered by giving him the number of car lengths he must travel.

\* \* \*

York, Pennsylvania, is about the same size as York, England, but apart from that they could not be more different. Whereas the English city, as one of only two archbishoprics in the whole country, was steeped in tradition, York, Pennsylvania was an industrial city famed for heavy engineering. Products familiar in Britain were made in factories in York: Allis Chalmers tractors, Caterpillar Tractors, Harley Davidson motorcycles. So vibrant had been the city's industrial past, it was still served by three separate railroads, Maryland & Pennsylvania, Conrail and York Rail. Successive economic recessions had decimated York's industry, but Harley Davidson and others survived into the new millennium. The Maryland and Pennsylvania served only one heavy industry, though the product was so massive and intensely engineered, movements were rare. Most of the railroad's traffic was inbound raw materials and consumer products, with a handful of outbound loads, mainly scrap metal.

Up till about 1980, the Maryland and Pennsylvania ran six crews regularly. Now, only the A1 crew worked Monday to Friday - or Monday through Friday, as is the better American way of expressing it. Thus only the three-man A1 crew regularly completed a five-day week. All other men on the roster - about ten, with me at the bottom – worked only when needed. Of those, the three most senior occupied a position analogous to relief signalmen in Britain, they were termed the Extra Board. The Extra Board was used to cover absences and, two or three times a week, to service customers between York and the town of Hanover at the end of the West Branch.

In early days of training, it struck me that American couplings which had been in use since the 1880s were superior to the hook and link system in Britain (and Europe). American automatic couplers comprised a pivoting knuckle at the end of a rigid shank. When two cars were brought together, two open knuckles met and closed upon one another like a handshake. In the process, a component within the coupler dropped behind the knuckle to lock it in the closed position, which was confirmed by appearance of a metal link about three inches long dangling beneath the coupler. To uncouple, a cut lever located on the corner of cars had to be lifted to disengage the locking mechanism.

As part of my five day's training I joined the Extra Board crew on a run to Hanover and had my first try at uncoupling. I turned a valve – the angle cock - to shut off supply of air to the braking system of the car to be left behind, then attempted to lift the cut lever, but it would not move. In those circumstances, I had observed that cars had to be bunched. "Er... you need to bring the cars together a bit," I said to the engineer over the hand-held radio. Nothing happened.

The Hanover brakeman, another of the large and furry kind, smiled to himself, and said over the radio, "I think he means 'a bit of slack'."

Thanks to the brakeman's clarification, cars moved together slightly, the cut lever lifted, and I could complete the uncoupling. "Okay ahead," I said. The train moved away. Two air hoses first stretched, then split apart explosively: ninety pounds of air pressure exhausted into the atmosphere from the car left standing, which action automatically applied brakes. Staff had to turn the head away when uncoupling, to avoid being splattered with flying dust.

I also learnt how to couple cars by giving the engineer signals to bring cars together slowly, and by halting the movement when the coupling made. The British hand signal to stop was two raised arms. In America the hand signal for stop was a side to side movement; by radio the words "far enough" or "that's good" were used. It was then necessary to ensure that the hanging metal link – the "pin" - was visible, because that meant the coupling had been successful. Two air hoses were cupped together and the angle cock slowly opened to feed air. The importance of proper handling of the air brake system for safe operation of trains cannot be over-emphasized. However, at this early stage in a career, appreciation of the ingenuity and sophistication of the air brake had to be left till a later time.

Two more days were spent training with the A1 crew, and one day on a coal train. About two Sundays out of three, the railroad received from Conrail a hundred-car coal train destined for a paper mill in Spring Grove, about ten miles outside York on the West Branch. I was seconded to the first of three crews that handled the train. At 03:30 prompt I joined the same men who had comprised the A1 crew. In the company's Princess Street Yard six locomotives coupled together throbbed noisily in blatant disregard of the day of the week and of the time of day. The bulky brakeman ordered me to sit with him on the rearmost of the six engines: "And don't touch anything!" Seated in the engineer's position, I looked at the bewildering array of controls, and nodded that I understood his directive. I sat tight as the six-locomotive consist made its way down the East Branch, through Poorhouse Yard, and onto Conrail trackage to couple to the waiting train. I could tell from radio conversations that several procedures were implemented before we set off.

As we threaded our way over grade crossings in the centre of York during the small hours, increased engine roar signified we were climbing. The track was straight, so I leant out of the window to watch. Ahead, six locomotives shot sparks into the darkened sky as they laboured to lift twelve thousand tons of coal train out of York. Six yellow-painted locomotives fighting for adhesion dug into rails. I was spellbound by the raw power, the noise, the colossal effort needed to move uphill such unimaginable weight. I looked back to see murky but uniform shapes of loaded coal hoppers reluctantly being lugged through the sleeping city. As dawn broke over York County we encountered another stiff gradient beyond the city purlieus. Again I poked my head out of the window to watch and listen in awe as a total of ten thousand horsepower of diesel electric traction proclaimed their authority over protesting freight cars being dragged behind them.

Once at the paper mill, the train was split into twelve or fifteen-car strings to be emptied by moving the cars one by one over a pit. A vibrator framework lowered onto the tops of cars hastened evacuation. The vibration was so violent I could never understand how the device's electric motor did not shake itself to bits. Conductor and brakeman took turns directing operations at the pit.

It took three crews twenty-four hours to empty the train and hand it back to Conrail. The legal limit for traincrews was a twelve-hour day, but in exceptional operating circumstances small companies such as the Maryland and Pennsylvania were given a dispensation to work sixteen hours, which we did sometimes. The first occasion I worked such a long day my wife thought I had got lost! In winter extreme cold froze the coal slowing down the emptying process. On many occasions an Extra Board crew had to return to the paper mill during the week to finish the train. In years to come, I would spend many hours watching dusty, crumbly, uniformly-black coal tumble into a waiting pit, many hours watching paper mill employees opening and closing pockets at the bottom of the cars, and many hours gazing at the never-ending succession of coal hoppers waiting to be unloaded. The majority of cars were coloured brown and marked Conrail, with a small number of Reading Railroad and others mixed in. They brought to mind lines from the signature tune of television's "Rawhide": "Don't try to understand them/Just rope, throw and brand them". The coal hoppers were like a herd of cattle, mostly the same with a few odd ones, but each an individual if closely inspected. Very occasionally a maverick would break loose, and you had a derailment. Throughout an American railroading career the Maryland and Pennsylvania coal trains would provide a significant part of my income.

To return to the first trip on the coal train, I arrived home about mid-afternoon. As I walked through the door my wife stood rigid with shock at the sight before her. "Have you seen your face!" she said.

"What's a matter with it?" I asked, perplexed.

"Go and look in the mirror!"

My face was covered with small round black spots, like a frightening case of measles. When I had leant out of the window to watch locomotives storming the grade, they had responded by pelting me with minute discharges of oil. I had spent the whole day looking like a painted clown, but nobody told me!

\* \* \*

On completion of five day's training on the Maryland & Pennsylvania I was furloughed. In Britain use of the word appears limited to military leave. In American railroading (and other employment) the word is dreaded: it means laid off. In England if a worker is made redundant it usually means the end of a career. To be furloughed in the States is not quite so final, a person could be called back in a week's time, or a month, a year, ten years or never. I was called back on average twice a week, only to be furloughed again immediately at the end of the working day, till the next time. Of course, they did not issue me a furlough notice on every occasion. The arrangement may better be described as being on call for part-time work. Compare being hired by the Maryland & Pennsylvania to work only odd days when it suited them with being hired on British Railways where for all intents and purposes I had a guaranteed job for life with at least a five-day week.

The disadvantage of working in furloughed status was that it lacked what the American labour market termed benefits. Many months would pass before I grasped what "benefits" meant. If the term were used in Britain it would mean holiday pay and payment for bank holidays – public holidays in America. In the States benefits meant the same, *plus* health care, because there is no National Health Service. So I had to purchase health insurance in the same manner as purchasing automobile insurance. Probably the only advantage of being furloughed was that I was under no obligation to accept a call to work.

With training behind me, a routine settled in of one or two day's work during the week and most, but not all, coal trains. On weekdays I usually worked as brakeman on the Hanover run but occasionally on the A1 crew. On the latter a good portion of the day was spent standing at number 1 switch in Poorhouse Yard whilst the conductor radioed directions for the train to go in and out of that track. The train rumbled by at slow speed imposed on it by waiting for Queen Street grade crossing barriers (gates) to lower at the western extremity of the yard and by the operating necessity of having to reduce speed to a crawl when making a coupling. Thus I had plenty of time to watch the parade of huge box cars go by. Some cars, such as those owned by Union Pacific Railroad, were emblazoned with lettering about two feet tall trumpeting the company's unmistakeable self-confidence.

Each railroad car was marked with the owner's initials, or reporting marks, and a serial number. Only by knowing what those initials meant could the splendour of American railroad names be enjoyed. Here is a selection of railroads whose cars were seen on the Maryland & Pennsylvania (whose initials were MPA) together with reporting marks: Ashley, Drew & Northern – ADN; Atchison, Topeka and Santa Fe - ATSF; Burlington Northern - BN; Chattahoochee Industrial – CIRR; Chicago and North Western – CNW; Corinth and Counce - CC; Dakota, Minnesota & Eastern - DME; Denver and Rio Grande Western – D&RGW; Elgin, Joliet and Eastern - EJE; Florida Central – FCEN; Kansas City Southern - KCS; Louisville, New Albany & Corydon - LNAC; Northwestern Oklahoma - NOKL. Similarly exotic names could be found in Britain prior to the 1923 grouping of railways into four big operators, but they fell short of the scintillating uniqueness, the tantalizing remoteness of American counterparts.

But many railroad cars, particularly box cars, were marked in a different, unofficial way: they were tagged. A tag was typically a small illustration, about eighteen inches tall, with a name, often dated with month and year, all placed near the corner of the car. Identity of those making the tags, be they trespassers, customer employees or railroad employees, was not known. Several tags appeared regularly on Maryland & Pennsylvania traffic. The Artful Dodger drew himself laughing and wearing a cloak and large hat. Bozo wore a ten-gallon hat. Proviso was modestly represented by a hanging medallion or something of that sort. Trademark of The Rambler Port of Beaumont Texas was a glass of champagne. Smokin' Joe's name was enveloped in exhaust from a simply-drawn locomotive. The Solo Artist drew himself against an elaborate setting-sun landscape. Sudz sketched a frothy tankard of beer. Water Bed Lou merely wrote his name. Unauthorized as they were, the arabesques were pleasing embellishments, unlike artwork of later years where trespassers daubed car sides with vast, garish, sometimes hideous but occasionally skilful paintwork disfiguring the equipment rather than adorning it. In cases where whole box car sides were coloured, a ladder must have been used and huge amounts of spray paint – and huge amounts of time. It is difficult to grasp how such blatant vandalism could become so acceptable that classes on how to execute it would be advertized, but I saw such an advertisement.

The Maryland & Pennsylvania brakeman position became the first permanent job I had ever had outdoors. Pennsylvania's continental climate drove temperatures up to the high nineties (thirty-eight degrees Celsius) in summer. Advice often repeated is drink plenty of liquids. I would amend that to say the only way a cooling effect can be felt is to drink as much water as you possibly can. Winter can see temperatures plunge down to single digits, which is thirty degrees of frost (minus sixteen degrees Celsius). How can cold get any colder than freezing? The answer is that in those regions the face tingles and the bitter cold passes through all clothing that can be worn - no matter how much – through skin to reach the bones. Lined coveralls (in Britain referred to as a boiler suit) known by the brand name of Carhartt were essential. A man kept physically busy however would normally generate enough heat, in fact working in those temperatures could be quite invigorating. A person such as I used to wearing collar and tie in previous occupations might have been expected to suffer in such extremes, especially if pitched into them in middle age, but in high school years I spent time on a farm handling sheaves of corn with much protective clothing in a sweltering summer and on frosty days harvesting turnips with bare hands. Those British schoolboy weather experiences were much less harsh but nevertheless gave a taste of exposure to the elements. Pennsylvania's ninety degree weather was more taxing than Yorkshire's seventy degrees, but the increased discomfort was not as great as might be expected, similarly with the cold.

By October 1989 I had been promoted conductor, initially to work coal trains, but in due course to conduct jobs during the week. I found the most enjoyable part of conducting to be breaking down a train – or busting up a train as the slang used to go – which meant sorting it into different categories. A railroad conductor acquires skill in making the most economical moves. In a simple example, consider a yard with three tracks, one of those tracks containing two types of cars, Y and Z, mixed up as follows: YZZYYZYZY. To sort them into their two categories, a novice would pick up all nine cars and proceed to sort them on the two remaining tracks. An experienced conductor would not move the hind Y car and would put all other Y cars with it, placing Z cars on an adjacent track, which would save one out and back move.

However I must confess to sometimes not seeing the easiest way of doing things. In this true example, cars arranged in this order ABCAB needed to be resorted thus: AABBC. With the engine at the right hand end, I set the head B car over to another track first, then BC on top of it, put back A, then picked up BBC and went back on top of AA. The quickest way would have been to set BC over first, set AB back, then pick up BC and back onto the top of AAB. The engineer let me know what he thought of my making six moves when four would have achieved the same!

From 1989 onwards, though happy working for the Maryland & Pennsylvania, I had to supplement modest income with other part-time work, notably in a warehouse distributing computer software. Domestic finances improved when my wife obtained a permanent word-processing position with a firm of solicitors – attorneys – which initially gave her health cover, at a later date extended to cover me. Fortunately, when income from all sources fell below a certain level, a safety net kicked in in the form of the American Railroad Retirement Board which, financed by railroad companies, bolstered earnings of low-paid railroad employees. Demand for railroaders fluctuated erratically, and the Railroad Retirement Board supplements existed to prevent trained workers drifting away.

By late 1990 our finances had stabilized sufficiently to purchase a house. We decided to set up home in York County reasonably close to the Maryland & Pennsylvania Railroad in the hope that a future with them would be bright enough to justify the move. Whilst house-hunting, a delightful stone-built cottage in a rural setting came on the market. "I want this house!" exclaimed my wife ecstatically, unhesitatingly. We bought it. Pleased with our purchase, life proceeded in a highly satisfactory manner for a few years, even if income fell short of the elevated level expected, strove for, dreamt of in America. It would change, and the Railroad Retirement Board would instigate that change.

# CHAPTER 3

# CONRAIL

"Telephone call for Mitchell Deaver," bellowed the public address system. Conveyor belts and conveyor rollers rumbled, rattled and roared transporting in apparent chaos computer software boxes and packages around a cavernous warehouse. Intended recipient of the call missed the summons owing to the din. "Telephone call for Mitchell Deaver!" yelled the loud-speakers once again.

I heard the second time and dashed to the nearest telephone to pick up the handset. "Who?" I asked after listening to words unintelligible. I pressed the handset against one ear and a hand against the other to shut out the warehouse cacophony.

"This is the Railroad Retirement Board," the voice repeated. "Conrail are hiring. I've got a number you need to call for an interview." For the first time in twenty years Conrail were taking on new traincrew staff. News had reached the Railroad Retirement Board, who were under an obligation to notify any railroader claiming assistance. It did not matter that a man was already employed by another railroad, the aim of diverting him to Conrail was to eliminate completely his reliance on Railroad Retirement Board financial help. I took down the number.

A week or two later about one hundred men and a few women gathered in a Harrisburg hotel conference room. The modest-sized town of Harrisburg is capital of Pennsylvania, little known outside the state and completely unknown to most of the rest of the world. An elegantly-dressed statuesque woman strode confidently into the centre of the conference room, a woman with such presence, if she were met in a corridor all would step aside. She fearlessly addressed a sea of faces. After briefly describing the job she said, "You will work holidays and weekends, on call any hour seven days a week, fifty-two weeks a year." She then paused before adding an aside, "Mm, at that point we usually lose a few!" Evidently no one had left. The woman proclaimed, "You will be engineers." To explain the significance of this statement, much like British Railways, American engineers and trainmen had traditionally followed separate lines of promotion. However, a 1985 union agreement stipulated that newly-hired trainmen would progress to the rank of engineer. The declaration to a room full of new entrants made it clear that advancement to engineer was not discretionary but a condition of employment.

All applicants were briefly interviewed and sat a comprehension test, then put through a short physical examination. Timing of the medical examination was crucial, for it would determine position on a seniority roster if the applicant were hired. Before long, I learnt my application had been successful. On Monday 22nd August 1994 I began a career on Conrail by attending classroom training.

* * *

The class instructor, a man built like an American football player and who might well have played the sport when a younger man, addressed sixteen people beginning their first day on Conrail. He said that twelve of us, including me, had been allocated to work in territory east of Harrisburg, four to work west. Aware that we had already been warned of unsociable hours, he said, "We don't ask you to work very hard, we just ask you to be here." What he did not say was that there was no differential in pay between working sociable hours and unsociable hours. British Railways had a different approach, the basic hourly rate applied only to duty from 06:00 to 18:00 Monday through Friday, all other work was at an increased rate. The Maryland & Pennsylvania contract struck a middle course in that rates of pay were enhanced for hours outside a five-day week and for working a public holiday. On Conrail there were no such enhancements, but the hourly rate was higher than both the short line and British Railways.

Once under way, classroom tuition repeated much of what I had been taught on the Maryland & Pennsylvania, including identical hand signals. From his front desk the instructor gave standard hand signals and asked the class to call out their meaning, which we did successfully until at one point he held his arm straight out but slightly angled upwards. "What's this mean?" he asked. Nobody knew. "Howdy!" he explained with a grin.

It was explained that operating rules in effect were those of the North-east Operating Rules Advisory Committee, Norac for short. Conrail, whose official name was Consolidated Rail Corporation, were members of Norac, as were Amtrak, officially the National Railroad Passenger Corporation. About thirty other railroads shared the Norac Rule Book.

A ring binder handed out to each of us contained separate segments on operating rules, the air brake, hazardous materials, safety rules and one called timetable. The timetable included information on stations, speeds and special instructions, and in that respect corresponded to the British Railways Sectional Appendix. I was puzzled by one aspect, and pursued it with the instructor. "Can I just ask you something?"

"Yes," replied the instructor.

"This whole book," I said, holding up the complete binder with one hand, "what's it called?"

"It's called the Operating Manuals."

"Okay. And this part here is called the Timetable?" I asked holding between fingers of the other hand a segment of the book.

"Yes, that is the Timetable," said the instructor patiently.

"But there's no train times in it," I said in pained expression.

Howls of laughter rolled round the class. The instructor did not laugh, but growled to one of the class close by, "I dunno, these Englishmen, you could just smack 'em couldn't you!" Raising his voice back to a normal oratorical level, the man in charge addressed the concern just expressed. "You see, Mr. Deaver, all freight trains are run as Extra. There is no timetable. At least not one that you will see. We try to run certain trains within a specified window, but we don't tell you about that. There is no timetable as such, Mr. Deaver." I thought I had raised a legitimate point and intended no humour, but the class saw otherwise and had fallen about in merriment. What classmates did not know - because I never revealed it to them - was that there was a far greater joke, one that has remained untold until publication of this book.

When aged about eight or nine years, whilst living in a North Yorkshire village, along with other boys I used to play trains. When looking for ways to metaphysically expand the game I first drew a map, a terribly-drawn map, of the supposed network of tracks and stations. A natural progression from the map would have been a railway timetable, were it not for the fact that actual train times proved hugely problematical. Writing down the number of minutes it took to trot from make-believe London Kings Cross station to make-believe York station produced a preposterously fast time of a quarter-hour for the supposed 200-mile journey. If real timetable times from Kings Cross to York were used I would have had to drag out a half-mile journey to about three hours, equally unacceptable. Another point was that in a real timetable train times seemed to be scattered thinly and randomly about a page, as if they were less significant than the page heading and station names. In a piece of original thinking unsurpassed in the annals of original thinking, a notion sprouted from the conscious like a toadstool from a midden that if train times were so apparently unimportant, why not in boy Deaver's timetable omit them altogether? So I produced, with all seriousness, a hand-written timetable in pencil giving not one single train time, the columns which should have contained them instead containing row after row of leader dots, interrupted only by occasional notations about shunting requirements and so on. The idea was that each barren column represented a train, the reader having to guess at which point in the day it would appear. Nothing could have been more useless, but it was just a young boy's play thing.

Forty years later and at 3000 miles' distance the author found himself face-to-face with an uncanny reincarnation of his schoolboy folly in the form of a Conrail official publication. The childhood foray into the impossible had been vindicated, there really was such a thing as a timetable without any train times.

Classroom tuition lasted six days, after which we were dispersed to a location of our choice for practical training. I elected Dillerville Yard, Lancaster, as it was closest to our York County home. At 09:30 hours on Tuesday 30th August 1994 I reported for duty.

# CHAPTER 4

# LANCASTER

On the Maryland & Pennsylvania the working day began with the locomotive moving off promptly in the shift's first couple of minutes. A start to the working day on Conrail was less decisive, to say the least. After reporting to the yardmaster I was told to take a seat and wait.

Bulky men strode deliberately and purposefully about Lancaster Dillerville Yard office. As on the short line, they were five or ten per cent larger than their British counterparts, as if to match larger dimensions of railroad vehicles they handled. Shoulders were broader, jaws heavier, paunches more expansive. If an American man was overweight, he heaved his way around like a giant cannonball. The British overweight man was, I am afraid, inclined to be flabbier. But it was the blistering self-confidence Lancaster men exuded that just about scorched me out of my seat. It was a self-confidence borne out of years handling huge tonnages of freight cars as if they were nothing more than match boxes, a self-confidence of knowing how to deliver the right cars to the right customer, of being in complete control of long and heavy trains. Men milled around exchanging platitudes as they arrived for duty or left for home. Conductors studied paperwork or awaited their turn to see the yardmaster. Over there a heated discussion took place with one man spearing the air with his forefinger to make a point. Collectively they had little time for new employees who possibly could not tell the difference between an Electro-Motive Diesel GP15 locomotive and an ex-Pennsylvania Railroad thirty-foot covered hopper car. In the midst of the hustle and bustle sat an Englishman nervously awaiting instructions.

At last a conductor approached: "Mr. Deaver?"

"Yes," I replied militarily.

"All right, we're ready to go," he said. "Grab your stuff and we'll get on the engine."

For the first week I would be training on what apparently was the best job in Lancaster, the WHLA80 which began its journey at Dillerville Yard, ultimately travelled to the town of New Holland thirteen miles away, and returned. Along the way it would serve a multitude of customers. It was the American version of the British pick-up train (or freight train stopping at intermediate stations) but was known on Conrail as a travelling shifter. But instead of the pick-up's handful of wagons seen in my Yorkshire home, our "pick-up" typically departed with forty cars and would take close to twenty-four hours to complete its work. Our crew would work for approximately twelve hours, after which another crew, the WHLA81, would take over.

The conductor, a slight man by American standards who sported a carefully trimmed moustache, directed me onto a nearby locomotive. It was one of two Electro-Motive Diesel Class GP38 engines coupled back-to-back. (By the way, the manufacturer Electro-Motive had, for part of its history, been a division of General Motors.) Two flights of steps leading to the cab were steeper than those met on the short line. The brakeman, a stocky man with a similarly trimmed neat moustache, told me to place my bag (containing manuals, wet-weather clothing and lunch box) in a corner. He was close to retirement and had chosen to work brakeman on the three-man crew rather than exercise seniority and take the conductor position. The engineer was a silver-haired man of astoundingly even temper, a quality admirably suited to the position.

Train WHLA80 had already been prepared prior to our coming on duty, so one would have thought the only thing to do was go. But railroading on Conrail was seldom so swift, in fact progress in Dillerville Yard was downright laborious. To begin, Lancaster yard was a dead-end configuration built on an old alignment that used to carry the main line through the city centre. Departures such as ours had to reverse out of the yard onto what was called the Number 1 Industrial Track. With the conductor hanging on the rear car giving radio instructions to the engineer, at about 10:00 the train shoved backwards. Pushing forty cars was not an exercise to be rushed. We eventually came to a stand clear of a facing switch – a switch that presented a choice of routes as opposed to one the other way round that merged two routes - which the brakeman re-aligned.

The conductor had to walk from the hind end of the train, but a ballast trackbed composed of coarse, fist-sized rocks made for poor walking. It was impossible to make rapid progress. Furthermore, the employer insisted we never rush. Conrail produced a training video instructing men on the ground how to walk. Movement always had to be at a slow pace, with feet slightly splayed outwards, and with constant vigilance for tripping hazards, projecting objects and the possibility any rail vehicle may move any time. I was used to working at a faster pace on the short line, thus more than once Conrail men had to correct me and insist I slow down. The simple task of walking was therefore not so simple, it took the conductor about twenty minutes to reach the head end of the train.

With the conductor on board, the engineer radioed the Dillerville Yardmaster for permission to leave. The engineer then switched channels to radio the block operator at Cork tower, about a mile away. To translate, a block operator is equivalent to a signalman, a tower to a signal box. The proper name for a tower is an interlocking station, but the technical term is seldom used. By the time Cork tower gave permission for the train to enter his territory, about one hour and twenty minutes had elapsed since going on duty. At least another thirty minutes passed as the train gingerly moved about minor tracks in the vicinity of Lancaster passenger station to come to a stand at a stop signal. Cork tower was (and still is) on Amtrak's Railroad. Amtrak was set up in 1971 to take over passenger train services from Penn Central and other railroads. The block operator at Cork quite properly held us whilst a passenger train went by on the main line, so that we were already two hours into our working day by the time we gained the main line which would take us to the New Holland Secondary Track.

In America a railroad junction or other place where it is necessary to switch trains from one track to another under control of signals has always been called an interlocking. The term is now used in Britain to refer to such an arrangement that is remotely controlled. Cork interlocking was exceptionally long, about four miles, being made up of three or four previously separate interlockings. We slowly traversed this string of connections to arrive at Cork's eastern extremity where we left Amtrak's property to re-enter Conrail's. The engineer obtained by radio permission from Cork block operator to use hand-operated switches to leave the main line. Oddly, the switches were within Cork interlocking and protected by Cork's controlled signals yet had to be swung by hand. I do not know why, probably to save costs.

About a mile later we made our first stop on the single track New Holland Secondary to shift a printing company which needed about ten cars in and out each day. Ample headroom without occupying grade crossings also made this location ideal for re-arranging the train. It would ultimately be blocked (grouped) into empty cars on the hind end, loaded cars for a food processing company on the head end, and all others between.

A trainee would normally cling to the side of the brakeman for guidance, but thanks to previous experience I was able to work as second brakeman, much to the delight of the entire crew. Though the brakeman's duties mainly comprised the undemanding task of throwing switches, a knowledgeable man could expedite work by always ensuring he was at the correct switch for the next move. The conductor's and brakeman's voices crackled over air waves constantly giving instructions to the engineer. "Ahead, over to the Main." "Okay back, ten cars to couple." Rules stated that the locomotive number should be used to identify a train by radio. After an hour or two, work at the printers was complete.

The matter of brake tests needs to be covered. Before trains left their initial terminal, all freight cars had to be inspected for defects and brakes tested by first applying then releasing them. On large railroads this was usually undertaken by employees called car inspectors prior to the crew coming on duty, which was the case with WHLA80. Cars picked up *en route* however had to be subjected to the same scrutiny, and were therefore responsibility of the crew, which added time to each shifting operation.

Train WHLA80 continued its day by servicing a couple more customers before arriving at a row of covered hopper cars on a sloping siding that curved away through ninety degrees. Under instructions from the conductor, empty cars were first pulled from the plant and coupled to the train left standing on the main line. The engines now had replacement cars of plastic granules in tow, and the brakeman radioed, "Okay back ten cars to couple." The engineer then commenced the operation of pushing six loaded covered hoppers, the most difficult cars to stop owing to their mass, into the customer's downhill siding. I watched anxiously as cars passed at a steady four miles per hour.

"Five cars to go," radioed the conductor. "Three. Two..." Two GP38 locomotives roared by as they shoved the heavy loads with air brakes fully applied. "One. Half..." The train slowed to a crawl as the engineer eased off the throttle. "Ten feet. Five. That's good!" The train halted with a perfect coupling thanks to the engineer's superb train-handling techniques.

Once the train was back together we moved further along the line to another customer needing supplies of plastic granules. So great was demand three separate buildings existed, each with sidings. Not all switches faced the same way, so a nearby run-around loop had to be employed to get round cars. Lengthy moves were of such complexity I could not follow what was happening. It had been a wearying day, so I was pleased to hear at about 20:00 hours that our work was almost done. A taxi arrived with the WHLA81 crew to relieve us, and to take us back to Dillerville Yard.

A further six travelling shifters worked out of Dillerville Yard, three of them venturing onto Amtrak territory as had the WHLA80. Five additional assignments that merely shifted the yard had to pick their way amongst arriving and departing travelling shifters.

From 30th August till 14th October 1994 I trained on most of the above-described assignments. During that time I noticed a couple of new hand signals. One brakeman conveying a message to his conductor raised his arms and clasped his hands above his head. Another brakeman moved his hands in small arcs at chest height as if stroking two ten-pin bowling balls, or something similar. When I asked the latter what it meant, he was dumbstruck at having to explain something so obvious as a hand signal that had been in use for decades. Eventually I coaxed out of him that the signal meant a blend of "everything in order" and "I've completed the task" and "all set". Clasped hands above the head was the original form of this unofficial but useful hand signal as practiced on the former Reading

Railroad, the lesser, caressing version was an adaptation by former Pennsylvania Railroad men. Dillerville Yard was located where the Pennsylvania and Reading Railroads used to cross one another.

\* \* \*

On Conrail and throughout working life in America the prime concern was to learn and execute the job to the best of my ability. Concentrating on the task in hand generally shut out extraneous thoughts, including self-consciousness about the unusual placement of an Englishman – a very English Englishman at that – in the middle of the quintessential American institution of railroading. The commission of mastering railroad operating practices, terminology and place-names and the minutia of which track led to where and whose permission was needed to use it and of where the key was located to open a rail loading dock in the middle of the night – consumed all mental capacity and left no room to muse over the oddity of a former British Railways employee deposited in the middle of Conrail. Inevitably the subject of that transplantation came up from time to time.

"What are you doing over here?"

"I married a girl from Lancaster."

"How did you meet her?"

"She was studying *cordon-bleu* cooking in England."

"Where did you meet her?"

"I chatted her up in a disco."

Eventually I deemed the last reply unworthy of the occasion and changed it to "We met in a London night club."

Similarly, as I concentrated on work I gave little thought to the difference in dialects. Grammar is identical, so mechanics of the language are the same, with consequent minimal risk of misunderstanding. However, interposition of a foreign dialect did not pass without comment. Most American women warmed to the British version of spoken English, but reception amongst males was mixed. Some men had no opinion on the matter, others were mildly interested in a different culture, a minority were irritated. Twice Conrail men were sufficiently incensed by the absence of rhotacism to snarl at me, "Cah? What's a cah?" There is marked contrast between the even metre of American spoken English and

27

the spluttering out of phrases found amongst British speakers such as myself. Concerning the calibre of English, in public speaking the British politician generally has the edge, but when comparing the population at large from both countries, a higher standard is found in America owing to a more forthright way of communicating. As critic Clive James wrote in *The New York Times* when discussing the literary world, Americans "expect honesty" in language. I recall asking someone from the States who he thought would win the next election. He replied, "I don't know." A British response would have been to extol the virtues of one or other political party, but that was not the question asked, the American answer was the correct one. (I recall an exception to the British proclivity not to answer the question: in an attempt to extract an opinion from him, former Prime Minister Edward Heath was asked on television what he thought the current Prime Minister would be considering. He replied, "Oh *I* don't know what Mrs. Thatcher will be thinking!")

The biggest dialectal differences reside in words. The improbable statement, "I'm going to queue up for a cheeky fortnight," would have to be translated as: "I'm going to stand in line for two week's naughtiness." It took a long time for my wife and I to conclude that the dessert known in Britain as jelly could only be translated into American by using its brand name, Jello. Pudding is used in Britain to refer to any dessert: in America its use is limited to describing a range of flavoured creamy confectionary. Though the word sidewalk is widely known, not many realize that pavement in America refers to the highway! A motor car bonnet is a hood, the trunk a boot. Soil is often called dirt. In America one would never run out of insults to hurl at one's enemies. Many such words have found their way into British vocabulary; they mean what they sound like: dirtball, dork, geek, klutz, nerd, scuzball, shmuck and wuss.

Regarding pronunciation, in America the aspirate in herb is silent but voiced in vehicle, the opposite to Britain. The American dictionary states gondola may be stressed either on the first or second syllable. In order to be understood in railroading I had to forsake the British version and always stress the second syllable because that pronunciation was universal. A gondola is an open car, like brick wagons that used to be seen in Britain. The usage has now crossed the Atlantic, but I do not know if the railroad pronunciation has. I *refuse* to change pronunciation of tomato! To stick with the British version requires effort, determination, stubbornness and callous insensitivity to bewilderment it causes in greengrocers.

In early days on the Maryland & Pennsylvania I said to men I could not understand their accent, to which they retorted, *"You've got the accent!"*

\* \* \*

Conrail's Lancaster Dillerville Yard was showcase for that indispensable ingredient in all vernaculars, humour. With the addition of trainees such as myself, in 1994 the crowded yard office was often bursting with discourse, much of it light-hearted.

Most Lancaster assignments did not complete their work within an eight-hour day. When the workload was so heavy that even the legal maximum of twelve hour's work would not see it off, conductors would say, "It don't look good," which, despite lack of grammatical pulchritude, conveyed to all who heard enormity of the task ahead. Some travelling shifters, such as those to New Holland, regularly worked twelve hours. On rare occasions when the workload was light and could be completed in less than twelve hours, a conductor fond of overtime might also say, "It don't look good," but did so ironically.

As I walked into the yard office one day the yardmaster asked me, "What job are you on?"

"WHLA75," I replied.

"You'll be in good company, that crew's not very good either!" quipped the yardmaster.

"Ran over a couple of squirrels on the way to work," said a brakeman. "It was just like running over a couple of hogheads!" Hoghead was slang for engineer, having its roots in locomotives at one time being called pigs; squirrel was a derisory term in general use. Using both pejoratives in one statement gave a clue to the brakeman's opinion of engineers. He continued the piercing but witty onslaught on fellow workers by slighting the character of one of them: "If [so-and-so] had run 'em over, he would've stopped to see what sex they were!"

An engineer chimed in, "And I'd have stopped to see if they had any money in their wallets!"

Conrail men were not shy about insulting one another. One addressed a colleague wearing a shapeless felt hat saying, "Did you find that hat?"

Though many Americans are given to such dry humour, they are not silly. The Scots, Welsh and Irish are fiercely nationalistic, and would not countenance ridiculing their homeland. But we English are so conceited about the supposed stature of our country we think the most ridiculous lampoons of ourselves run not the slightest risk of tarnishing a perceived spotless international image. People like me readily launch into episodes of arrant tomfoolery with not a care what others think. However, only a minority of Americans are prepared to sacrifice their and their country's dignity by descending into the absurd. For example, in a discussion about a long-abandoned route, one man argued a train could still go in that direction but would only be able to cover a short distance – meaning that if the track were cut and slewed the locomotive's running off the rails and sinking into soil would quickly halt the excursion.

There was a time when the Lancaster trainmaster needed to find out which lockers belonged to whom, so he put a note on each reading, "Give your name to the trainmaster." One by one men went to his office, announced who they were, and promptly walked out again!

Sensing in me an appreciation of quirky humour, an engineer in a quiet moment between moves told me of a list compiled in high school days of silly names, the type used in fictitious books such as *Simple Exercises* by Stan Dupp and Sid Downe. The list included the following that were new to me: I. Will Beebac, Wendy Boyce-Cumhome, Rhoda Bustatown, Amos B. Goinow, Norman D. Invasion, Shirley U. Jeste, Maxie Mumspeed, Frances Nextaspane, Amanda B. Recondwith, Yul B. Sorrie, P. Anna Stoole, N.E. Timeatall, Carrie D. Way and Tamara Zabetterday.

A small number of men were prepared to bend their innate sense of humour in the direction of the odd British version now surfacing sporadically on the Conrail system. "I can't remember people's names sometimes," said an engineer.

"I can't remember my own name sometimes," I joked. "I've gotta look at my driving licence."

"So you can remember what you look like as well?" enquired the man with a grin.

"Yeh, make sure I'm shaving the right person in the morning," I replied.

# CHAPTER 5

## ENOLA

To move a train on any part of the Conrail network – or Conrail system to use the proper American term – required authority from someone or other. The yardmaster gave authority in Lancaster yard. To enter the New Holland Secondary Track the WHLA80 required permission from the train dispatcher in charge of it, the Port Road Dispatcher, who at that time was located in Philadelphia. The dispatcher issued his authority on a standard form called a Form D. Thus the method of operation on the New Holland Secondary Track – and on all other lines described as a secondary – was Norac's Form D Control System, which had no equivalent in Britain. The nearest was Radio Electronic Token Block where the signalman issued a token by computer as authority to use a track. If the dispatcher was located in Philadelphia, the question arose how did he get a Form D to a traincrew in Lancaster? The answer is that all crews carried blank Form Ds whereby the dispatcher could dictate his instructions by radio. In the case of the New Holland Secondary, conductors usually telephoned the dispatcher for a Form D before leaving the yard office.

Only train dispatchers could initiate a Form D. Block operators, such as those employed in Cork tower, were subordinate to dispatchers, and part of their duties was to hand over a dictated Form D on the dispatcher's behalf. Sometimes block operators were seconded temporarily to remote locations where the passing of a Form D was often done at speed, with the operator attaching the form to a triangular string loop through which the conductor thrust his hand to pick up the document. Thirty miles per hour was normal for the operation, and conductors had to clench the fist to avoid painfully catching the string loop with finger nails! Compare this fast exchange with the walking-speed handing over of tokens on British single-track branch lines.

Form Ds were multipurpose. Another use was to grant authority to work in the wrong direction over a line signalled for traffic going the opposite way, or, to use the official American term, to operate against the current of traffic. To use a dictated form was far more economical than the British remedy of appointing a pilotman to accompany every train. During the 1990s, both in America and Britain, each track of double-track main line was used in one direction only, in the majority of cases anyway. As may be guessed, it was right-hand running in America. Such single-direction arrangement was referred to as Rule 251. Since the 1990s in both countries more and more lines have been converted to bi-directional working, in America known as Rule 261.

On one job I trained on in Lancaster we worked against the current of traffic over Amtrak's main line. Once we arrived at Cork tower, the conductor suggested I collect the Form D from the operator. Accordingly I climbed the tower steps to reach the operating floor. The building was equivalent to a small British panel box, but in place of a control panel stood a large table-like structure (which contained the interlocking mechanism) with handles on the front rather like old-fashioned automobile starting handles but somewhat smaller. Handles turned 180 degrees to the left or right to operate signals and switches.

Another assignment I trained on was the WHLA85 which serviced many industries packed closely together on the ten-mile long Columbia Secondary Track. The Columbia Secondary butted onto Lancaster Yard's Number 2 Industrial Track, the exact boundary marked by a four foot high sign in the grass lettered vertically FARM, white letters on a blue background. The object was known as a station sign. It is important to note that the term station in America has a far wider meaning than the passenger station it refers to in Britain. In America, station means any identified location on a railroad. Thus a station may be a passenger station, site of a former passenger station, an interlocking, siding, former siding, lineside detector, state boundary, or any other feature deemed important enough to be recognized as a station.

One day, Form D authority had been given to the WHLA85 to work as usual the Columbia Secondary in both directions. After several hour's intensive switching we left the Columbia Secondary at its western limit marked by station sign EY located in the town of Columbia. It had been the intention to run round the train and return to Lancaster, but plans abruptly changed. "We're not going back to Lancaster," said the brakeman.

The first emotion on receiving this intelligence was panic. My car, a 1989 strawberry-red Ford Escort, was stranded in Lancaster. "Where are we going?" I gulped.

"Enola."

"Why?"

"All these cars are for Enola," said the brakeman, "and the engines are due to go to Enola for service, so they've decided we're just going to take the whole train there."

"When do we go back to Lancaster?" I asked, beginning to worry.

"They'll deadhead us back," was the reply.

Deadhead meant we would be transported at the company's expense, still being paid whilst doing so. The term derived from an earlier era when men were taxied on a steam engine that was not in steam but towed by another that was, the former referred to as having a dead head of steam. The equivalent procedure in Britain would be use of a suitable passenger train service - on the cushions, as it was known. (I learn that in post-privatization Britain, freight operating companies sometimes provide a vehicle for train drivers to "deadhead" themselves to and from locations.)

Meanwhile, train WHLA85 set off from Columbia on its thirty-two mile trip to Enola. Locomotives had only three seats, so I offered mine to the brakeman, but he was happy to stand. He was one of those special Americans who participated in the venerable practice of extracting oral refreshment from leaf of the tobacco plant; a standing position better suited the ceremony. As the train rattled along, the brakeman stood facing me, one hand gripping a handrail that protected stairs down to a toilet in the nose of the engine, the other hand holding a plastic cup. The tobacco rite generated an excess of fluid which had to be discharged. Outdoors the ground provided a ready and willing depository, elsewhere a receptacle had to be used.

The brakeman periodically transferred overflow into the cup. I watched with rapt attention a ritual I had never seen in Britain, novelty of the occasion given extra poignancy by the plastic cup steadily filling up. The locomotive dashed along at forty miles per hour ignoring slight imperfections in the track that caused it to buck and roll, that jiggled men in their seats, that made the cup's ever-increasing liquid slop about disconcertingly. I remained transfixed on the brakeman and his chalice. He watched me watching him, not really knowing why I was doing so. For ten minutes two men were locked in silent eye-to-eye contact, as if in some drawn-out atmospheric French film. Puzzled by the engagement, the brakeman eventually asked, "Do you want some tobacco?" I declined his kind offer. Shortly, the indulgence ceased, and the cup and contents were disposed of.

On the Columbia Secondary we had operated under the Form D Control System. On passing EY we had entered Cola interlocking, and in so doing came under Interlocking Rules, which had some provisions in common with British Absolute Block Regulations. Beyond Cola, Automatic Block Signal System rules applied, which meant obeying signals that functioned automatically - much in the manner of British Track Circuit Block Regulations.

Signals were of the position light variety to the designs of the former Pennsylvania Railroad, being originally inspired by three-position semaphore signals. Thus three amber lights in a horizontal row meant stop, officially STOP SIGNAL. The Norac Rule Book defined a signal instruction as an indication and used capital letters to name it, a practice I shall copy. However, I feel the word indication is too vague, and henceforward will use the term signal message in its place.

Three amber lights in vertical display meant CLEAR: proceed at authorized speed. Three lights at forty-five degrees sloping from bottom left to top right was APPROACH: be prepared to stop at the next signal. In future I will refer to three lights sloping bottom left to top right as a diagonal display. All three signal messages were backed by a fifty-two inch sighting disc with the central amber light common to all. They were learnt instantly.

In Britain, if there is a train ahead in the next automatic block section, the signal protecting that section will show red, which means stop and stay stopped. In identical circumstances, the Norac signal will say STOP AND PROCEED, meaning, once the train has made a stop, it may proceed at restricted speed bearing in mind there is probably another train ahead. The upshot of this is that all main line signalling, not only on Conrail but probably in most of America, is *permissive*. That even passenger trains may enter an automatic block section already occupied by another train to my mind is the most significant difference between British and American signalling. In Pennsylvania Railroad signals, STOP AND PROCEED is a horizontal display of either three amber or two red lights, differentiated from STOP SIGNAL by a number plate or yellow marker light on the signal post. But, oh the other signal messages!

As we neared Enola we met a signal with two sighting discs, the upper arm – as it was known – was horizontal. The lower arm sloped forty-five degrees from top left to bottom right. It meant RESTRICTING: proceed being prepared to stop within half the distance that can be seen, at no more than fifteen miles per hour. For many weeks I sought the logic in this bizarre array of lights, until it occurred to me it was almost identical in appearance and meaning to a British upper quadrant semaphore signal authorizing entry into an occupied permissive block section.

\* \* \*

First sight of a new landscape is unique. One is able to take in everything at once, a bush just twenty feet away, a building in the middle distance, far off hills, as if all were painted on a single flat canvas or captured on photographic film. After such an initial visual sweep of Enola Yard, I was able to focus on what interested me most, which surprisingly was not a vast expanse of sidings (some full of cars, some not) but a distant horizon where the sharply defined outline of what our high school geography mistress would have called a truncated spur was engraved into the blue sky. Suggesting glaciation, upper slopes of the the eastern side of the Susquehanna River valley began gently, then suddenly changed to an almost vertical cut into a promontory, after which the gradient eased again towards the valley bottom to produce a classic U-shape. Closer inspection of this profile at a later date revealed natural contours had been made steeper by roadworks. Thus the moment of arrival at a place I had heard so much about, a complex that in the 1940s had been the biggest railroad yard in the world, was stolen by the arresting appearance of a remote hill!

Train WHLA85 was deposited somewhere in Enola Yard, I cannot remember where, and after waiting a short while in the yard office, a taxi arrived to take us back to Lancaster. I had little opportunity to make sense of the yard layout, especially after being distracted by a rock formation far away! It was not my first visit, the induction class had visited Enola Yard to be instructed on couplings. On that occasion I was so disorientated I had to ask where the Susquehanna River was in order to establish points of the compass. The yard actually ran north to south, parallel to the river, but the official operating direction was east and west.

The problem with Enola Yard was that it was four miles long. At no point could an observer see the whole yard. To grasp its layout, it is best to start with four building blocks. As we arrived in the yard on WHLA85, sixteen tracks of the Westbound Receiving Yard fanned out to our right. At their far end, they would have come together in the West Hump and fanned out to thirty-five tracks of the Westbound Classification Yard had not the West Hump recently been closed and partially ripped out. The Westbound Classification Yard was mainly still intact, but underused. Entering Enola Yard from the opposite direction, fourteen tracks of the Eastbound Receiving Yard on the right were still busy, but the Eastbound Hump and Classification Yard had long been taken away leaving behind a melancholy windswept emptiness. As WHLA85 had travelled through the yard we had passed ghosts of the forty-four track Eastbound Classification Yard in the form of rusty indentations in dirty ballast. What appeared to be tumbleweed bowling along this death valley emphasized the bleakness. (How far did the weedy spheres travel, one wonders?)

Thus the four units of Westbound and Eastbound Receiving and Classification Yards took up most of Enola Yard. They were flanked by four long tracks to the east (nearest the river) known as the Old Line, and four long tracks to the west known as the Coal Yard. In the centre of everything was Enola Diesel House where locomotives under test roared like caged animals in zoological gardens.

The yard office was known as the Brick Office, or sometimes just The Brick. Why, I do not know. Was it to differentiate from another built of straw, or one of clay and wattles made? The building was run down and needed a spring clean. Some rooms were dilapidated. The upper floor appeared to be abandoned dormitories. Eventually, a new, smaller, modern yard office was built. The old Brick Office was demolished in April 1998, cobwebs and all. I recovered one of the bricks from the rubble. Railways and railroads are notorious for clinging to obsolete terms, perhaps because dated expressions generate a warm and comfortable feeling amongst those using them. As a result, the brand new yard office in Enola continued to be called by the name of its grimy predecessor, the Brick Office.

\* \* \*

Enola Yard's West Hump closed whilst I was still working on the Maryland and Pennsylvania prior to joining Conrail. News spread like wildfire that Enola Yard itself had closed, but that was an exaggeration. With the closure, numerous activities supporting the West Hump - the assembly of traffic in the Receiving Yard, the disposal of traffic in the Classification Yard – also ceased. A great number of jobs were lost, though the rest of the yard remained in use as a crew change point, for storage, and for swopping blocks of cars in incoming trains. Status of the Diesel House remained unchanged.

The original Enola Yard belonged to the Northern Central Railroad. Apparently Enola was the name of a four-year old daughter of the man who sold land on which the yard was built. The adjacent town took its name from the railroad yard. The Pennsylvania Railroad effectively took over the yard when it acquired a controlling interest in the Northern Central in 1861, and rebuilt the yard in 1905. At one time, the Enola Yard Extra Board ran to several hundred employees. The Pennsylvania Railroad, once the biggest employer in the state, became part of Penn Central Railroad in 1968, which in turn became part of Conrail in 1976. In the 1990s Conrail, current custodian of Enola Yard, was still an important employer in the area. (Drastically altered employment patterns in the 2000s are evinced by the fact that the Walmart retail chain is said to be the biggest employer in the United States, Wellspan Health the biggest employer in York County, Pennsylvania.)

Enola West Hump closed because it was outdated. It relied on men located in towers manually operating retarders to slow cars on their descent from the hump. Work that used to be undertaken at

Enola's West Hump was transferred one hundred miles to a modern hump at Allentown where information about each car was fed into a computer which decided which track to send it down and how much retardation to apply.

To men whose jobs depended on the West Hump, its closure was devastating. Overnight, their source of income vanished. To remain employed by Conrail, they had to exercise seniority within the company and obtain another position. The most senior men probably found alternative work in nearby Harrisburg or Shiremanstown Yards by displacing less senior employees, by bumping them, as it was known. Quite a number of men chose to travel to Lancaster Dillerville Yard, about forty miles away. For some, opportunities on Conrail presented themselves elsewhere in Pennsylvania, in the towns of Reading and Allentown. Further afield lay Baltimore in Maryland State. A man with little seniority could remain in the Enola and Harrisburg area, but he would have to begin working on long-distance freight trains: to go on the road. For those with the lowest seniority in Enola, closure of the West Hump probably signalled an end to a railroad career.

Whilst working in Lancaster I witnessed two emotional outbursts directly attributable to the closure at Enola.

One day a middle-aged man burst into the yard office and immediately went on the computer placed there for men to view assignments. One by one, he flicked through screens that displayed which men at which seniority level held which positions. After he had completed the exercise, with a physiognomy lined with anguish, he said to himself and to anyone listening, "Eighteen years, and still can't hold Lancaster." He fled the yard office with tears in his eyes, victim of the Enola closure.

A member of Conrail middle management visited the yard office one day, a routine visit, as far as I could see. He was seated at one of the messing tables in the locker room, when a brakeman learning of his presence approached him. "Do you know [so-and-so]?" asked the brakeman, referring to the senior executive widely believed to be architect of the Enola closure. The manager nodded that he did know the senior executive. "Well, I can tell you," stormed the brakeman, "that he is a no-good, rotten..." The brakeman then proceeded to heap insults on the senior executive of the vilest possible nature, accusing him of the most deviant sexual activities imaginable. The brakeman's face grew redder, his eyes bulged larger, his torso curved ever closer towards the man forced to listen to years of pent-up anger erupting in a lengthy, imprecation-strewn tirade that silenced all other conversation in Lancaster Yard office. The middle manager slowly leant backwards to recoil from an avalanche of foul language, until the brakeman burnt himself out, stopped ranting, and stomped off, knowing that history could not be re-written no matter how much he wished it could. After the brakeman left, the manager quietly returned to studying papers in front of him.

# CHAPTER 6

# READING

Training in Lancaster Dillerville Yard continued, including spells on travelling shifters that served nearby towns of Lititz, Manheim and Marietta. Surprisingly, a second week was spent on the New Holland travelling shifter. A couple of weeks saw duty on Lancaster Yard jobs. The initial training period at last came to an end with two more days in class on 17th and 18th October 1994, after which we were considered qualified to work as brakemen. The second day finished officially at 15:00 hours, and as tuition drew to a close we were told our fate. I had to report to Reading at 23:00 hours that night.

It will be a surprise to fans of the British Great Western Railway to learn there is another town called Reading famed for its railway history. Reading, Pennsylvania, is also located in Berks County. Not Berkshire abbreviated to Berks., but simply Berks, pronounced to rhyme with works. American Reading was home of the former Reading Railroad whose trackage, centred mainly on Reading and Philadelphia, once sprawled across much of the eastern part of the state. Like Penn Central, it, too, went bankrupt, and became a constituent of Conrail.

It appeared Reading Yard, known as Spring Street Yard, was desperately short of brakemen. I ought not to have been surprised at how little time I was given off duty. By now I had learnt a railroader may be called back to work only eight hours after he had completed his previous assignment, provided that previous assignment was less than twelve hours. The time of day did not matter, nor how far a person had to drive, nor how weary he might be, nor how many times he had doubled-back that week. To work he must go. I went to bed as soon as I arrived home from class, slept as much as I could, set an alarm for 21:00 hours, and left home about 21:30 for the sixty-mile drive to Reading.

Conrail provided directions, which I followed faithfully. At a few minutes before 23:00 I made one last turn onto a patch of higher ground and came to a stand in the middle of a black void. In every direction, save the direction from which I had just driven, nothing could be seen on this vacant plateau. It was as unsettling as falling down a pit at midnight. I took a few steps this way, then that - not too many for fear of stepping off a cliff.

Headlights then appeared from below. A vehicle stopped a few feet from mine. Someone to the rescue, perhaps. "Hello!" I called out.

"Is that you, Mitch?" said a voice.

"Yeh. Who's that?" A tall shape approached, whose owner I now recognized as a fellow classmate. "Is that you, Dave?"

"Yep, that's me. What are *you* doing here?"

"Supposed to report to the YHRE65, but can't even see the yard office, never mind the train. Can't see *anything*," I complained.

"Seems a bit strange," said Dave, who surveyed the inky black nothingness that surrounded us, then added, "Surely we both couldn't have taken a wrong turn. Let's try and find something."

Dave and I, unlike others in our class, had prior railroad experience. He had worked as engineer on a southern railroad, but had been furloughed. I of course had worked five years with the Maryland and Pennsylvania. I had had an additional eight years with British Railways, but those eight years may as well have been spent at sea for all the experience counted in America. Dave and I had been described as the "slickest" of the new intake by men in Lancaster Yard, who chose to ignore the fact we had both been around trains for many years. Either the Lancaster men refused to believe we had previous railroad employment, or they considered it of no value, or they considered holding a position on Conrail such a privilege all other vocations were inconsequential.

To return to Reading, and to the predicament in which two newly-hired men found themselves, we set off in opposite directions to find a way out of the black hole. After a short while, Dave called out from somewhere, "Over here Mitch. The road goes down a slope." A rough road dropped steeply, turned a sharp corner, and duly brought two lost brakemen in front of the yard office which had been hidden from view by unlit buildings and other obstacles. We reported to the yardmaster and apologized for our tardiness. Dave learnt he would be working at an outpost about a mile away; he had to be shown the route by someone in another vehicle. (That may have been the last I saw of my former classmate, for he grew impatient of not being promoted engineer, and left Conrail.)

Most yards of any size had a midnight shifter. Crews reported for duty at 22:00, 23:00 or midnight to work all through the night. Though I had had very little sleep and had been dispatched to a place I had never before seen in my life, mercifully two factors were favourable on this first day of true employment on Conrail. First, the conductor was one of the best conductors I ever worked with. His instructions over the radio were slow, deliberate, clearly audible, and reinforced by constant enquiries to make sure I understood. His voice matched his demeanour: even and unhurried. The second advantage was that Spring Street Yard was easy to learn. In the southern part of the yard, where we would spend most of the night, tracks 16 to 21 branched off a straight lead at evenly spaced intervals – a lead (or ladder) was a track that connected several other tracks. Most yard switches were marked with the track number, but if sidings were laid out methodically the job was so much easier.

After hasty introductions and the sketchiest outline of the night's work, we set about shifting cars.

"Take 'em ahead, over to 19," said the conductor. "I've already got number 19, Mitch."

"Roger," I acknowledged. As the last few cars went by me, I said, "Three cars. Two. One. Half. That's good." I then threw back number 21 switch to re-align for the lead. "Lined up for 19, okay back, eight cars to couple."

"Four cars," said the conductor as the train neared him. "Two. One. Half. Ten feet. That's good."

And so it went on all night. Back and forth from this track to that, picking cars up, setting cars off. I did not know why. I just did as I was told.

The three-mile long Pottsville Branch ran alongside the eastern flanks of Spring Street Yard. In Britain, a branch was usually a shortish single-track line leading to a dead end. On Conrail, a branch was more likely to be what in Britain was called a secondary route, one that was not as important as a principal line. A Conrail secondary track was more like a British branch line. The two terms were almost reversed, but not quite. At some point in the Reading night, a long train came to a stand on the Pottsville Branch and deposited the front part of its train on a track that ran parallel to the Pottsville Branch, the Number 2 Running Track. "What's that train?" I asked the conductor.

"Oh, that's a road job," he replied.

At the time I assumed the train had come from somewhere like New York, but would eventually learn it was an Allentown to Harrisburg train.

As we soldiered through the night it was relatively easy to see as the yard was well lit. But railroad lighting penetrated only so far - as far as a street adjacent to the Pottsville Branch and licensed premises that stood in it. Beyond that, for all I knew there could be a desert, a lake, a golf course, I had no idea. A massive wall covered in black wallpaper surrounded the entire railroad yard, just like the island on which we had found ourselves when first arriving.

Then something wondrous happened. Dawn broke. To the west, a jumble of railroad architecture slowly materialized out of the murkiness. To the east, beyond the Pottsville Branch, street after street of Reading city centre emerged from a receding tide of gloom. Beyond the streets a substantial tree-covered ridge took shape about half-a-mile away. As we shifted cars in nascent daylight, I marvelled at the transformation, at the beauty of the wooded ridge, at the bursting into life of another urban day, at the stark difference between being able to see and not being able to see. Finally, there appeared a curious red building embedded in the woody hill side. It was the well-known pagoda. An enterprising individual had decided to erect a building to oriental design, one that, in another country, would have got no further than the in-tray of a town and country planning officer.

A coffee in the middle of the night had produced a temporary spike in energy, but as dawn materialized so did hope that the day would soon be over. As the crew gathered in the yard office at 07:00 hours, I had about as much bounce in me as a punctured rubber ball. The conductor went back and forth clutching papers. "Are we done?" I asked hopefully.

"Just talking about another little job to do," said the conductor.

"But aren't we finished at seven?" I asked desperately.

"Our time's up at seven, yes, but sometimes we get a bit of overtime, if there's the work," explained the conductor.

"How long are we going to work till?"

The conductor studied my features momentarily before replying. I had told him of the quick turn-round from rules class. Perhaps he could see I was capable of very little more. Whether or not these considerations influenced a decision, his face did not betray. "Maybe another hour or so, we'll have to see," he said.

It was not uncommon for Conrail midnight shifters to continue working beyond normal finishing time. It seemed that a measure of overtime was built into the shift to entice men to work otherwise unappealing hours. This theory was reinforced by the converse circumstance of a Lancaster yard shifter that reported for duty at a pleasant 06:30 hardly ever working overtime. Still, I could not understand why anyone would want to continue working after dawn if they had been up all night. Perhaps I had become so conditioned on British Railways to finishing the signalman's night shift before 07:00 hours that to work longer seemed more like a penalty than the bonus Conrail men perceived it to be.

No matter which side of the Atlantic Ocean, night work was unavoidable on the railway. The difference was the majority of British trains were passenger trains running only during the day. I got the impression British Railways would run freight during the day if they could, but if unavoidable, ran it at night. Working round the clock of course made best use of such assets as diesel locomotives. The majority of American trains were freight, and it was of little consequence to railroad managers what time of day trains ran as long as they kept moving. A box car took about five days and nights to travel from California State to New York State. There was no reason to double that journey time by stopping traffic just because it was dark outside. To work in the American freight railroad industry is to say, yes, I am willing to work at night because those wheels must keep turning.

To return to the first night, now morning, in Reading, at about 07:15 I hastily grabbed another cup of coffee and poured it down. We hopped on the locomotive and headed northwards to shift premises located in the middle of the yard. There were only three tracks in the building, numbered 2, 4 and 6, which were widely spaced, presumably because 3 and 5 had been removed. My simple job was to throw switches, but that simple job grew progressively harder as the brain no longer properly functioned. The shift ended at 08:15. I slumped into the car and, grateful to sit down, drove home.

In order to find my way out of Reading, I had to read backwards Conrail's instructions to get there, which was not easy in the circumstances. Eventually I was on Route 222, a dual carriageway main highway between Reading and Lancaster, which would deposit me on Route 30 for the last leg of the journey back to York County. But mental and physical fatigue took its toll.

I suddenly opened my eyes to see Route 222 hurtling towards me. I had lost consciousness, but recovered it. I had blacked out, I do not know for how long. It surely cannot have been for too long, for I was still on a straight course, still with hands on the wheel, still on the highway moving forwards. If I had remained unconscious for much longer I would certainly have left the road.

I would have liked to have said that I learnt a lesson. But there was no lesson to learn. Long hours and demanding, unpredictable work schedules were inescapable. Zero seniority granted the new man no choice. Even with a few years' seniority long night shifts prevailed which were frequently so wearying that when I stopped at a certain set of traffic lights on bright summer mornings I shut my eyes to rest them, but was still able to see lights change through closed eyelids.

\* \* \*

The complicated arrangement of tracks in and around Reading was a riotous construction of triangles upon triangles. The American term for a triangular railroad configuration was a wye. If the Reading layout were pictured as a capital letter A, then the single track Pottsville Branch was the right-hand slope of the letter as far down as the horizontal. The left-hand slope as far down as the horizontal was the double-track Reading Line. The horizontal in the letter A and everything below were segments of the Harrisburg Line. The right-hand base of the letter A continued eastwards as the double-track Harrisburg Line to Philadelphia. The left-hand base reached over to the right-hand base but also had an offshoot of the Harrisburg

Line that struck out eastwards independently to rejoin the main line seven miles away at Bird interlocking. This single track Rule 251 offshoot was nicknamed the Turkey Path, apparently a corruption of the original owner's name, Turk and Path, and another excellent example of the longevity of obsolete railroad names.

On Conrail, but not on Amtrak, if an interlocking had one or more Rule 261 tracks feeding into it, then its name was prefixed by CP. CP stood for Controlled Point, meaning that it was a location where the direction of traffic on a Rule 261 line could be changed. Which brings up the curious case of Center interlocking. One Reading wye comprised the three interlockings CP-Walnut, CP-Oley and Center. The double-track Rule 251 Harrisburg Line came into Center from the west favouring the interlocking not being prefixed CP. However, single lines that could be used in both directions came in from the other two interlockings, and it was only because Interlocking Rules were in effect on those two lines that Center, pedantically, avoided the prefix CP. The question is then posed why were those single lines dubbed Interlocking Rules and not Rule 261? We were never told; I can only surmise it was to prevent two trains occupying these short lengths of track at the same time which Rule 261 would permit.

The labyrinthine layout of Reading was invaluable to the Harrisburg East Dispatcher who controlled it. Stationed in Philadelphia, the dispatcher could use the complicated formation to regulate, to reshuffle, to re-route and to change the order in which trains ran. Trains destined for Allentown and north New Jersey State (to serve New York City) normally travelled up the left slope of the letter A. To allow one to overtake another, a slower train could be routed along the horizontal and up the right slope, the Pottsville Branch. But the dispatcher had yet another option for New Jersey trains, he could send them to Philadelphia and, once in that city, have them diverted northwards along a route called the Trenton Line.

*A Railroad Atlas of the United States in 1946* by Richard C. Carpenter reveals that in 1946 the majority of lines in Reading belonged, not unsurprisingly, to the Reading Railroad, and that the general pattern was as described above. Despite the Reading's dominance, it did not enjoy a monopoly. Pennsylvania Railroad tracks ran almost parallel from Philadelphia to Reading in a fashion often repeated in America: the Reading ran along one side of a river valley, the Pennsylvania the other, the river in question being the Schuylkill River. It is a mark of how lucrative railroads used to be, how cheap their costs were, that two rivals could co-exist side by side. By the 1990s, the Reading alignment had obviously proved its superiority, for only fragments of the Pennsylvania remained, in the form of industrial sidings connected at various points to the Reading Railroad route.

* * *

I worked three more shifts, long shifts, during my first week in Reading. One shift was spent at the outpost where my classmate had been sent on the first night in Reading, a factory that built chassis for a major automobile manufacturer. The factory not only provided employment for local residents, but required a Conrail crew to be on hand to shift as required. The completed chassis, or frames as they were called, were loaded onto flat cars to make a short journey via the Richmond Street Industrial Track to Spring Street Yard for onward transmission. The frames had numerous holes of various sizes, for bolts or connections, different dimensions for different vehicle models. "Do they ever get the holes wrong?" I asked.

"One time they did," said the conductor.

"So the whole lot came back?"

"Yep," said the conductor.

"Were they able to alter the frames or did they have to re-make the whole batch?"

The conductor replied that he did not know, but looked at me with mild surprise that I should have homed in on what must have been an extremely costly, embarrassing and much talked-about mistake. What the conductor did not know was that in the 1970s when preparing work orders for a small factory in Liverpool I bore the crushing responsibility of having to get things right first time. When watching scores of precisely manufactured frames go by on flat cars in Reading I could see that, despite utmost care, sooner or later human error would creep in.

In the second week in Reading, work declined so much I applied to the Railroad Retirement Board for financial assistance. It was possible several employees had been on holiday in the first week, and returned the second. I should of course say they were on vacation.

48

Does not the word holiday sound much more joyful though? It has a happy ring to it, that captures the elation of being away from work, but is at odds with its origins: there is nothing holy about two weeks in Benidorm! Vacation sounds like a medical procedure, but roots of the word far better qualify it. My wife and I continue to use the word holiday, but only between ourselves, because in America it is an abbreviation for public holiday, or bank holiday.

In a third week in Reading I was put back training – on the WHRE29, a travelling shifter whose primary work was to convey traffic between Reading and Pottstown, which required a twenty-mile journey in the Philadelphia direction. On the first occasion we picked up speed after leaving Reading, I held onto my seat. I had not done fifty miles per hour on a freight train since an unofficial ride on a steam engine when a boy!

Like Lancaster men, those in Reading were fond of verbal horseplay. In a friendly disagreement one said to the other, "Have you ever wondered what it'd be like looking through bandages!"

The other replied, "Have you ever wondered what it'd be like looking through bars!"

I was quietly sitting at a locker room table when a man burst in. He puffed himself up for a fight, and angrily addressed another seated, "Why, you lousy rotten stinking..." He continued the invective with a stream of unspeakable sexual allegations much in the manner of the brakeman in Lancaster Yard. I prepared to duck for cover.

"Hello there Steve. How yer doing?" was the calm and friendly reply from the man sitting down.

"Not so bad John. How's yourself?" said the first. It had all been a joke.

Notwithstanding the free entertainment, it was clear that being stationed in Reading would produce little work. The telephone rang at home one day to address the problem. "I tell you what we're going to do, Mr. Deaver," said the supervisor in charge of trainees, as if we had been engaged in a lengthy debate on what we were going to do, "we're going to put you out on the road. The crew dispatcher will be contacting you. So we're taking you out of Reading."

I and several others were placed out on the road to learn long-distance freights, much to our surprise, even shock. Whilst training in Lancaster, one man had said, "What we can't understand is, what are they going to do with you all?" For a week or two, it appeared the man's concern had been well-founded. However, as time went by, Conrail ran into periods when they were desperately short of traincrews, particularly for road work. The hiring of large numbers of new recruits in 1994 was justified.

# CHAPTER 7

# ON THE ROAD

At about 19:30 on Wednesday 16th November the telephone rang. "M.C. Deaver?" asked a deep gravelly voice.

"Yes," I replied accurately.

"Need you for the Pie-say Six. Nine-thirty, Harrisburg," I thought the crew dispatcher said.

"Need me for the *what*?"

"PICA6."

"P. I. C. A. Six," I repeated deliberately.

"That's right. Nine-thirty, Harrisburg," confirmed the crew dispatcher.

"Right. I'll be there." What did PICA stand for, Perishable Insulated Cargo Aboard, Pallets In Containers, Assorted?

Working long-distance freight trains usually meant staying in a hotel at an away-from-home terminal, so I rammed a change of clothing into a black bag that already contained Rule Book, work gloves, wet-weather clothing, switch keys and other miscellaneous items, adding afterwards a rapidly prepared lunch box. Donning work boots, I kissed my wife farewell and left for the fifty-mile drive via Interstate Highway 83 to catch the cryptic PICA6 train in Harrisburg.

Men filled Harrisburg yard office, men going on duty, men going off duty and others of uncertain status. I approached a couple of individuals saying I was with the PICA6, but was met with a shake of the head. A third attempt was successful. The man stared at me, briefly doubting that someone with a foreign accent could work for Conrail, but since I had quoted a correct train identity, he decided my credentials must be in order. "Yes, that's us," he said. "I'm the conductor. My name's Steve." After I had introduced myself and said this was my first job on the road, the conductor, a wiry man with pronounced facial features and wearing a cowboy-style hat, explained he had some sorting-out to do, excused himself and assured me he would return shortly.

Five minutes later the conductor came back to say, "Actually, we've got a four-man crew. The engineer has a trainee with him, he takes priority, you see. There are only seats for three on the engine. You won't be able to be with us on the lead engine, safety and all that, so you'll have to ride on the second engine." The conductor sensed disappointment. "I'll tell you what I'll do, I'll give you my maps so you can follow as we go along," he said encouragingly. He then changed the subject, grinned, and said, "There's detectors out there that'll be talking to us. You'll hear 'em!"

The conductor was referring to lineside devices that detect if a train has an over-heated axle box – a hot box – or something dragging, or that its loading is too high for the route. The conductor had been victim of the Enola closure in that he, not having sufficient seniority to move to a yard like Lancaster, had been forced out on the road. He seemed amused by machines that talked over the radio to traincrews, and keenly shared that delight.

"Okay, Mitch, we're ready to go," said the conductor a little later.

In addition to such items as safety glasses and work boots, it was imperative road crews ensured they had necessary paperwork before departing, for there was no turning back. Documentation for each hazardous material car within the train was vital. Equally important were current bulletins. British Railways printed a booklet known as the Weekly Operating Notice (the WE1 version covered the North London Line) that contained advice on temporary speed restrictions, temporary track work, permanent changes to infrastructure plus general information. Conrail printed the same material in typed daily bulletins, except that general matters appeared in periodic publications called division notices. At this stage I did not know enough to make a selection from stacks of bulletins in the yard office. Just before we left, the engineer came over to speak, "Once we set off, we'll probably keep going till we get to Abrams." Perhaps Abrams was the A in PICA6.

I followed three others through the yard office door, over a small crowded car park – and across a series of tracks. The rule stated a stop must be made to look both ways before crossing each track. When we arrived at main lines where our train was patiently waiting, the conductor directed me to take a seat on the second locomotive. That would be the last I would see of him for quite some time. Train PICA6 left Harrisburg pulled by diesel locomotives 3000 horsepower Class GP40-2 number 3279, 4000 horsepower Class B40-8 number 5063 and 3000 horsepower Class SD40-2 number 6961 hauling a train of mixed freight, sixty-six loads and eighteen empties, all weighing 7937 tons. As a rough guide it was considered advisable to have one horse power for every ton of train, so on this occasion we had adequate power.

In darkness and with another locomotive directly in front, I did my best to follow progress on maps given me by the conductor. They were originally work of a Conrail engineer who had gone to enormous trouble copying railroad infrastructure onto scale topographical maps. The work had become so invaluable, particularly with the influx of new employees, that the rights had been sold to the employer. It was not that Conrail did not have plans of its railroad, but that they were not in useful form; civil engineers' drawings would be too large a scale.

Double-track main lines sped us away eastwards from Harrisburg and its environs. Conditions under which I rode made our exact position difficult to determine. Now and again a milepost would peer out from the gloom to pinpoint unequivocally where we were, otherwise only a large built-up area, such as the city of Lebanon, provided firm evidence. Reduced speed of twenty-five miles per hour was mandatory owing to a succession of grade crossings in that city; higher speed would not have allowed barriers to lower in front of highway traffic in time. Barriers were very similar in design to those in Britain and elsewhere in the world, but were generally called gates.

Within Lebanon was an interlocking called Wall, which I would pass many times in the future. Each time I looked for the large wall that named the interlocking, but never saw it. Eventually I learnt the interlocking had been named not to honour brickwork but a nearby town called Cornwall. It was explained to me that some years ago an exercise took place to shorten often unwieldy interlocking names. In many cases an abbreviation was adopted, but in the case of Wall the last syllable was taken.

A couple of miles east of Lebanon was a cluster of dwellings known as Prescott. The Harrisburg Line station pages listed Prescott as a station, as does *A Railroad Atlas of the United States in 1946.* As previously stated, a station means any identified railroad location. Maybe there used to be a passenger station at Prescott, or maybe just a siding. Now there was nothing, except houses at a distance, which I came to recognize as Prescott by the few lights coming from them. Some weeks hence I rode for the first time in daylight and failed to recognize the location! Two miles further down the track Myerstown hot box detector talked to us on the radio. "Conrail. Myerstown. Pennsylvania. Track Two. No Defects. Total axle count 354. Over." Compiled from prerecorded segments, the message came over as a lifeless monotone. Detectors counted axles. At the first detector, traincrews checked that the axle count corresponded to paperwork. Thereafter, detectors confirmed nothing had been left behind along the way. Either engineer or conductor responded by gabbling over the radio, "PICA Myerstown Track Two no defects out." Or something of that order. On a future occasion I quipped to an engineer, "Wouldn't you think those people in Myerstown would get fed up with that detector going off all night." In response, the engineer just stared at me.

We continued to burrow through darkness, unrelenting darkness – darkness that searched out every last corner of the locomotive cab rendering everything invisible. I opened my brown plastic lunch box for a snack. It was full of darkness too, I had to poke around for food. When I switched on locomotive cab lights to study maps, all I could see through the window was my own reflection; it was not possible to read maps and look outside at the same time. At times I just gazed into the night. Little could be seen, save for lights twinkling from scattered dwellings - a bathroom light, a security light, a street light. It seemed as if those nocturnal lights represented souls, countless souls, each life magnificent in its uniqueness, each no less complicated, no less prone to exhilaration or pensiveness than our own lives as we hurtled by on PICA6. Yet all those lives were unworthy of our contemplation because we were in too much of a hurry to think about them.

Familiar territory came into view as we travelled between Reading and Pottstown, after which we were once again in strange surroundings. A siding led to Limerick nuclear power station. At one point I joked to an engineer, "I suppose you're going to tell me you used to deliver there hundred-car hopper trains of uranium."

The engineer in question looked at me blankly, then said, "When they were building the power station, the siding was used to deliver equipment." Not used to having jokes or drollery inflicted on them, men were frequently perplexed by a humorous comment. After a moment's thought, most would respond with a smile if nothing else. I do not know if there is enough uranium in the world to fill a hundred-car train.

I peered into darkness for landmarks as we rolled along at forty or fifty miles per hour. The former passenger station at Royersford, still largely intact, was a pleasing surprise. The 1946 atlas showed the station open for business in Reading Railroad days. Speed then gradually dropped, until we reached Black Rock Tunnel where two lines became one to pass through it. Home signals of CP-Phoenix positioned either side governed which trains went through the tunnel first. Speed remained lower until irrefutable evidence in the form of large numbers of sidings announced we were at Abrams Yard. But we kept going, leaving Abrams and its busyness behind. When the engineer had said to me, "We'll probably keep going until we get to Abrams," I thought he meant that Abrams was our destination, but he only meant that we would probably be held up there. Now, I had not the slightest idea where we were going, with no one to ask.

Further mileage created a distinct feeling of the landscape closing in on the train. Surroundings becoming more urban as we followed the Schuylkill River valley downstream gave the impression we were descending into a hole. A few miles after Abrams this tunnelling illusion became reality as we plunged beneath an edifice of strikingly modern, even futuristic design. The railroad retained its original alignment but was now perfectly ballasted, free from rubbish - trash – and immaculately lined with smooth concrete walls and ceiling. Next, the Conshohoken dragging equipment detector spoke to us. The scripted radio message ought to have been: "Conrail. Conshohoken. Pennsylvania. Track Two. No defects. Over," but when the baritone voice had originally recorded the word Conshohoken, some wag in the background had exclaimed, "Whoopee!", an interjection that had been preserved for ever. The engineer on PICA6 felt it his duty to faithfully repeat the detector, so included "whoopee" in his response!

Train PICA6 passed through another single-track tunnel, Flat Rock Tunnel, guarded by home signals of CP-Rock, to emerge on a narrow ledge shared not only with a major highway, the Schuylkill Expressway, but with high voltage electricity power lines on pylons. Crammed between the river and its steep valley side, there was insufficient room for three utilities to run side by side, so in another arresting sight, electricity pylons straddled the railroad with legs splayed outwards like traditional Thai dancers. So closely did the pylons' shape match the poise of Thai dancers I was reminded of the art every time a train passed beneath them.

Milepost six was passed at West Falls Yard. We were getting close to the end of the line, or the end of the Harrisburg Line anyway. Grappling with the twin constraints of ignorance of our ultimate destination and having spent the entire night for all intents and purposes blindfolded, I nevertheless deduced we were somewhere in central Philadelphia. In the small hours we travelled for a short distance over the southern end of the Trenton Line that ran from Philadelphia to North Jersey.

By the time we neared a station called Belmont, it seemed as if we were at the bottom of a dark canyon. This irrational feeling was to an extent justified by Belmont's being close to the Schuylkill River, which in turn was close to sea level at that point. Subsequent visits to Belmont confirmed absence of artificial lighting from any source, surrounding tall trees making it indeed a dark place at night.

Principally because I had been unable to keep up with radio channel changes, I was completely unaware that a Form D had been obtained for the Shore Secondary, which we entered after beginning to climb out of the Belmont abyss. For about four miles the Shore Secondary ran alongside Amtrak's Northeast Corridor, of which it had once been part. Included in its length was the intriguingly named station Monty. At a station identified as Shore – actually an interlocking on Amtrak – the Shore Secondary and the Northeast Corridor parted company. Soon after, two events occurred simultaneously: the train stopped and dawn broke. Similar to the experience in Reading, I felt as if we had emerged from subterranean captivity. Outside, the conductor beckoned me onto the ground. "We're going to make a set-off here," he said.

"Do you want me to get the switch for you?" I asked, anxious to be useful. The conductor agreed. Paperwork indicated twelve of the eighty-four cars were for Frankford Junction; it was safe to assume that was our location. Remainder of the train was for Pavonia (which sounded like a fictional central-European country) wherever that may be. The set-off made, we were again on the move.

Shortly afterwards, we entered a massive steel construction rising to dizzying heights above us: the Delair Moveable Bridge. Built by the Pennsylvania Railroad in 1896 as a swing bridge, re-built in 1960 as a vertical-lift span and now subject to a ten miles per hour speed restriction, the towering structure took the railroad across the Delaware River. After the bridge, a sharp right-hand curve pointed the train in the opposite direction to which it had been travelling: we had completed a U-turn. Low speed prevailed as PICA6 trundled along trackage obviously not to main line standard. We halted outside a yard office. The conductor called up, "We're done. Grab your stuff."

"Where are we?" I asked.

"Camden."

"What happens to the train?"

"The yard crew will take over and break it down. It's their train now," replied the conductor.

We had crossed the state line on the Delair Bridge to arrive at Pavonia Yard, Camden, New Jersey. PICA stood for Pittsburgh – Camden. Six was the last digit of the train's original departure date, 16th November.

After this initial trip I would always have a soft spot for Camden, in part because it was the first outing on the road, in part because it reminded me of my previous London home where Camden was a well-known suburb.

At that time, 1994, the PICA was crewed by Harrisburg men who took the train east and deadheaded back. The balancing working, the CAPI, was manned by Philadelphia men who similarly deadheaded back. It had been decided that on this occasion we would deadhead back to Harrisburg by Amtrak train. The crew was taxied from Pavonia Yard to Amtrak's palatial Philadelphia 30th Street Station where, having been supplied a special authorization number, we were given free passes at the ticket office.

Four men in railroaders' work clothing (British Railways and Amtrak provided uniforms, Conrail did not) stood around waiting for the Harrisburg train. We placed our bags, which we called grips, at our feet. The conductor, engineer and trainee engineer launched into esoteric railroad conversation, perhaps about seniority. I moved away to sit down and enjoy the art decor of 30th Street Station, an expression of unassailable confidence Pennsylvania Railroad had had in itself and in the ability of its cathedral-like station to lure passengers. Ten fluted pillars numbered in embossed gold characters soared 120 feet to support a ceiling of 372 recessed squares coloured milk chocolate and orange. Twelve additional pillars stood sentinel at ends of the station concourse. As if wishing to both complement and compliment the architectural masterpiece, fashionably attired passengers dashed from this corner to that corner, from ticket office to escalator, from friend to colleague, all done with urgency, the hallmark of a city-dweller. Others sat on station benches with noses buried in paperbacks or the *Philadelphia Inquirer.* What kind of jobs did they all have? Where were they going, and why? Did travelling alone by train suggest being unmarried?

Before long we boarded our train and were swept efficiently back to Harrisburg. Another taxi conveyed us from the railway station to the yard office, where we completed timecards and finished at 12:15 hours on Thursday 17th November. When I arrived home, in high spirits I telephoned the supervisor in charge of trainees to tell him of my first trip out on the road: "It was the most exciting day yet on Conrail!"

At about 23:00 hours that evening the telephone rang. "M.C. Deaver?" asked the crew dispatcher.

"Yes," I replied.

"Need you for the PICA7, 1 o'clock, Harrisburg."

We were going to do it all again!

\* \* \*

Writing about being on the road prompts a discussion on going to the toilet. I will use the children's terms number one and number two for more palatable reading.

Railway and railroad companies would of course have been ecstatic if the same genetic make-up that drew people to work for them also brought on a condition that negated need to use a lavatory, but since that was not the case carriers had to address the matter.

British steam engines were fitted with a urinal on the tender front. I understand the fireman's shovel was used for a number two. In present-day Britain shifts incorporate a physical needs break as most freight train crews comprise only a driver (engineer). In America no such break is provided, road trains just keep moving. When in my normal place on the lead engine of a train and needed to do a number one, I used the toilet in the nose of the locomotive. I endeavoured to hold back if needing to do a number two, but if unavoidable would walk back to the toilet on the second engine, train speed permitting. An engineer would have to wait till the train was brought to a stand before he could do either. Somehow, engineers' needs seemed less. It is of course possible to control workings of the alimentary canal by what is ingested and by how much is ingested in the period leading up to an expected call time, and perhaps engineers were inclined to take those kind of precautions more than conductors. Mind over matter might also play a role in controlling natural bodily functions. At night circadian rhythms suppress activity.

When a locomotive was new the toilet was of course spotlessly clean and fragrant. As the machine aged, despite the carrier's best efforts at cleanliness, the toilet acquired an ineradicable stale bouquet which one learnt to tolerate. Slight olfactory discomfort bothered men little, but one could not help but be sympathetic towards the small number of female railroaders who, though even better at restraint than male engineers, had to use the same facilities.

In yard work a man might readily stand behind a box car to do a number one; such convenience is not available to a woman. Railroads generally were not designed for the opposite sex, but have had to be adapted to meet requirements of non-discriminatory law. And male employees have had to learn to tone down conversations and avoid language that could be construed as sexual harassment. It is these considerations that caused some men to say about female railroaders, "They don't belong out here." However, it seems likely the principal if unspoken objection to women occupying positions traditionally held by men – in the railroad industry and elsewhere - was that it lay siege to the sacred shrine of male superiority.

To conclude in a lighter vein, if, in the Austin Powers series of comedy films the joke of naming Dr. Evil's lieutenant as Number Two was intentional, it was probably widely missed. And back to railroading, in York Windsor Street Yard I recall taking advantage of a parked locomotive to do a number one when an engineer friend came round the corner of the engine and said, "I knew I'd catch you with your pants down sooner or later Deaver!" Of course I had only my zipper down.

# CHAPTER 8

# HARRISBURG

Centrally placed Harrisburg was declared capital of the State of Pennsylvania (or to give it its correct title the Commonwealth of Pennsylvania) at expense of the bigger and better known cities of Philadelphia and Pittsburgh located at the Commonwealth's eastern and western extremities. As with all state capitals, Harrisburg is home of the state governor and of the state legislature that copies the national government in having a Senate and a House of Representatives. When I moved to the United States in 1988 I saw the fifty states as a layer of government additional to that I had known in the United Kingdom: state governments occupied a new position between national and county level. A local level existed below county level in both countries. I have never been able to evaluate how much English county responsibility was handed up to state level in America. Since 1988 an intermediate level of government has been introduced in Scotland and Wales and reintroduced in Northern Ireland, so that the United Kingdom of Great Britain and Northern Ireland is more like the United States of America than it used to be, in that respect anyway. The country of England retains only three layers of government: national, county and local. But enough of governmental matters.

To recognize the unquestionable pre-eminence of Harrisburg as a railroad centre, it is necessary to pull back and look at physical geography. Prehistory was kind to Britain in that it placed a central strip of high land, the Pennines, in line with orientation of the country, bequeathing railways (relatively) easy routes to race north and south either side of the backbone of Britain. Nature was not so obliging to the United States, which is orientated the other way, and where areas of high land running north to south down each side of the country obstruct ready passage. The Appalachian Mountains lay in the east. Mountains often collectively referred to as The Rockies but which properly include the Sierra Nevada and the Cascade, Coast, Wasatch and other ranges occupy the west. Far more formidable than the Appalachians, the western ranges greatly hindered both pioneer settlers and railroad builders. Nevertheless, a 100-ton steam locomotive could no more climb steep slopes of the Pennsylvania Blue Mountains than could a Conestoga wagon. So, before the Rocky Mountains could be tackled, a way had to be found through the Appalachian Chain. Harrisburg provided that way, courtesy of the incision made by the Susquehanna River, as described in the chapter on Enola. True, other routes availed themselves, but the Harrisburg route from Pittsburgh projected a straight line, or very near a straight line, to the cities of Philadelphia and New York. The gateway was adopted by the Pennsylvania Railroad as route for its main line.

At one time the biggest railroad in the world, the Pennsylvania Railroad took on the mantle of exemplar for all others: it called itself the standard railroad. Its four-track main line following a straight course whenever possible would remind British enthusiasts of principal routes into London once owned by the Great Western Railway, the London, Midland and Scottish Railway, the London & North Eastern Railway and the Southern Railway. But just as British Railways underwent drastic surgery during the Beeching era, unfavourable trading conditions during the 1960s forced the Pennsylvania Railroad into a merger with the New York Central Railroad (and with a lesser party, the New York, New Haven & Hartford Railroad) to eventually form Penn Central Transportation Company. The unhappy marriage ultimately ended in bankruptcy. Following intervention by the United States Government, Conrail took over Penn Central and others including the Reading Railroad on 1st April 1976.

Pittsburgh to Harrisburg was and is one of the busiest freight corridors in the United States. From Harrisburg, trains fanned out to the New York area, the Philadelphia area, Baltimore, Hagerstown, Allentown and to Delaware State. I was told New York and Philadelphia traffic at one time took the still four-track main line through Lancaster, or an alternative route, now abandoned, via Enola. That was no longer the case. New York and Philadelphia merchandise was now routed via the former Reading Railroad line, turning one way or other at Reading. New York traffic ended its journey in that part of New Jersey State directly across the Hudson River from New York City, known on the railroad as North Jersey.

A vital hub in Conrail operations, Harrisburg re-fuelled and re-crewed trains. As eastbound trains approached Harrisburg from the Pittsburgh direction, decisions had to be made as to which had priority into Harrisburg. The running order had to be established about two hours before estimated arrival, so that relief crews could be given two hour's notice to report for duty. My experience was that the complex decision-making process worked remarkably well.

Whilst few trains ended their journey in Harrisburg, many stopped to exchange blocks of cars, particularly intermodal traffic. Intermodal trains carried time-sensitive goods in either trailers secured to flat cars or containers secured to flat cars. The British term articulated lorry is translated in America to rig or to tractor and trailer, the latter expression normally only associated with farming in Britain. Success of intermodal business depended on trains running to time, even if traincrews were not told what that time was. If intermodal trains ran late, carriers, as railroad companies were often called, were subject to hefty penalties, so men and management in Harrisburg gave their all to dispatch intermodal trains in a timely manner. The supervisory task was not easy, as revealed by lined features and chain-smoking habits of trainmasters held responsible for operations. One can imagine telephone conversations if things did not go right.

"And why was the intermodal train thirty minutes late leaving Harrisburg?"

"Well, we had a new guy helping because the regular guy was sick, and the new guy's radio packed up," replied the trainmaster.

"Doesn't this man know his radio has got to be in good working order before he starts a shift?"

"He says he hadn't used it much recently, so he thought there was plenty of charge in the battery," answered the trainmaster.

"Don't we issue these new guys with spare batteries?"

"Yes, but because he was working in the yard he didn't think he needed to carry a spare."

"This still doesn't explain why the train was thirty minutes late leaving Harrisburg."

"The guy was way down the yard when his radio gave out. He couldn't radio for help, so he had to walk back to the yard office. We gave him a lift back to where he was, but all this took time."

"Is this man still working for us?" asked the voice testily.

"I don't think we could put him on the street just for his battery running out," replied the trainmaster wearily.

The above conversation is pure fabrication, though I personally had some unpleasant experiences with radio batteries. The imaginary exchange is intended to illustrate what I sensed to be tremendous pressure on trainmasters to keep intermodals on time.

I was hired to work east from Harrisburg, which meant serving North Jersey, the Philadelphia area, Baltimore, Hagerstown, Allentown and Delaware State. Many trains were timed to arrive in New York and Philadelphia areas by dawn so merchandise could be delivered that day to satisfy the cities' voracious appetites for consumer goods. The PICA was just one example; I would see many more.

Once men were hired to work either east or west out of Harrisburg, they could not change sides without first resigning and starting afresh with zero seniority. I do not think anybody ever did. Those working west were often referred to as Middle Division men, a relic from Pennsylvania Railroad days. From what I could see, there seemed to be little interaction between east and west men, as if a Berlin Wall separated them. A similar state of affairs existed when I was signalman on the London Midland Region of British Railways. If I had wanted to transfer to, say, the Eastern Region, I would have had to resign and start over. Like the Berlin Wall, both immovable barriers eventually fell, allowing British signalmen to move anywhere in the country, and Harrisburg traincrews to work either east or west. Harrisburg yard office was principal signing-on point for what was termed the Harrisburg Consolidated Terminal (which included nearby Enola and Shiremanstown Yards) and would be where I would most frequently report for duty.

* * *

Harrisburg yard office was always called GI8. Nobody knew why. There was no GI7 nor GI9, nor GI1 for that matter. The story was told that two officials were discussing naming the yard office. One said to the other, "Let's go and get a bite to eat. Have you thought of a name for the new yard office yet?" to which the other replied, "Gee, I ate!" which elicited a response from the first man, "Right, that's what we'll call it, GI8." A more plausible explanation is that GI stood for General Inventory, and GI8 was the eighth building on the list, all others having since disappeared.

I was working in Harrisburg one day when I heard the yardmaster say over the radio, "Yardmaster to the Thirty-one crew."

"Thirty-one crew," they replied.

"What are you doing at the moment?"

"Talking to you on the radio," the crew replied.

"I meant what work are you doing right now," said the yardmaster with mock irritation.

It was clear the yard crew enjoyed a good working relationship with their supervisor, otherwise impertinence would not have been tolerated.

On another occasion in GI8, two men entertained all who listened by impersonating each other's dog. One said, "You should see his dog, it waddles along like this." He then feigned staggering one foot at a time as if grossly overweight. The stocky victim of this lampoon responded by saying, "You should see *his* dog." He then imitated a dog panting, and between pants saying "Penn State, Penn State!" alluding to the other man being a fan of Penn State American football team.

Another amusing incident, though not funny at the time, involved a train on which I was riding being held up behind another on one of the long sidings in Harrisburg Yard. Radio conversations revealed the train ahead needed a replacement air hose, so I set off with a spare hose from our lead engine, together with what in Britain is called a spanner, in America a wrench. Not long after setting off, the radio informed a hose had been found, so I dropped mine but kept walking in case assistance were still needed. A car inspector in his vehicle saw this and thought I had dropped the hose through weariness, so he picked it up and brought it to me. I had not the heart to tell him it was no longer needed, so had to carry it to the point of repair and all the way back again to the locomotive.

Seasoned yard conductors had to suffer new employees. Sometimes the most straightforward moves were beyond comprehension of new brakemen who had no grasp whatsoever of yard layouts, who had not the foggiest idea what conductors were trying to do, nor why. I recall a conductor telling me, "Over to number three," and being in such a state of confusion I could not absorb what he said. Seeing my bewilderment, the conductor patiently elaborated on this most basic shifting instruction: "After we pull out of this track, we're going to put some cars on number three track." Yard conductors, especially those of Penn Central or Pennsylvania Railroad origin, were the most solid and reliable of men, square in feature, stance and disposition, plodding in mission, unruffled by irregularity, expert in finding economical moves, masters of all nuances and variables in their work and forbearing beyond the call of duty when dealing with ineptness of new employees.

At a later date, when shifting skills were better developed, curiosity drove me to ask a conductor, "Why are we taking these cars from number five track to number seven?"

"'Cause the yardmaster said so," came the reply.

"Yes I know, but why?"

"'Cause he's the boss," was the matter-of-fact explanation.

The conductor misunderstood. I was trying to uncover a reason for the move. Maybe it was to consolidate traffic for the same destination, and to make room for more inbound cars. I took the matter no further.

Working in Harrisburg Yard may have had its moments of levity; learning its layout did not. Again, the initial difficulty was orientation. The highway route from the centre of Harrisburg City took so many twists and turns by the time I arrived at GI8 I had no idea which way I was facing. Harrisburg and Enola Yards sat either side of the Susquehanna River which flowed north to south at this point, but because Pittsburgh through Harrisburg to the east coast was obviously west to east, both yards were considered running west to east for railroad purposes. I eventually rammed into my recalcitrant brain that if I stood in front of GI8 facing tracks, to turn left would be looking to the railroad's east even though the compass said south, to turn right, towards the hills, would be looking west even though the compass said north. The first forty-five years of life had locked me into the British north-south way of thinking, reinforced during youth by ever-present ranges of hills so aligned. To find myself now in a country where emphasis was primarily west-east required that I completely re-calibrate. Assistance came in train identities. Trains with a numeric identity heading east had even numbers, for example TV2, those heading west odd numbers, such as TV1. Trains heading north on the Buffalo Line (covered by men working west) had even numbers, southbound odd numbers. This was universal practice in America.

Once this most basic aspect of railroad operations – knowing in which direction a train was heading - had been mastered, the layout of Harrisburg Yard could be tackled. I will ignore the compass and use official directions. To begin, Harrisburg Yard was bounded by CP-Rockville in the west and CP-Harris in the east. The most southerly track, the one nearest the Susquehanna River, was the Single Track of the Pittsburgh Line. At CP-Harris the Pittsburgh Line ended and the Harrisburg Line began. The Pittsburgh Line Single Track ran between the two aforementioned interlockings without connecting to any other track. Next to the Single Track was the Controlled Siding, a term which meant signals at each end controlled entrance and exit. (The British equivalent would be a goods loop, though the American models were usually much longer.) Both the Single Track and Controlled Siding came under the control of the Harrisburg Terminal Train Dispatcher. Midway, the Controlled Siding had two hand-thrown switches that let into Harrisburg Yard proper, switches which were subject to special procedures to operate them.

The remainder of Harrisburg Yard was run by the yardmaster. Whereas Enola Yard could be reduced to four basic components, the layout of Harrisburg Yard was a tangle. If one took up a position to the east of CP-Rockville at about milepost 108.5, the list of tracks from south to north would read Single Track, Controlled Siding, Eastbound, 5-and-5, 6-and-5, Westbound, Old Westbound, New 2, New 14, 2, 3, 4, 4A, 5 Spur, 5, 6, 7, 8. Upon taking up a position two miles further east, the list of south to north tracks would read Single Track, Controlled Siding, 3 Relay, 4 Relay, 8SK, 9SK, 11-and-2, 12-and-2, 13-and-2, 15-and-2, 18-and-2, 19-and-2, Eastbound, 5 Relay,

6 Relay, 7 Relay, Westbound, 13, 14, 15, 16, 17, 18, 24. At other positions between CP-Rockville and CP-Harris the south-to-north list would be different yet again. GI8 yard office stood about half-way. In front of it, a grid of switches permitted trains to cross east and west from just about any track to just about any track. The overall layout resembled a sheaf of corn tied in the middle.

New employees used to complain, "Why don't they re-number the tracks in order?" The response was that, whilst it would make life easier for the small number of trainees, it would make work difficult for a far greater number of employees who had been using the present numbering system for decades.

Nomenclature such as 8SK and 9SK was baffling. "What's SK mean?" I asked one conductor.

"Nobody knows," he said. "At one time it must have stood for something, but nobody can remember what."

Logic seemed lacking. On another occasion I asked, "Why are the tracks numbered 11-and-2, 12-and-2, and so on? It doesn't make sense."

"That's just how they're numbered," was the unhelpful explanation.

Within Harrisburg yard four smaller yards were identifiable, numbered 1, 2, 4 and 5. I suspect tracks 11-and-2, 12-and-2 were at one time 11-*in*-2, 12-*in*-2, and that frequent usage resulted in their being known as 11-'n-2, 12-'n-2, which over time were corrupted to the present names.

Many classmates began their training in Harrisburg Yard, much of it in daylight, and they became familiar with it. Having spent my formative weeks in Lancaster, Harrisburg Yard was never fully mastered. Some corners remained unknown. In the future, when I was responsible for moving trains over the criss-cross of tracks in front of GI8 – particularly at night and particularly when handling intermodal trains – I would keep my map firmly in hand to avoid mistakes. The yardmaster, from his elevated position in the stilted yard office, could see this. One night, he instructed me over the radio, "Mail9 engines, okay from the Westbound through the Lower Crossover, Eastbound, West Extension to Number 1 Fuel Pad – if you can find your way."

* * *

Harrisburg Yard became setting for two momentous face-to-face encounters, the first with a signal. Pennsylvania Railroad position light signals so far described have been what in Britain were described as running signals, in America as high signals: those that govern normal movement on main lines. Lesser signalling functions were carried out in Britain by, in mechanical form, disc ground signals, in electric form, small position light signals. The Pennsylvania Railroad equivalent of British position light ground signals were very similar in construction, and were termed dwarf signals. They stood about two feet tall, were triangular in shape, and displayed, for example, two horizontal white lights for STOP SIGNAL.

The Pennsylvania Railroad designed a third type of signal, intermediate between high and dwarf, known as a pedestal signal. Men working east out of Harrisburg had to know the railroad a few miles into west territory, to CP-Banks on the Pittsburgh Line, to CP-Stoney on the Buffalo Line. A train had to be taken to CP-Stoney. On arrival at the high signal on the Buffalo Line Single Track, we applied hand brakes, alighted and waited for a taxi back to GI8. Home signal for movements from the Buffalo Line Controlled Siding was a pedestal signal. (Home signal in both Britain and America means the first in a series of controlled stop signals – controlled as opposed to automatic.) I walked over for a closer look at the extraordinary object. It stood about six feet tall, and looked as if two dwarf signals had been stacked on top of one another, then both mounted on a three-foot stem. In their aspects, pedestal signals mimicked high signals, save that they used two white lights in place of three amber lights. Thus STOP SIGNAL was two horizontal white lights, CLEAR two vertical lights. When both upper and lower parts of pedestal signals were illuminated, the aspect took on the appearance of a domino piece.

Pedestal signals were used where speeds were low but where a dwarf signal would be inadequate, and were also used where space restrictions disallowed a high signal. I heard of no other railroad producing an intermediate between high and dwarf signal. British practice permitted a tall siding signal, a miniature semaphore arm on a full-sized post, which filled a similar niche.

A second momentous encounter brought to life a character whom a Briton could be forgiven for believing existed only in fiction, the hobo. We had a consist of four engines, and before departing GI8 the engineer asked a favour, that I walk through each of the engines to ensure all were set up for normal running rather than idling mode. I readily agreed to this simple task of checking locomotive isolation switches. On arrival at the last engine, a man sprawled out on the cab floor stopped me in my tracks. My first thought was a sick colleague. I spoke to him. He did not stir. I shook him. "Wha... wha..." he said.

"Are you all right?" I asked.

"I'm okay," he said in slurred speech of someone who had just emerged from deep slumber.

"What are you doing here?" I pursued.

"Nothing. You know, just riding," he replied nonchalantly.

Only then did I realize he was a hobo. For a moment I did not know what to do. Hobos had not been discussed in class, but then I remembered we were told to escort trespassers off the property. A violent confrontation did not seem in the offing, so I said, "You can't stay here. You're going to have to get off."

"I won't harm anything, man, you know, just hopping a ride," he said.

"I know, but you might get injured. We're gonna have to get you off," I said, inventing an excuse.

"Where am I?"

"Harrisburg."

"Pittsburgh?"

"No, Harrisburg."

"Where's that?"

The hobo had not heard of Harrisburg. I told him it was about one hundred miles from Philadelphia, and repeated that he needed to get off the train. With great reluctance, he heaved his weary self off the cab floor and, with some help from me, negotiated engine steps to alight at ground level. He was a well-built individual, clean shaven and not at all shabby – in fact his appearance was quite respectable. Nevertheless, the eviction had to be completed so, applying gentle pressure to one arm, I escorted him across the GI8 parking lot to the access road, much to the amusement of traincrews going to and from work. "I'm going to have to get back to the train," I said to the man. "Follow this road to the main road, then turn right and head for Harrisburg city centre. There's a place there that'll give you something to eat, and maybe give you a hand with things." Bewildered, he studied me momentarily, half smiled, turned and trudged off down the road to begin the next phase of his uncertain life in a place called Harrisburg, Pennsylvania.

# CHAPTER 9

## JITNEY

The American word jitney seldom sees the light of day in Britain, at least I never heard it. Neither have I encountered its use in the States outside Conrail, where currency may or not be further limited to Eastern Pennsylvania. It must have been early days in Lancaster when, at the end of the day's work, someone said to me, "We'll have to wait for the jitney to pick us up."

"What's a jitney?" I asked.

"Taxi."

I was told the word jitney originally described small motorized rail vehicles that used to convey brakemen back after riding cars down a hump, though it is not clear how the jitney avoided oncoming railroad cars nor how it made its way back to the far end of the hump yard to pick up more men. As used in the 1990s the word applied both to Conrail work trucks that ferried employees around a yard and to commercial vehicles that deadheaded crews to and from remote locations which could be as far away as a couple of hundred miles. Vehicles on such long hauls were neither the familiar British black hackney cab nor the yellow taxis seen on New York streets, but a vehicle referred to as a van. Since my childhood days a van had always meant a small enclosed delivery vehicle, but in 1990s America it was a vehicle seating six or eight, half way between a large saloon car and a minibus, typified by the Dodge Caravan. The British equivalent was termed a people mover. In America the design was later superseded by sports utility vehicles.

In Harrisburg the separation of jitney duties between shuffling crews around yards and conveying them elsewhere was strictly observed, with external haulage being contracted to a local taxi firm. That contract included a shuttle service when required between Harrisburg and Enola Yards. A crew could work a train from Enola to Philadelphia, stay in a hotel, and bring a train back from Philadelphia to Harrisburg, but because they had signed on in Enola they needed a ride back there for their vehicles. In such cases the tour of duty strictly speaking ended in Harrisburg where the timecard should have been closed and where the crew would have had to hitch a ride on the next train to Enola in their own time. Conrail granted a concession however in allowing the timecard to be kept open and providing transportation to Enola. Such a service would be announced by the jitney driver bursting into GI8 with the esoteric proclamation: "Two for the Brick!"

Sometimes when learning the road I would work out with one crew and come back with another. In one case we arrived back in Enola and obtained a jitney ride to Harrisburg. On arrival at GI8 I searched for my red Ford Escort. I could not find it. Then I remembered Enola had been my original signing on point. A jitney had to take me back again!

We seldom had to wait long for the local taxi company, even for a short hop across the Susquehanna. The firm was not allowed to park vehicles on Conrail's property; I do not know where they waited in the wings. Service was not so splendid in North Jersey, where I understand taxi drivers, who inexplicably were all Egyptian, took their vehicles home. It was from home that they were called to work. On two occasions at Manville Yard, about twenty-five miles from North Jersey terminal, I had to wait about two hours. Presumably the driver had been called from home somewhere in the greater New York City metropolitan area and took that long to reach Manville. Whilst we waited I read the notice boards top to bottom, walked round and round the office block for exercise, looked at the boring notice boards again and sat at the messing table with head hung in hands in despair. One crew waited at Manville for a record six hours. After three or four hours had passed and a couple of angry telephone calls had been made, what can one do? How long can a person continue waiting before frustration reaches distressing levels?

Despite occasional lengthy waits, men I worked with displayed a penchant for deadheading one way rather than staying in hotels, with a preference for working out and deadheading back. I grew to detest deadheading mainly because I had a long drive to and from work, but also because I thought it wasteful. I might have been the only railroader of that frame of mind. In the case of Allentown work it also seemed that more money could be made by staying in the hotel.

"You see, if we stay in the hotel, we stand a good chance of two ten-hour days, one out, one back. So that's sixteen hours at basic rate and four hours overtime in total," I said to an engineer. "But if we deadhead one way, we only get the equivalent of about eleven-and-a-half hours at basic rate."

"I know that," said the engineer, "but you're back home sooner when you deadhead one way, and you're out again quicker for another trip, so you're better off."

"Yeh, but if you take into account the cost of gas (petrol in Britain) to and from work, which is quite a lot in my case, and you also take into account that we get a meal allowance when we stay in the hotel," I argued, "I think we make more money not deadheading."

"I tell you what," said the engineer somewhat disturbed by this logic, "if that's what you believe, you stay away from me with that kind of thinking!"

The engineer obviously stuck to the widely held belief that deadheading one way was more remunerative. Weary of highway travel, I was unreceptive to the idea. A solution of moving closer to Harrisburg was not countenanced because the property my wife and I had bought was a unique stone-built cottage of chocolate-box prettiness, irreplaceable.

An example of deadheading one way would be a coal train from Harrisburg to Allentown with footboard relief at each end. Footboard relief was where one crew alighted and another immediately took over. (Such a trip between two terminals with no work along the way was sometimes referred to as a straight shot.) For the purposes of examining the hypothesis that staying in hotels generated more income than deadheading, I am going to assume an average overall time for an Allentown deadhead-one-way trip of eleven hours, that Harrisburg Consolidated Terminal to Bethlehem Allentown Consolidated Terminal one-way trips took on average ten hours, that time at home between trips was an average of fourteen hours and that time in the hotel averaged ten hours. On the basis of these admittedly grand assumptions it transpired the theory held up: about six per cent more money was earned by staying in the hotel than by deadheading. Even if the arithmetic were unchallenged, most crews would argue that staying in hotels was not worth the extra cash, they would rather go home after every shift.

* * *

Jitneys and the personnel who drove them were a vital part of Conrail's operations. Jitney drivers knew that. Some aspired to the dizzying heights they perceived traincrews occupied. Whilst on the GI8 access road one day, a jitney driver exclaimed, "There's a roadrailer just leaving!"

The engineer had to correct the driver. "That's actually an intermodal train." Roadrailer trains comprised highway trailers strung together mounted on special trucks that raised them a few inches above rail level. As intermodal trains often included trailers tied down to flat cars, the driver's mistake was forgivable.

If a jitney driver seriously wanted to join the ranks of those he ferried around, theoretically there was nothing stopping him. When one driver complained of being desperately poor, I said to him, "Our wages are not too bad. Why don't you get a job on Conrail?"

"I couldn't," the man said sadly. "I'm illiterate." My heart went out to him.

A misunderstanding arose with another man. As we loaded our grips into his van, he complained of being overworked. "Are you getting harassed?" I asked.

"Harrist, where's he going?" My British emphasis on the first syllable caused confusion.

A language problem again arose concerning telemetry markers, devices that, in addition to displaying a flashing red light, radioed to the locomotive what the air brake pressure was at the rear of the train. Too many devices had accumulated in Enola. Several had to be urgently taxied to Pittsburgh, and a jitney driver was duly instructed to pick up telemetries from Enola. On arrival at the Brick Office he told the yardmaster, "I'm here to pick up two lemon trees."

An Allentown jitney driver new to the job called at the motel to pick up a Harrisburg crew. When asked where they wanted to go, the crew said to the Wawa, a convenience store where crews regularly bought provisions for the journey home. After the men disappeared into the shop, the driver thought his task was complete and drove back to Allentown Yard leaving them stranded. Nobody had explained he was supposed to *wait*. Imagine the crew's shock when they emerged to find no jitney.

The Wawa chain in Eastern Pennsylvania was popular amongst Conrail crews. The retailer's extensive range of nourishing snack foods were ideal to munch on when riding. I typically bought a coffee, a sandwich, a container of fruit and occasionally indulged in a bar of chocolate. The convenience stores, which took their name from the town of Wawa which was a native American word for wild goose, were just as much part of Conrail's life on the road as were jitneys.

A female jitney driver in Lancaster had several piercings about her face that were plugged with rings and pins, as was the vogue. The chauffeuse must have taken her adornments very seriously, evidently travelling great distances to have them done because she confided in us that she had had some done up north and was thinking about having some done down south.

Self-mutilation in the name of fashion was always a mystery to me. Tattoos have been around a long time, but in the 2000s enjoyed a resurgence in popularity amongst younger people. Earrings enjoy similar longevity, but jewelry fastened to a woman's eyebrows, nose, lips and tongue – facial ironmongery that can hardly be said to enhance her appearance - has seen an explosion in popularity. In the 1990s the phenomenon of branding took hold whereby young men had a limb stamped with a hot branding iron.

To return to the subject of jitneys, when I first took rest in North Jersey it was surprising to find we were treated like royalty, initially being conveyed from sidings to office by yard jitney, then yard to hotel by taxi firm. But working the road I soon became accustomed to being chaperoned about, which not only kept trains moving but which provided income to some jitney drivers who would otherwise have none. Crews and jitney drivers came to know one another well enough to allow a measure of amity to develop, inasmuch as amity may be allowed to develop in the gritty business of railroading. Several stories have been worth repeating, but The Tale of the Incontinent Taxi Driver has had to be omitted as it is too sordid to repeat. Even in this book.

# CHAPTER 10

# NEW YEAR'S EVE

The final weeks of 1994 saw increased demand for brakemen in Harrisburg Consolidated Terminal, so I was taken off learning the road and placed on an extra list resulting in several turns on three-man crews. Another position filled was utility man, a floating brakeman who worked with different two-man crews, but only ever with one crew at a time. In such circumstances the utility man had to identify himself: "This is utility man Deaver, I'll be a member of your crew." A utility man assignment in Harrisburg had me working with an intermodal train crew. I relied heavily on the yard jitney driver's familiarity with operations to be in the right place at the right time to make cuts and throw switches.

In November I had passed an examination for promotion to conductor, an accomplishment that had bearing on events as the year drew to a close. I had worked on Thursday 29th December, had not been called on Friday the 30th, and had been hoping to spend Saturday New Year's Eve with my wife, when the telephone rang.

"Mr. Deaver?"

"Yes."

"Mr. Deaver, my name is [so-and-so]. I'm the Chief Crew Dispatcher. We have a bit of a problem." At that point I wondered what on earth was in store. "We need to run a train to Pittsburgh but we can't find a conductor. Now, we know you're not qualified to work west, but you are a qualified conductor, and what we can do is have a qualified engineer with you who'll act as conductor. You see, the union agreement says that we must have a member of both the UTU and the BLE on each train. So we wonder if you'd help us out here

by being the UTU representative on this train." (UTU is the United
Transportation Union, BLE Brotherhood of Locomotive Engineers.)

Swaying with shock, I said, "Just... just hold on a minute." I
covered the handset and turned to my wife who had been drawn to
the odd conversation. "They want me to go to Pittsburgh."

"I thought you weren't allowed to go to Pittsburgh," she said.

"I'm not, normally. This is something special, something to do
with the union contract."

My wife shrugged her shoulders. Clearly disappointed, she said,
"Well, I had planned a New Year's Eve meal for you, but I suppose
it can wait."

After a few more quiet words were exchanged with my wife, who
by now had become resigned to bowing to whims of the railroad, I
was able to tell the Chief Crew Dispatcher I could do it.

"Thank you very much Mr. Deaver. I'm going to put you on to
the crew dispatcher now who'll give you the details."

The assignment was Mail3 Harrisburg to Columbus, Ohio State,
on duty at 12:30. Having been forewarned of an overnight hotel stay,
I set off with full grip and lunch box. At GI8 I met the other two crew
members. The engineer proper was a mild mannered middle-aged
bespectacled man who greeted the interloper with a smile. A younger
man, the surrogate conductor, remained distant. It is only now as I
write this narrative that I see a possible explanation for his coolness:
had I not acceded to the Chief Crew Dispatcher's request, both the
conductor pilot and engineer would probably have had New Year's
Eve at home with their families. The two men nevertheless advised
me on paperwork and guided me to the train. I was allowed to occupy
the conductor's position in the front of the cab, directly opposite the
engineer. The conductor pilot took a back seat. The engineer lent me
his Rule Book which of course included station pages for the complete
Pittsburgh Line - enabling me to reply to various lineside detectors
that talked to us along the route. Locomotive consist comprised Class
SD40-2 numbers 6454, 6500 and 6992. The train consist was seventy-
nine cars totalling 5530 tons with an axle count of 410.

The 275-mile journey began by crossing Rockville Bridge, first of
several items of American railroad lore we would see. A few minutes
later, I noticed the engineer look back over his shoulder at the train,
but attached little significance as it was part of both engineer and

conductor's duties. He then beckoned me over, and pointed towards the rear window. I looked back to see far away rear of a train crossing Rockville Bridge. "That's our hind end," said the engineer.

"Is it really!" I exclaimed. The train was two miles long. Tiny freight cars creeping along at great distance looked like a model train set and seemed unconnected to the locomotive on which I was travelling. But they were, and in skillful hands of the engineer they remained that way. The next icon on this exceptional journey was the town of Altoona, whose railroad tracks hustled and bustled like a busy market place. We paused there from 17:00 hours till 17:09 to attach two helper engines for assistance up the gradient that lay ahead. Otherwise known as a pusher engine, such assisting power is referred to as a banker in Britain because it assists in pushing up banks. Even with modern motive power, helper engines are still employed at certain locations in America. Use of bankers was widespread in Britain during steam engine days; the Lickey Incline south of Birmingham still sees banker duty during the 2010s.

Shortly after leaving Altoona we met the Horseshoe Curve, famous not just in Pennsylvania, nor in the United States alone, but known amongst railway enthusiasts the world over. I had heard of it whilst still in Britain long before any hint of moving to the States; little did I know one day I would be riding round it. Such is the standing of this piece of railroad infrastructure it is classified a National Historic Landmark. As train Mail3 entered the right-hand horn of the horseshoe, the engineer announced the fact in case I failed to notice. The conductor's seat afforded a view down into Kittanning Valley whilst the train made a long steady left-hand sweep round the monument. Dusk settled. As the head of our train exited the left-hand horn of the horseshoe, the engineer pointed across the valley to the tail end just entering the right-hand horn, where we could see two helper engines hard at work. Not long after the Horseshoe Curve we plunged into Gallitzin tunnel, which at the time was being heightened to take double-stacked containers on intermodal trains. A stop from 17.47 to 17.53 at a location identified as MO allowed the helper engines to detach.

Darkness prevailed for much of the journey. Burying my face in the rule book following progress in order to respond to talking detectors robbed me of the rare opportunity to study the scenery, the people, the architecture, the industry, the atmosphere of Western Pennsylvania, though such a survey, of course, would be hampered by the tenebrous mask of a mid-winter's night. Nevertheless, I doggedly drew my finger down station pages keeping track of every interlocking, every detector, every station that was a station just because it was a location. The avalanche of new place-names tested concentration. As night wore on, the never-ending list of stations on the Pittsburgh Line began to lose the aura in which they had initially bathed. Lineside features no longer stood out like castles on a Scottish loch, but leaned drunkenly against a backdrop of uncertain landscape – signals, interlockings, sidings, all drooped as novelty wore off and weariness settled in. Though I was merely a token union representative on this assignment not expected to master the railroad in one trip, I lamented fleeing perspicacity.

This difficulty in focussing mercifully came to an abrupt end when the city of Pittsburgh burst into view. In high school we were taught the city was an important steel-manufacturing centre. By the time I moved to the United States, that reputation had faded as Pittsburgh, along with all other steel towns in the western world, suffered severe decline owing in part to the oil price-induced slumps of the 1970s and 1980s, in part to competition from emergent economies. But that appraisal had ill-prepared me for the splendid view of new Pittsburgh now presenting itself, a city filled with sparkling futuristic towers that glistened like polished candelabra. Paying little attention to the railroad still streaming towards me, I gazed at what looked like a luminous hand-painted film set, a gloriously shining crystal city. It took another shock to tear my concentration away from city lights and back to the railroad: we sailed through Pittsburgh passenger station without a stop.

"I thought all these trains just went as far as Pittsburgh?" I said to the engineer.

"Conway," he replied.

"But," I persisted, "I worked a PICA. I thought the PI meant it started off from Pittsburgh."

"They all start from Conway. It's about another twenty miles further on."

"I wonder why they don't call it COCA instead of PICA?"

The engineer shrugged his shoulders. It was an unchallengeable fact that Conrail chose to designate these trans-Appalachian trains PI even though Pittsburgh was some distance from Conway Yard. By contrast, Conrail sometimes differentiated between trains for Enola and Harrisburg, only a few miles apart, by the letters EN and HB.

So on we rolled to Conway. As our destination drew close, a fine misty drizzle developed, so I donned waterproof clothing including a southwester, ready to work in the elements. Those preparations proved unnecessary. The train stopped at CP-Freedom at 21:15, where we got off and were bundled into a jitney with no time for me to remove waterproofs.

As we travelled to the hotel, I said to the conductor pilot, "I suppose we had better be prepared to be out on our rest." Since we had been on duty less than twelve hours, the telephone could ring at 03:15 for a return trip.

"No, no, no," he assured. "On these long trips you're not normally out on your rest. It's going to be at least sixteen hours before we go back."

With that comforting news, I relaxed, sank back, and allowed the taxi seat to swallow me up for the ride to the hotel.

* * *

Three men pleased to be finished work expeditiously tumbled out of the jitney and strode towards the hotel reception area to find a party going on, a New Year's Eve party! Security personnel, who may have muttered something under their breath, could do nothing to prevent our entering, the Conrail contract had to be honoured, party or no party. The engineer and conductor pilot in obvious but respectable work clothing made their way to the reception desk to book in, but in so doing had to pick their way through fluttering giggling young women in cocktail dresses and high-spirited inebriated young men in fashionable attire. I, in my bright yellow rain-wear and still wearing a southwester, followed. A hotel under-manager whose task it was to scan all arrivals to ensure clientele were only of the highest calibre to enjoy a party the hotel was laying on despaired at my two colleagues in their workaday clothing, then slumped apoplectically into a chair at sight of a North Sea fisherman.

After booking in, I raced to the room, freshened up, changed, and returned to the bar to celebrate New Year's Eve. The hotel offered a buffet meal for $7.44, of which I took full advantage. Neither of my colleagues came to the bar, but I struck up conversation with another whom I was somehow able to recognize as a fellow Conrail worker. After a few drinks together, he left, possibly because he was expecting to be called out earlier than I was. As midnight approached, I leant against the bar nursing a glass of beer, enjoying the spectacle of drunken young people shaking off last of their inhibitions. Close by, a pleasant young woman remarked how much she would like to be with a man that night, or words to that effect. Happily married, I was content to watch others in the process of searching out a mate, to observe a man confidently say the right words to generate a broad smile of approval from the woman he had chosen to pursue. I mentally kicked the man off the dance floor to take his place, to briefly relive heady bachelor days of chasing the opposite sex. Excitement of those times twenty years ago was heightened by never knowing the outcome, never knowing at which point on an emotional spectrum that spread from icy rejection to effervescent glee a woman might respond. Yet, as memories clandestinely took me back, I was free from the underlying unsatisfactoriness of that rakish existence, free from the loneliness.

Just the right amount of excessive drinking – enough to relax one completely but not too much to make one ill – can occasionally, as happened here, induce a state of euphoria. Not only was I in the middle of an extraordinary train journey, I had, courtesy of a Pittsburgh hotel, travelled back in time and relived misspent youth whilst contemporaneously enjoying benefits of a stable marriage. A television suspended above the bar showed the midnight ball drop in New York City. I shook hands with those close by, and gazed across the dance floor at couples dancing to slow music. A sloppy grin of contentment passed across my face. A mild state of reverie was interrupted by the bartender who tapped my elbow and handed me another bottle of beer. When I asked who bought it, he pointed to a man across the other side of the bar, who grinned and waved a small wave. I unquestioningly mouthed a thank you and happily accepted the beer. In other circumstances, one would have been wary, but I think the man was genuinely delighted to see it still possible for a fellow being to reach a state of absolute bliss, and thought the achievement worth rewarding.

The free bottle of beer was the last I drank before retiring. Once in the hotel room, I collapsed on the bed, only to find the room spinning round. I sat upright, laid down again when the same sensation occurred, and sat upright again to stave off nausea. To find a room revolving after drinking an excess of beer was an experience not unknown to the author, though I had never analyzed it. Had I attempted an investigation, the initial assessment that the room was rotating would have been dismissed as structurally improbable. A second idea, that eyeballs were rotating 360 degrees within their sockets would soon be dismissed as anatomically impossible. A theory that eyes were not spinning at all but were habitually moving to one side and being brought back to a central position by a blink could never be tested, because one could not simultaneously experience the condition and observe it in a mirror.

Investigation or no investigation, at about 01:00 hours it was clear that sleep was out of the question, so I switched on the television. On the road, sitting on a hotel bed against the headboard with television remote control unit in hand was a common pastime. Up and down the television channels I flicked, compelled to do so for fear of the sickening room-spinning alternative, though I found little of interest. I halted at one channel, unable to discern the subject matter. I concluded it was a lesson in bread-making, with close-up of the baker kneading dough. When a third hand appeared, I decided it was a wrestling match. When that assessment did not match the action, after a period of bewilderment, it became clear the surging screen was a film suitable only for limited audiences.

\* \* \*

Skating up and down television channels on NewYear's Day found actor Peter Ustinov narrating with extraordinary eloquence a BBC programme on classical music. I make no pretence at being knowledgeable on the subject – when listening to BBC radio I coloured with discomfort when in the 1970s Robert Robinson said on "Stop the Week": "Oh, you *stayed* for the Debussy!" - but I do enjoy listening to it from time to time. A further consideration is that on New Year's Day 1995, perhaps the mind needed purging.

The programme discussed, with passages, the music of Beethoven and Bach, but also covered more obscure topics, the most memorable being a story from the period when conductors kept time by thumping the floor with a large staff, and where one hapless conductor missed the floor, struck his foot, failed to seek treatment, and unfortunately died from his injuries, a rare occupational fatality.

The return trip from Pittsburgh to Harrisburg would be a train of mixed freight, on duty at 17:30 hours. When reporting to the hotel lobby, I was surprised to find a different engineer. He introduced himself and explained: "On this pool, they allow the engineer more time in the hotel than the conductor. You know, he has more responsibility. Often, the conductor hasn't much to do. Usually, he just gets on at one end and gets off the other, so they reckon he can make do with less rest."

During the course of the round trip, I learnt another peculiarity of the Conway Pool. A pool, as far as railroading is concerned, is a number of employees whose work is limited to certain routes. The Morrisville Pool, for example, comprised about eight crews – a paired engineer and conductor – who worked solely between Harrisburg Consolidated Terminal and Morrisville, north of Philadelphia. The Conway Pool differed not only in engineer and conductor not remaining together, but in the fact that it was double-ended: one pool was based in Harrisburg, one in Conway. The question then arises, if a crew is required in Conway, does the crew dispatcher call a Harrisburg crew from the hotel, or a Conway crew from home? The answer is that it is done on a two-to-one basis: two crews are called from the hotel, then one crew from home.

With the pilot acting as conductor and myself as brakeman, we assembled the train in Conway Yard. A train of mixed freight is slower and less important than a mail train, and consequently not given priority. Some men disparagingly refer to mixed freight as junkers, ignoring the fact that an assortment of cars creates jobs for others to sort them, and further jobs to get single-car loads to their ultimate destination. As night progressed, it seemed unlikely we would have sufficient time to make it all the way to Harrisburg within the twelve-hour legal limit imposed on traincrews, because we would probably be held back in favour of faster trains. (Railroaders employ a number of terms to describe reaching the twelve-hour limit: blowing up, outlawed, Cinderella time.) We were instructed by the train dispatcher to end our journey at CP-Port, near the town of Newport, some twenty-five miles from home. After applying necessary hand brakes to secure the train – tying it down is the expression used - we deadheaded to GI8 and were off duty at 06:00. Twelve hours may be exceeded provided the extra time is for deadheading purposes only.

\* \* \*

The one and only train excursion to Pittsburgh afforded an excellent opportunity to study the Pennsylvania Railroad position light signals, to compare them with British signalling. There is a major difference. British operations employ directional signalling, in other words, controlled signals at a junction indicate in which direction the train will go. Colour light signals point the direction by means of a row of white lights, or a platform number or similar information is displayed. Semaphore signals are arranged in tree-like formation to copy the layout of the junction. Directional signalling is not used in America, speed signalling is. Thus controlled signals at a junction do not indicate direction but the speed at which a train must travel - depending on which route is lined up. Diverging switches are traversed at different speeds, Limited Speed is forty or forty five miles per hour, Medium Speed thirty miles per hour, Slow Speed fifteen miles per hour.

Usually comprising upper and lower arms, position light home signals display STOP SIGNAL unless changed by the train dispatcher. If cleared for the straight route a home signal will show either CLEAR or APPROACH. If cleared for a diverging route and the next signal ahead is displaying a proceed aspect, position light high signals exhibit three horizontal amber lights over three vertical amber lights MEDIUM CLEAR or horizontal lights over flashing vertical lights LIMITED CLEAR, depending on speed of the diverging switch. If, for a diverging move, the next signal after the interlocking shows STOP SIGNAL, then the home signal will show horizontal lights over diagonal lights SLOW APPROACH or horizontal over flashing diagonal MEDIUM APPROACH.

In both Britain and America it is no use trains approaching a junction at full speed only to find the home signal at stop or the junction aligned for a diverging movement for which speed must be reduced. Advance warning is given in the signal preceding the junction signal, known as the distant signal. The equivalent of APPROACH is given in a distant signal in Britain by a yellow semaphore arm in the horizontal position, or a colour light exhibiting yellow. For a diverging move at a British junction the distant signal is either kept at APPROACH and the home signal changed to a proceed aspect when the train gets close, or the distant indicates by various means that a diverging route is set. For an upcoming diverging movement, Norac position light distant signals will show diagonal lights over diagonal lights APPROACH SLOW, diagonal over vertical APPROACH MEDIUM or diagonal over flashing vertical APPROACH LIMITED.

Whilst the geometry of Pennsylvania Railroad position light signal messages do not change, newer versions replace three horizontal amber lights with two horizontal red lights and three vertical amber lights with two vertical green lights.

# CHAPTER 11

# NAMES

Excitable, loquacious, witty – all described the conductor with whom I would be working in the next stage of a Conrail career. For the first few days of 1995 I did not work at all, till the supervisor in charge of newly hired men telephoned to say I would be going out on the road again, this time with a clear directive to *learn* the routes in preparation for being a road conductor myself. I would be attached to a crew on the North Jersey Pool that covered traffic between Harrisburg Consolidated Terminal and North Jersey Consolidated Terminal. Men often referred to the destination as Joisey, or more accurately Jyoisey, mocking the dialect in that part of the country. The first train would be PIOI6, on duty at Harrisburg GI8 at 14:45, Saturday, 7th January. By now I knew that PI stood for Pittsburgh, even if the train did start from Conway.

On arrival, I quickly made contact with the conductor and, determined never again to be utterly lost, thrust under his nose a copy of Rand McNally's *Handy Railroad Atlas of the United States*, and demanded to know: "Where are we going?"

The conductor laughed, turned to the engineer, and said approvingly, "Look at this, he's brought a railroad atlas with him!" He took the book, flicked through its pages, and after studying it briefly, said, "Now, it doesn't actually show where we're going, Oak Island Yard. It's round about here," he said pointing to the map, "in the Newark area. Anyway, the train's out there, we'd better get going." With that, the three-man crew made their way to the train patiently waiting on the main line, and clambered aboard. In charge of ninety-seven loads and twenty-six empties totalling 11,949 tons was Class

C40-8W number 6085, Class SD50 number 6743 and a Norfolk Southern Railway locomotive Class C39-8 number 8614. One of the two principal North American locomotive manufacturers, General Electric, prefixed two-axle truck diesel locomotives with a letter B, three-axle with a letter C, echoing the now obsolete British diesel wheel arrangement terms of Bo-Bo and Co-Co. The other principal diesel manufacturer in North America, Electro-Motive Diesel, used a different classification system.

Slowly but surely we pulled away. By now I had made several trips eastwards on the Harrisburg Line, so quickly recognized many features. But that would not be enough. To qualify on the route, I had to know not just the obvious stations, such as interlockings, but every unimportant, obsolete or irrelevant station on the 176.3 mile journey to Oak Island.

On the single track that connected CP-Harris to CP-Capital, we passed two stations, Wye Track Leading to Lurgan Branch and Paxton Street Industrial Track. A station known as 19th Street lay just beyond CP-Capital. Each of these lesser stations identified what Conrail called breaks in the rail, in simpler language, switches - though a diamond crossing would also be considered a break in the rail. At CP-Capital the railroad opened out to double track; we took the right-hand track. Both tracks were Rule 261, meaning we could have taken either, but train dispatchers usually kept to right-hand running unless circumstances compelled otherwise. In Britain a pair of main line tracks were usually called the Up Main and Down Main, the former normally going towards London (or towards the head office of the company that built the line) the latter away. In America a pair of tracks were called 1 and 2. I have never been able to ascertain how they were chosen. It is possible Track 1 went towards the original railroad's head office. Conrail's Harrisburg Line from Philadelphia to Harrisburg was the former Reading Railroad's main line. A train travelling from the major city of Philadelphia towards Reading would use Track 1, which supports the hypothesis. Track 1 continued on past Reading to Harrisburg, but that is by the way.

So we, on OIPI6, were travelling on Track 2. Unbelievably, I found it extremely difficult to remember in those early days which was Track 1 and which was Track 2, but could do so after a moment's thought. I would discover I was not alone amongst railroaders. Furthermore, it is common to muddle two things that are close. Whilst most have no difficulty recalling seven-digit telephone numbers, some confuse left and right. Eventually, I devised a mnemonic. When going away from Harrisburg, the train was travelling *to* Philadelphia (or North Jersey or Morrisville), hence Track 2. When coming back to Harrisburg, we had *won* the battle, hence Track 1. In four-track territory, numbers 1 and 2 were retained for the main tracks, 3 and 4 were used for the other two. In British four-track railway, additional tracks were identified by Up and Down Slow, or Up and Down Relief, or Up and Down Goods, or others.

Next stations after 19th Street were Ruth, Roadrailer Switch, CP-Beaver and CP-Tara. Nearer Philadelphia, but not on our route, was the name Tillys. How charming, I thought, that Conrail should use female names to identify physical characteristics. Charming, until I learnt they were nothing of the sort. Ruth was merely truncated Rutherford. Tara was derived from the Swatara Creek. Only Tillys, location of a crossover, remained unsullied; no one knew its origin; no nearby settlement carried that name. The only explanation I heard was that Tilly might have been name of a track foreman who installed the crossover.

After CP-Tara, the station pages read Hummelstown Detector, Hummelstown itself, Brownstone, Hershey (home of the famous chocolate bar) and Derry. A mile or two further, on one of the early North Jersey trips, the engineer turned to me and said, "Where are we now?"

The unexpected interrogation made me sit bolt upright and glare at the railroad ahead. I saw a grade crossing about a mile away. After a second's thought I said, "Just coming up on Palmyra."

The engineer chose not to acknowledge veracity of the statement. "This is Landis. Over there -" he said, pointing to north of the line, " - you can see what's left of the trackbed where a siding used to curve off. You can't see it now in the dark, but you can see it in the daylight. Landis. You're supposed to know all these places." The engineer drummed into me that the train had just passed a location identified in station pages, and that I was not aware of the fact. Landis had at one time been a break in the rail. After that, I kept my eyes fixed on the road ahead to hide the pain of disgrace.

On a later trip, the same engineer asked me, "What's the speed through Tara today?"

"Forty miles per hour. Same as it always is," I said with a look of disdain at his asking the obvious.

"That's what I like about this guy," he said to the conductor with a grin. By making the effort to master the railroad I had eventually earned his respect.

To return to the first outing on the North Jersey Pool, beyond Palmyra we encountered Millards, Annville, a detector of the same name, Cleona, West Lebanon and Wall interlocking sans wall. The city of Lebanon came next, then Avon, sleepy Prescott, Myerstown and its detector, followed by Richland which, I was told, earned a place in the Guinness Book of Records as a geometrically perfect intersection of highway crossroads and railroad. The official list of stations on the Harrisburg Line continued with Sheridan, Womelsdorf, Robesonia, Wernersville, Sinking Spring detector, CP-Sink, Sinking Spring and Lawn. CP-Wyomissing Jct., which somehow escaped the editor's scalpel, permitted us to leave the Harrisburg Line and run up the left-hand side of Reading's letter A. The Reading Line, on which we now travelled, presented four interlockings in a row – CP-Tulp, CP-Belt, CP-West Laurel, CP-Laurel – then offered CP-Blandon and its detector followed by stations Fleetwood, Lyons and Bowers. The single track between Laurel and Blandon was said to be the busiest on Conrail. Fleetwood, or just to the east of the village, was a lay back point. American train dispatchers have the ability to verbally halt trains by simply calling on the radio, a procedure not available to British signalmen, at least not in the time I worked there. If STOP SIGNAL were displayed at CP-Blandon for a westbound train owing to an eastbound train using the single track, then the dispatcher would instruct the westbound to lay back at Fleetwood to avoid blocking grade crossings between Fleetwood and Blandon. No such crossings stood on the approach to Fleetwood. A point of interest about the Laurel area was that some years ago a train derailed and fell into an adjacent flooded quarry. The freight cars were still there, submerged under many feet of water.

I wondered how I would ever be able to remember the next four communities (plus a detector) that were virtually joined together, until I realized they were a simple rhyme: Topton, Hancock, Mertztown,

Shamrock. Then came Alburtis interlocking and Macungie, which sounded like something blocking a Scottish drain. Three stations bore the name Emmaus, a Greek-sounding name of biblical origin. Had the train, after passing Rock Cut, proceeded towards Allentown Yard, it would have negotiated both CP-Burn and CP-Allen interlockings. It appeared I was the only person who thought of a handy mnemonic in the form of the George Burns and Gracie Allen Show; maybe everyone else was too young. But PIOl6 turned right at CP-Burn, passed East Penn Junction, and headed towards the end of the Reading Line, where it joined the Lehigh Line. At that nexus lay a station (and its detector) which we shall skip, because the name had such an impact on the author a special chapter is devoted to it.

Under way on the Lehigh Line we passed Florence Yard, Freemansburg, CP-Richards and its nearby detector, Glendon, Abbott and CP-Easton. The next station was the border between New Jersey and Pennsylvania formed by the Delaware River, abbreviated in the station pages to NJ/PA State Line. Once Alpha and Conn were cleared, we ran into a stretch of the Lehigh Line that included amongst its stations several British or British-sounding names – welcome relief for this foreign traveller bombarded with alien names – *Bloomsbury* and its detector, CP-West Portal, Bellewood, CP-Pattenburg, *Jutland* detector, *Lansdown, Flemington Junction, Three Bridges,* Neshanic detector, Read Valley and its detector, *Royce,* CP-Port Reading Jct., *CP-Bound Brook, Middlesex* and its detector, *New Market* and its detector, *South Plainfield,* CP-Potter, *Clark* and *Cranford.*

Some detectors monitored height of passing freight cars. On one occasion a high car detector went off for a westbound freight from North Jersey bound for the Lehigh Line. Some confusion arose because, even though the traincrew reported the matter, the train was allowed to proceed. The result was that an oversize load hit a bridge and demolished it. The bridge was at Three Bridges, instantly re-named Two Bridges by traincrews!

Most station names in this survey were obviously derived from nearby towns and villages. Eventually I would have to recite every one. But many other communities existed along the way not recognized as a railroad station. In later times I acquired an appetite to know those places, partly through simple curiosity, partly through envy of seasoned engineers who seemed to know every stick and blade of grass along the way. One of those unsung settlements stood between Lansdown and Flemington Junction, Sunnyside by name. O to have an address in Sunnyside! Would not a smile break across the face of anyone opening a letter from Sunnyside! Sadly, it would not be. American residential addresses omit village names and comprise only three lines: name, street, postal town plus zip code. The British equivalent would add at least two lines, the village name, such as Sunnyside, and the county.

A siding at Clark gave access to the – sounding very much like British vernacular - Bloodgood Industrial Track. An engineer told me that a cluster of sidings at Cranford called Staten Island Junction used to be where Conrail interchanged traffic with the Staten Island Railway which had ferried the cars between Staten Island and the mainland. The sidings were now out of use and overgrown.

Whilst travelling on this part of the Lehigh Line I recall complaining to the conductor, "You know, I've got to be able to remember all these little sidings along here."

"I don't have to know them, I'm qualified!" quipped the conductor.

His flippancy was in part justified, inasmuch as a Harrisburg-based conductor would seldom need to enter industrial sidings served by a local travelling shifter. Should the need arise maps would assist. Having said that, there would be future occasions when I would have to set off a hot box into an unfamiliar siding.

\* \* \*

Much of the Lehigh Line after the state border had been both rural and single track. Port Reading Jct. had heralded a more urban landscape. By the time we reached the next station after Cranford, CP-Aldene, the big city was upon us. Houses huddled closer together. Littered streets and scuffed kerb-stones spoke of heavier usage. For a trainee conductor once fond of city life New York's magnetism pulled hard. Close proximity of the metropolis influenced the remaining ride to Oak Island Yard, particularly regarding signalling, discussion of which can no longer be delayed.

Signals previously described have been of the position light variety designed by the Pennsylvania Railroad. Signals installed by such as the Reading and New York Central Railroads were of a completely different type known as colour lights. Conrail inherited multiple signal designs, all now covered by Norac rules. Once train PIOI6 left Harrisburg, the route featured nothing but colour light signals. Red, yellow and green meant exactly the same as in Britain: STOP SIGNAL, APPROACH, CLEAR. But after that, the British signalling enthusiast is shocked by American colour lights that can, and frequently do, display more than one colour. This is achieved by multiple signal heads, each carrying red, yellow and green lenses.

For example, red-over-red-over-yellow means RESTRICTING, red-over-red-over-flashing yellow means SLOW APPROACH, red-over-yellow-over-red means MEDIUM APPROACH, yellow-over-green-over-red means APPROACH MEDIUM.

Whilst working in Reading and on our way back from Pottstown on WHRE29 we encountered yellow-over-red-over-green APPROACH SLOW. "That's what we like to see," said the conductor, "A Christmas tree!". His joy was twofold. The signal meant that we were not going to be held up at CP-Walnut and should soon be finished. And he liked the colourful display!

From CP-Potter onwards the railroad was double track Rule 261. As we approached CP-Aldene one would therefore have expected to see home signal for Track 2 on which we were travelling and home signal for Track 1. But only the latter was visible. Track 2 home signal could not be seen until rounding a bend immediately before the interlocking. In another country this would be an outrage. In Britain, sighting committees that include a traincrew representative are called to approve each new or changed signal. In a location like CP-Aldene either the home signals would be re-sited further back along the track so both were visible at the same time, or a banner repeater would be provided for Track 2 to give advance warning. A banner repeater comprised a circular framework containing a black bar, illuminated at night, in the horizontal position when the following signal was at stop, tilted forty-five degrees for proceed. No repeaters of any design existed under Norac rules. I feel that if any improvement could be made to American signalling it would be through adoption of the banner repeater. Should a crew member complain about sighting such as that at CP-Aldene, the complainant would be told that he or she was paid to be qualified on the railroad which included knowing exactly where each signal was. Moreover, he would be reminded the distant signal indicated what the home was displaying. But I would argue a home signal is especially important. The train dispatcher is able to throw it back to STOP SIGNAL in an emergency. Furthermore, another train could accidentally overshoot a home signal and put all others in the interlocking back to stop, as would a runaway train. In my view a home signal needs to be clearly seen at a distance.

Another important difference between British and American signalling was again illustrated by arrangements at CP-Aldene. Although the entire Lehigh Line was under overall control of the Lehigh Line Train Dispatcher, from Aldene eastwards signals and switches were controlled by the block operator in NK tower. In this two-tier arrangement, operators dealt with routine matters whilst the dispatcher oversaw. The man in a traditional British signal box enjoys much greater autonomy than his American counterpart the block operator.

New Jersey Transit's Raritan Valley Line fed commuter trains onto the Lehigh Line at CP-Aldene, after which signals were closer together to keep traffic moving in the rush hour - further evidence of New York City's influence. Conrail signals were normally about two miles apart, those here were about a mile apart. I think the standard in Britain was one thousand yards.

On a future occasion during the morning rush hour, our train halted at Aldene's home signal showing STOP SIGNAL. Resigned that we would be stuck in suburbia for some time, I joked to the engineer, "If I walked to that house over there and knocked on the back door, I wonder if they'd give us something to eat. 'Hey, I work on Conrail. Our train is stopped at a signal, and we're kinda peckish. Could you make us a chicken sandwich please?'"

"Yeh, and plenty of mayonnaise," said the engineer with a grin.

"And could I have a few potato chips to go with it?"

"And a pickle for me," said the engineer, "but not too big, 'cause they give me indigestion."

"And a napkin," I added. We guffawed at the preposterousness of intruding into someone's home to ask for a sandwich, and then having the gall to be fussy about its preparation!

One mile further on, at CP-Roselle Park, we encountered a rarity: gauntleted track. Roselle Park's home signals on Track 2 had an additional lens, a lunar white light which, if illuminated, routed a passenger train about a foot closer to an island platform to avoid a large gap. This was achieved by having two sets of rails interwoven; Conrail trains always took the outside track. The special signal was described by Norac as "not in conformity".

With signals looming into view almost too quickly for traincrews to react, we passed CP-Townley, a place called Hillside, then NK tower itself, a small unimpressive building whose duties included routing passenger trains off the Lehigh Line onto Amtrak. With just one more interlocking, CP-Valley, out of the way, we were in Oak Island Yard where Tracks 1 and 2 of the Lehigh Line became yard tracks under control of Oak Island yardmaster.

Harrisburg crews bringing PIOI into Oak Island usually left it on one of the long tracks that fanned out from CP-Valley, or maybe put part on another track, such moves marking the end of their commitment. On this occasion we deadheaded back to Harrisburg in the dark. On another occasion we arrived at Oak Island in bright daylight that transformed New York's skyline, about six miles away, into a row of incandescent dominoes. As we were making our way to the jitney, the conductor nudged me, pointed to the Empire State Building, and said, "See that monkey climbing up that building over there!"

\* \* \*

The Jersey Pool was single-ended, worked entirely by Harrisburg crews. For whatever reason staff in North Jersey did not hold Harrisburg men in high esteem. They called them Hammies – not a derivative of Harrisburg, but a reference to the city's inhabitants' partiality to a meal of ham and green beans which they, the Harrisburg men, used to keep on the boil in local dormitories called The Meadows. (Accommodation in The Meadows was apparently terrible.) An expression of North Jersey's opinion of Harrisburg men could be found scrawled on the gentlemen's toilet wall: "What's the definition of a Hammy? Someone who, if he twice counted his body parts of which there were a pair, would come up with a different answer each time." I have paraphrased the graffiti.

North Jersey Consolidated Terminal was a tangle of yards and connecting tracks, a consequence of competing railroads – Pennsylvania Railroad, Lehigh Valley, Central Railroad Co. of New

Jersey, Delaware, Lackawanna & Western - vying for the region's lucrative business. The terminal was chopped into several constituents based on original railroad properties, each with a different person in charge. When moving from one part to another, traincrews had to be absolutely certain whom to contact for authority to proceed, and on which radio channel that person could be found. It followed that knowing current position was vital, which in turn meant knowing more names, such as WA-2, Oak, Pike, Garden, PN, Peddie Ditch, Portside and 91 Bay. Oak was controlled by Oak Island yardmaster, Pike by the block operator in Upper Bay Tower. As it was unclear who controlled the connecting track between Oak and Pike, a wise traincrew would ensure they had clearance from both men before entering that track.

If a left turn were made at CP-Valley rather than continuing straight into Oak Island Yard, a train would reach the seven-mile long Passaic and Harsimus Line, a name that could be mistaken for one of Shakespeare's lesser known works. The Passaic and Harsimus led to South Kearny Yard which would whet the appetite of any connoisseur of peculiar names. One stretch of track was called the Eyebrow owing to its curve. Another was called Grape, another Government Lead. The gourmet of improbable names would take further delight in Karny, the title of an interlocking. There may be explanation for the discrepancy in spelling between Karny interlocking and South Kearny Yard. A reprint of the Victorian British Ordnance Survey map of London and Windsor spells Willesden as Wilsden, Wembley as Wembly. It appears that in times gone by spelling of place-names was not considered crucial. (Spellings chosen for some British signal boxes were unfortunately not the ones to survive.) In Karny interlocking, Conrail may have inherited a fossilized spelling.

As with all culinary expeditions, the best is saved for last. A moveable bridge within Karny interlocking was called Point/No Point. *Point/No Point*? It may as well have been named Cabbage/No Cabbage for all the sense it made! What is the point of calling anything Point/No Point?

# CHAPTER 12

# NEAR MISS

The Jersey Pool turned quickly. It seemed I had no sooner completed a round trip, driven home and slept, than I was called out again. No time was available at home to study the route. We deadheaded a lot. One day, as our crew left GI8 yard office to board a waiting train, we passed another Jersey crew, bewhiskered and drawn, staggering out of a jitney having just deadheaded back. Amongst them was a classmate; he glanced at me with a visage lined with anguish. It was clearly too much for him; he must have left Conrail for I cannot recall seeing him again.

A low point for me occurred on Friday 13th January 1995 when I was telephoned at about 01:30 hours to be on duty at 03:30 for a Roadrailer train. It was a bitterly cold night, and shortly before departing I went outdoors to warm up a second-hand Ford Escort we had bought. As I turned to go back indoors, I noticed the car creeping down the slight incline of our driveway – a faulty handbrake had been repaired but was still not functioning properly. Aghast, I opened the car door and began climbing back in the slowly moving vehicle. Then something hit me on the side of the head preventing me from getting in. Stunned and helpless, I watched as the vehicle rolled out of control towards our newer Ford Escort. With little noise the first Escort bumped into the side of the second Escort and stopped. I climbed into the errant vehicle, turned off the engine, and pulled on the handbrake as hard as I could. I sensed blood trickling down my face.

I raced indoors, called my wife from slumber, and in an agitated state, explained incoherently what had happened. The crew dispatcher had to be called. "I can't come to work," I said hurriedly. "I've had a mishap. I'm not able to work."

"Oh, marking off sick on call," he said.

"No... no," I pleaded. "I was getting ready to leave... I was coming to work, when I had a bit of an accident." I tried to explain that I was not calling in sick because I did not feel like coming to work, but was genuinely incapacitated.

"I'll have to put you down as marked off sick on call," said the crew dispatcher unsympathetically.

My wife hurriedly dressed for a trip to the emergency room. At the hospital reception desk, the lady asked, "What can I help you with?"

With blood streaming down my face, I replied, "I've hurt my finger," and held up a perfectly undamaged index finger. You see, I had seen too many James Bond films where, on the verge of annihilation, the hero always managed a witty rejoinder and, of course, lived to confound his adversaries another time. Neither my wife nor the receptionist was amused by the remark.

(This perverse tendency to play the fool in dire circumstances came to the fore again many years later when I had to attend a hospital emergency room twice with the same unpleasant condition. On the second occasion I said to the nurse, "You know I was in here five days ago with the same thing?" She replied in the affirmative. "Well, does that mean I get rewards points?" The nurse grinned broadly, but we both concluded health care did not work like that.)

To return to the 1995 emergency room, a nurse asked me what had happened. "Well, I don't really know," I began. "I had started the car to warm it up, and it began rolling down hill. I opened the door to jump in, and the door somehow smashed into the side of my face."

Soon after, a doctor arrived and asked the same question. I gave him the same answer, but was irritated at having to do so. On reflection, the dual interrogation was probably deliberate policy to ensure I was consistent - to rule out suspicious circumstances. The doctor, wearing green attire, examined his peevish patient. I said to him, "Don't you wear white coats any more?"

"I'll go and change if you prefer," he said cheerily.

A day later I telephoned the crew dispatcher to mark up from being sick, and in due course reported for duty with bruised cheekbone and stitches over one eye. It was quite some time before I could discern what had actually happened. It appears the culprit was a small sign I had constructed saying "Private Property". Motorists used to turn round in our driveway. When the Escort had begun to move and I had tried to jump in, the open car door, the sign and myself had become entangled in the dark. To this day, I do not understand how the car door struck with such force. As for the vehicles, the rubber front bumper of the errant Escort had collided with the front tyre of the stationery Escort causing no damage whatsoever. All in all, it was a lucky escape. The "Private Property" sign was hastily discarded.

* * *

In North Jersey, British airline staff used the same hotel as Conrail traincrews. One night, when flight attendants crowded the lobby area, I could not resist introducing myself as a fellow Englishman and commenting on the similarity of our jobs in taking rest away from home. Addressing them collectively, I then said, "What's new in England?"

The solitary male attendant replied, "[So-and-so] of [such-and-such football club] got sent off the other day." I had hoped for one of the women to reply with a juicier morsel from the world of politics or entertainment.

My diary is unclear, but I think it was Friday 27th January that proved to be another eventful day. It began brightly by again being entertained by British airline staff. Whilst awaiting transport for the OIPI8X at about 19:00 hours, a young woman declared: "I'm gonna need an early call to put my make-up on."

The male co-pilot said facetiously, "*I'm* gonna need an early call to put *my* make-up on!"

"That's why you're divorced," retorted the woman.

A gaggle of high-spirited female flight attendants, all of whom spoke with London accents and all of whom were by no means unattractive, flitted about the lobby area celebrating time off work. One took keen interest in a hotel porter, one left with a male flight attendant about one foot shorter than she was, others waited for a bus.

To return to railroad matters, the jitney took us first to buy provisions, usual practice when emerging from a hotel, then took us to Oak Island Yard whose dismal rubble-strewn approach underneath

Routes 1 and 9 overhead bridge always reminded me of films about a post-nuclear holocaust. Before long, we were under way.

It will be recalled interlockings that do not have a Rule 261 bi-directional track feeding into them are not prefixed with CP. Alburtis is one such interlocking. That fact has no bearing on what follows but is re-stated because the interlocking's name is repeated several times.

Some time in the middle of the night and about a mile from Alburtis, a transmission came over the radio. I was not yet sharp enough to instantly recognize it, and thought the voice said, "Mercy, mercy, mercy!" The engineer fortunately knew that those words were, "Emergency! Emergency! Emergency!" and immediately applied brakes to bring OIPI8X to a stand. The message communicated unequivocally to other trains in the vicinity that a train had suffered an undesired emergency application of brakes. The sender completed the emergency transmission by identifying his train and by stating on which track he was travelling, Track 2.

To grasp the seriousness of an undesired emergency application, it needs to be explained first that emergency application is an everyday part of railroading. It happens each time cars are cut off from a train: as the train pulls away, air hoses part company and ninety pounds of air pressure is exhausted to the atmosphere placing the vehicles left behind in emergency. Very infrequently, an engineer will find it necessary to initiate an emergency application on the whole train if, say, an obstruction suddenly appears ahead. Slang for such action is dumping the train, or putting it in the hole. However, if the train itself and not the engineer initiates an emergency application, there are several possibilities. One of the cars in the train could be what is described as a kicker, in that its air brake mechanism is faulty causing an emergency application when only a normal application of brakes should have taken place. Another possibility is that some cars with long coupler assemblies can stretch air hoses too far apart allowing air to escape, which in turn implements an emergency application. The most serious case is when a train, for whatever reason, breaks in two.

On the night in question, the engineer of OIPI8X called his opposite number to find out what the problem was, and was told that the train had gone into unexplained emergency, and that the conductor was walking the train, which was proper procedure. After a time, that conductor called the train dispatcher with his report. Because the conductor was some distance away and using his hand radio, we could not hear very well, but well enough to realize that in front of us was a train wreck.

Train OIPI8X had stopped a few hundred yards before passing the train in distress. When it became apparent we were not going to move, with the conductor's permission I left the engine to investigate. The stricken train was a consignment of iron ore loaded in *ex-*Pennsylvania Railroad short open hopper cars called jennies. Iron ore is very heavy, so heavy if it were fully loaded into a normal forty-foot hopper car the car's structure would be insufficient to carry the weight. So the shorter jennies were specially designed. Dwindling demand for ore owing to decimation of the steel industry and increasing use of recycled metal had removed any incentive to build replacements. So jennies were seeing out their last days in the few remaining iron ore trains. (The design was so old that by the end of the 1990s they were no longer seen; presumably most if not all had been withdrawn.)

Continuing my reconnaissance, it was found the train had broken not into two parts but three. About a dozen cars were still attached to the engines. Maybe a hundred yards further back was a group of about eight cars. Maybe another hundred yards back, just inside Alburtis's interlocking limits, the beginning of the rest of the train could be discerned in the dark. Immediately in front of the third portion, laying in the gauge (between the rails) was a coupler shank - the draw-bar that carries the coupler knuckle.

The first four cars on this third segment of the train were derailed. The front truck (that is to say, the wheel assembly) was missing from the first car, so the jenny pointed downwards into the ground. The second jenny had three trucks underneath the car body, the third truck obviously coming from the car in front. It appeared the emergency application succeeded in stopping wheels from turning, but could not counter tremendous momentum in car bodies densely packed with iron ore, which kept moving for another fifteen feet or so with such force they ripped away from trucks carrying them. Railroad cars are not fixed to their trucks, but merely sit on centre pins that allow trucks to swivel freely. Clearly, centre pins had sheared. It seemed likely that the train initially broke in two at the location of the ripped out coupler, and the jolt of an emergency stop was sufficient to cause a second break in the front part of the train. The third segment stopped immediately, as it was on a rising gradient, the first two segments kept going some distance on a falling gradient.

Physical properties of a trainload of iron ore moving at fifty miles per hour, which was the speed limit through Alburtis, are formidable. Alburtis is situated on a hill: gradients fall away either side. It is easy to understand how the strain of cresting the summit proved too much for the aging jennies, resulting in the coupler shank being rent from its housing. The torn-out shank was located at the summit, or very close to it.

I stared at the wreckage. The sudden stop had compressed and buckled the iron ore jennies. They stuck out over Track 1. Had we been a minute or two earlier, the twisted metal would have struck the OIPI8X engines, slicing through the cab on the conductor's side. I can only hope that I could have dived out of the way in time. Mercifully that had not happened, but there remained a minor concern. Alburtis interlocking's home signal for Track 1 still showed green for our train. Although wreckage had not spilled onto Track 1, the protruding mangled metal was foul of it. The dispatcher did not know that. I radioed. "OIPI to the Lehigh Dispatcher. Over."

"Lehigh Dispatcher. Over," came the reply.

"This iron ore train on Track Two, the wreckage isn't actually on Track One, but it's sticking out over it. It's fouling Track One. You've still got your home signal at green for us. Over."

"Roger," came a quick response. Instantly, the signal changed from green to red.

I wandered about the mess for some time, till the conductor called on the radio for my return. We were instructed to tie down the train and deadhead back to Harrisburg.

* * *

The Alburtis incident shook me, but fifty years of constant change including being grafted from one continent to another had witnessed innumerable dramas, so that a near-miss, whilst an uncomfortable reminder how dangerous railroad work could be, did not lessen determination to push ahead with training on the Jersey Pool. Still, the prospect of memorizing the entire 176 miles from Harrisburg to

North Jersey was daunting. Material available was not the best for study purposes. Scale maps provided by Conrail, copies of which I eventually obtained, showed physical characteristics wonderfully, but necessarily cramped complicated layouts into a small space, and contained much superfluous material. Station pages of the Rule Book methodically listed all necessary facts and figures, but on separate pages.

When I was a boy in Yorkshire, England, I walked alongside the local railway line, a distance of five miles. I can still remember where every signal was, and have no difficulty in recalling the handful of "breaks in the rail": I was "qualified" on that piece of railway. Now, in 1995, I had to memorize 103 stations, 111 siding and crossover switches plus numerous power-operated interlocking switches.

The first step in tackling what seemed to be an insurmountable problem was realization that the railroad could only be mastered by splitting it into sections. The second step was to prepare my own diagrams showing station names, track layouts, speed limits and rules in effect (Rule 251, Rule 261, etcetera) overlaid, so all could be found together, instantly retrievable. Maps that took shape on my desk at home were in essence expanded signalling diagrams. I always had been a budding cartographer so enjoyed preparing them.

Like British signal box diagrams, my maps were not to a constant scale. For most stretches of railroad, a scale of thirty millimetres to one mile prevailed. In crowded locations, the scale was increased to whatever was necessary. A simple line represented track. One arrow in the track denoted Rule 251, two opposing arrows Rule 261. Title of the controlling train dispatcher and on which radio channel he could be found was written (in what is described in Britain as longhand, in America cursive) across the top of every page. Next, stations were printed in large letters above the track, other information in small letters. Speeds were shown along the foot of pages. Special instructions, listed in the Rule Book as Station Page Information, were printed near the location to which they applied. Material not essential to qualifying, such as every grade crossing and every automatic signal, was omitted. Where line direction was east and west, tracks were drawn horizontally on landscape pages, north and south vertically on portrait pages. All sheets for one line were stapled together, and a face page added. The Harrisburg Line comprised sixteen pages.

No two pages were alike. Each was a picture, as in school geography lessons. And that is how I was able to memorize them. I stared and stared at them till the picture imprinted on the brain. On 28th January 1995, I qualified on the first stretch of Conrail territory, from CP-Harris to CP-Wyomissing Jct. But it may have been too late.

During the month of January I went to work on the Jersey Pool ten times, covering mainly the OIPI, PIOI and Roadrailer trains. Of particular note was PIOI7 of 18th January, a train of 152 cars totalling a massive 15,126 tons that needed C36-7 number 6621, SD40-2 numbers 6441 and 6991 and SD50 number 6826 – a total of 13050 horsepower – to pull it. On 9th January we took to South Kearny Yard a train of empty intermodal flat cars; we speculated they were surplus to requirements after the Christmas rush, and were being moved about Conrail merely to get them out of the way. On only two trips did we take a train east, stay in the hotel, and bring a train back west. In all other cases we either took a train east and immediately deadheaded back, or deadheaded to Jersey, took rest, and brought a train back. Described thus, the schedule seems not too demanding, but in truth was very tiring, so tiring I could not initially put my mind to learning the railroad. The rationcinative process that led to preparing my own maps, which in turn enabled me to finally qualify on a portion of the route, all took time.

The employer may have grown weary of paying out relatively high wages that the Jersey Pool generated to a trainee who, after four weeks, had qualified on only fifty miles of track. On 5th February I and others were taken off the Jersey Pool.

# CHAPTER 13

# MORRISVILLE

Road crews working east from Harrisburg saw some of the biggest and most famous cities in the United States. New York: probably the most thrilling city in the world whose districts of Broadway, Central Park and Manhattan are known to everyone. Philadelphia: city of brotherly love, home of the Liberty Bell and home of the Philadelphia Sound for those who remember it from 1970s discotheque days. And Baltimore, whose soaring vowels bestow on the city an irresistible *cachet*. All are magical, fantastic, the stuff of television programmes and Hollywood films, quintessential American cities this Briton thought he would never see but ones for which Conrail now offered a free ticket. But *Morrisville*? I am sure Morrisville is a very nice town even if it does share its name with several other communities in America, but why was it constantly the topic of conversation in Harrisburg GI8 rather than more glamorous candidates?

The explanation for Morrisville's popularity lay in the agreeable manner in which the pool that served it worked. Three trains ran daily from Harrisburg to Morrisville, a mail train, a trailer-van train (both intermodal trains) and a mixed freight. Given that the mixed freight originated in Conway Yard, a guess that it was called the PIMO would be a correct guess. The arrangement in 1994 was that crews who took trailer-van train TV2M eastwards mid-evening stayed in the hotel and brought back MOPI early the following afternoon. Crews who took Mail8M eastwards at about 02:00 stayed in the hotel and brought back TV1 that evening. Crews who took PIMO eastwards during the day deadheaded straight back. A separate regular job looked after the westwards mail train, Mail9. In 1994 the Morrisville Pool had,

I think, seven crews. They enjoyed probably at least twenty-four hours at home before being called out again. Most working days were less than eight hours, and demand for crews eased off somewhat at weekends. The Morrisville Pool was highly prized, though not highly remunerative.

Conrail's mail trains bore no resemblance to the overnight mails that ran with military precision on British Railways. When I worked at Kensal Green Junction signal box in London, each weekday morning at about 06:00 hours we had to completely turn round the mail train that ran between London and Scotland via the West Coast Mail Line, so that devices that picked up and dropped off mail bags on the move would always be on the outside. These travelling post offices, as they were known, handled letters. Trains of different coaching stock vehicles handled parcels. All this British Post Office traffic was eventually lost, but in the 2010s, some returned to rail. The American Post Office currently uses rail transport very little. Conrail's mail trains were intermodal trains that used the term "mail" to emphasize speedy delivery.

To look now at the route to Morrisville, trains from Harrisburg used to travel on Amtrak's Harrisburg to Philadelphia line. At Glen interlocking they turned left onto what was known as the Trenton Cut-Off, not because it bypassed Trenton but because it bypassed Philadelphia and re-joined the main line near Trenton, New Jersey State. After Amtrak priced Conrail off its passenger lines, the freight carrier routed Morrisville trains onto the Harrisburg Line as far as CP-Norris, just east of Abrams Yard, where they made a left turn to travel briefly on metals owned by the Southeastern Pennsylvania Transport Authority, SEPTA.

The SEPTA oasis is extraordinary in being a small sliver - only about a half-mile - of commuter line inserted into a freight route. Moreover, that half-mile is packed with all manner of railroad paraphernalia resulting in the map I eventually drew being one of the most exquisite. The problem of qualifying on a foreign railroad's territory was solved on Friday 5th May 1995 when SEPTA officials made a special appearance in Harrisburg for that purpose. Thirty engineers and conductors, plus one trainee in the form of myself, squeezed into a small room in Conrail's Harrisburg office for tuition. How did Conrail keep trains running that day? The visitors handed out copies of SEPTA's timetable and a map which they discussed in detail. The territory included a half-mile spur to Elm Street Station which was available for turning engines. An official dwelt at length on special instructions for Sawmill crossover, close to Norristown Transportation Center station, though it seemed highly unlikely Morrisville trains would ever use it. But I did on one occasion turn engines on the Elm Street spur.

Leaving SEPTA, Morrisville trains entered the Morrisville Connecting Track which ran past a night club. During nocturnal hours traincrews could watch night revellers coming and going, including young women in snug sweaters, in economical skirts. On one occasion when we unusually passed the establishment at about 08:00 hours, dismayed at missing the nightly show I said to the engineer, "Perhaps we might see some good-looking cleaning ladies."

The mile-long Morrisville Connecting Track ended at CP-King. What used to be the Trenton Cut-Off was now two separate lines, the Dale Secondary from CP-King to Glen interlocking, and the Morrisville Line from CP-King to Morris interlocking on Amtrak. Morrisville Yard, now sadly stripped of many tracks, occupied land immediately before the Amtrak junction.

Interlockings were located at the eastern and western ends of the Morrisville Line, but in the twenty miles of single track between were just one little-used switch and one grade crossing. That sparsity did not prevent an unpleasant occurrence when, at that solitary grade crossing, a Morrisville crew hit a highway truck. The truck driver was found to be driving under the influence of alcohol, but survived. His vehicle was destroyed. Somehow, his wife arrived at the scene, took stock, then promptly told him she was getting a divorce, an excellent example of the fragility of marriage these days.

Twenty miles of featureless single track on the Morrisville Line was even bleaker than the picture already painted, for one simple reason: a complete absence of wayside signals. This curt statement requires a lengthy explanation.

The Pennsylvania Railroad at one time experienced severe delays on the Harrisburg to Pittsburgh line owing to thick winter fogs. The message STOP AND PROCEED authorized a train to pass an automatic signal and proceed at restricted speed, restricted speed meaning be prepared to stop within half the distance that can be seen. In thick fog, that was hardly any distance at all, so trains crept along at snail's pace for two miles till the next signal, which by that time was invariably at CLEAR. The company wanted a system to advise engineers as soon as the next signal improved, so trains could immediately pick up speed. They devised, it is believed somewhere in the 1920s and 1930s, the Cab Signal System, which provided a display in the locomotive cab of the conditions under which a train was occupying track. To put it another way, the cab display showed what the signal to the rear would be showing were the train itself not occupying the track. If a first train passed an automatic signal, the signal changed to STOP AND PROCEED. If a second train then passed that STOP AND PROCEED signal, its cab signal showed RESTRICTING. If the first train later cleared the block, the cab signal for the second train went up to APPROACH, because that is what the signal to the rear would show were that second train itself not in the block. At that point, the second train could accelerate, simply being prepared to stop at the next signal. The cab signal would still show APPROACH even when the train came to a stand looking at a STOP SIGNAL, because the cab signal showed the previous signal message, not the message of the signal ahead.

The multifarious Norac signal messages were grouped into just four for cab signal purposes: CLEAR, APPROACH MEDIUM, APPROACH and RESTRICTING, the last included STOP SIGNAL. The Cab Signal System employed a spinning device, nicknamed a coffee grinder, at each signal to send an electrical pulse down the rails at 180 beats a minute for CLEAR, 120 beats a minute for APPROACH MEDIUM, seventy-five beats a minute for APPROACH and no signal for RESTRICTING. A sensor under the front of the locomotive picked up the signal and transmitted it to a twelve-inch tall display in the middle front of the cab – where it could be seen by both engineer and conductor.

If a cab signal dropped from one message to another more restricting, the system emitted a loud warble, which the engineer had to acknowledge, usually by depressing a pedal on the floor of the cab. If he failed to acknowledge, the system automatically applied brakes and brought the train to a stand. It eventually must have occurred to authorities that if wayside signals were taken away between interlockings, trains could run quite safely on cab signals alone.

Referred to as Rule 562, this was in fact the case on the Morrisville Line, and at other locations. When Rule 562 was in effect, as an extra precaution the system was modified so that the cab signal would display RESTRICTING for about a mile before reaching a location occupied by another train.

The Pennsylvania Railroad was so pleased with the Cab Signal System that they installed it on their entire signalled network, where it is still in place today under ownership of descendant railroads. Amtrak has made several improvements to the system, including provision for signalling over high-speed switches. So refined are Amtrak's changes to the Cab Signal System they go a long way to meet requirements of a concept called Positive Train Control which is being implemented in America during the 2010s to increase rail safety.

\* \* \*

If I had fleeced Conrail on the Jersey Pool I was punished for it by being placed not on the Morrisville Pool proper but on the Mail9, the effective date being 7th February 1995. Mail9 ran during the night Monday to Friday, and was covered by two crews, each alternately working Monday, Wednesday, Friday and Tuesday, Thursday. Crews either deadheaded to Morrisville and worked back, or took light power – light engines - from Harrisburg Consolidated Terminal, in the latter case train dispatchers ensuring they had a clear run to avoid running out of time. The light engine move was puzzling; three Morrisville trains each direction daily ought to have assured balanced working of motive power. Men of course preferred to deadhead, but had no say in the matter. Whether crews deadheaded or worked light power, the crew dispatchers called the assignment as combined service, meaning men were paid for mileage covered, rather than time worked. One hundred and thirty miles was the equivalent of one day's pay. The distance to Morrisville was coincidentally 130 miles, so Mail9 crews received two days' pay each time they worked whether they deadheaded or not. On the subject of mileage, the distance from Harrisburg to Conway was 275 miles, so I was paid over two days' pay for the New Year's Eve trip.

Mail9 did not provide vast income, but it did give both crews the weekend off. I took advantage of that free time by returning to the

Maryland and Pennsylvania to work, when available, the Sunday coal trains. I signed no contract with Conrail that forbad working for another railroad, or working for any other company for that matter. Breaching the hours of service law was never a risk because time between coal train and Mail 9 assignments was always about twenty-four hours.

The engineer on the Mail9 crew to which I was seconded was a former Penn Central man, the conductor a former Reading Railroad man, a combination that produced an interesting discussion. "All these jobs should be ours," said the engineer. "They're our trains."

"But you're running on our railroad, John," retorted the conductor.

"Listen Steve, these Morrisville trains used to come over the mountains, then along the main line through Lancaster, then turned onto the Trenton Cut-Off for Morrisville. That's all Pennsy rails. The entire Morrisville Pool should be Pennsylvania equity."

"You're living in the past," said the conductor. "We're all Conrail now. We've gotta share the goodies."

"Reading men have got no right to be working in Morrisville," insisted the engineer.

"You couldn't get to Morrisville if you didn't use our railroad!" pointed out the conductor.

Neither man gave ground. Most of the 130 mile route from Harrisburg to Morrisville comprised former Reading Railroad metals, the Harrisburg Line as far as CP-Norris, plus half-a-mile of SEPTA. Equity was a term used by unions to state which jobs belonged to which men when railroads merged or were taken over. The engineer had Penn Central prior rights, which meant he would have a prior right for any position established as Penn Central. An older man originally employed by the Pennsylvania Railroad would have prior prior rights. The conductor enjoyed Reading prior rights. Hired by Conrail, I had no prior rights. Hereon, I shall refer to either Penn Central or Pennsylvania Railroad equity as simply Pennsylvania equity.

A less heated discussion took place another night on the matter of Pickett's Charge during the 1863 Battle of Gettysburg. I remember very little of the exchange between the two men so, with help from the book *Gettysburg* by Colonel William C. Oates of the Confederate side and Lieutenant Frank A. Haskell of the Union side, I will reconstruct a discourse.

"But you see, John," said the conductor, "the Union held an excellent defensive position on Cemetery Ridge. The Confederates had to attack them uphill. And the Confederates were out-manned."

"Numbers are not the only factor in war, Steve, it's tactics," said the engineer.

"I think the Confederate army made some tactical errors at Gettysburg," said the conductor. "They failed to take advantage of a position at Round Top Mountain, for example."

"Even so, they broke through the Union line," said John.

"And they were repulsed," said Steve.

"Let's ask the new guy what he thinks," said Steve. "What do you think, Mitch, was General Lee right in charging the Union line in Gettysburg?" I opened my mouth with the intention of saying I did not know enough about the subject to comment, but before any words came out the engineer interrupted: "I'll tell you what Mitch thinks, he thinks that with proper support from other divisions Pickett's Charge would have succeeded and the Union would have been defeated at Gettysburg." And so, with no contribution from me, the argument raged even though the die had been irreversibly cast on 3rd July 1863.

In 2013 my wife and I visited Gettysburg. Without planning, we made off over grassland rather than following tourist by-ways to arrive at an imposing sculpture of a man on horseback. It was General Robert E. Lee. After admiring the monument, again with no scheme, we took another grassy path and struck out towards more monuments. Upon studying those monuments we realized we had, without knowing, retraced the path of General Pickett's men on that fateful day.

\* \* \*

Attached to railroad work were several benefits not immediately apparent, one of which was a prestige that invited admiration, envy and even idolatry amongst followers. At one point in British history it was the dream of every schoolboy to be an engine driver. Then there is the aura surrounding an American freight train, so visually arresting, passers-by find it difficult not to turn a head when a brightly-coloured somewhat noisy mile-long cavalcade goes by. And not to be lightly dismissed is the railroader's personal feeling of accomplishment at having moved such a scene-stealing leviathan successfully from one city to another.

On a less grandiose scale, after exiting a siding on the Maryland & Pennsylvania, as conductor I swiftly closed the switch, locked it, climbed on the rear steps of the engine, walked along the gangway and gave the go-ahead signal to the engineer with an economical wave of the hand. As I completed the series of short sharp tasks and the engine began to move, I looked down to see a female car driver trying to suppress a smirk of amusement at what she perceived to be an arrant display of showmanship, but which was really no more than a particularly efficient moment in a routine day's work.

In America many young boys waved vigorously at each passing train. I would gaze at them and remember how I used to do the same thing in England, until an engineer shouted at me: "Wave back at the kids!" Henceforward I followed standard procedure and returned every child's wave, but in a restrained, almost indifferent manner, to maintain the awe with which boys beheld those in charge of a train. An engineer told a story of a boy asking if the locomotive had a steering wheel. "No," replied the engineer, who then painstakingly described how: "The ridge on the inside of the wheel, called the flange, ensures the engine keeps to the rails, so whichever way the switch is lined the train will go." The youth obviously found this carefully reasoned explanation unconvincing, for his response was, "Mister, you're full of crap!"

When time came to work as a qualified conductor I would discover Morrisville had much to offer. Conrail secured for accommodation a pleasant, quiet motel in nearby Levittown, one that provided breakfast and a good range of television channels to run up and down. If no other room were available, the motel management had to place Conrail personnel in higher priced rooms, such as one containing a jacuzzi. Not familiar with such contraptions I managed to half flood the bathroom when water jets shot over the tub side.

As conductor, once in the motel room I made out the outbound journey timecard. I went straight to bed as soon as clerical duties permitted for the uncomplicated reason of being tired. Some men preferred to first enjoy a substantial meal, and stay up for a while to ensure they were called from slumber, fresh and alert. That plan was always a gamble, for it assumed time spent in the hotel would be more than eight hours.

The Morrisville Pool in the mid-1990s worked predictably, with more than the minimum eight-hour stay in the motel, so crews had chance to take fresh air. Step by step I explored the surrounding urban area, a few tentative streets at a time to avoid getting lost. As I write these words many years after the experience, memories of streets surrounding each motel have become muddled. Invariably located on wide busy four-lane highways - colloquially referred to in America as a main drag – all motels looked the same. In the case of Morrisville I eventually discovered a lengthy and stimulating walk through the nearby town of Bristol, along streets of stylish architecture to the banks of the Delaware River where one could while away time gazing across the wide, serene, curving, slow-moving waterway.

Morrisville supplied even more. When summoned from the motel about midday for the MOPI, crews often called for a take-away meal at a cafe which served the most scrumptious home-cooking ever! MOPI, less urgent than intermodal trains, was not usually ready when crews arrived at the yard office, so time was available to devour the mouth-watering dish rather than pick at it as the train went along.

When I first worked MOPI assignments they began in Morrisville Yard. Later, the point of departure was changed to USX Yard two miles away, a yard as extensive as Morrisville itself. The handful of tracks at the northern tip of the USX complex of which Conrail had exclusive use provided a perfect railroading setting. Because crews were operating entirely within yard limits no wayside signals limited operations, and because we were too far from Morrisville Yard no other radio transmissions interfered. We had to ourselves the entire railroad as far as the eye could see, and could assemble the train in whatever fashion we wished without having to obtain permission for every move, as was the case elsewhere. In other words, we had complete freedom. In the summer of 1998 more than once I partook of the delicious local fare, then worked the MOPI in USX yard. So enjoyable was this combination of good food and immensely satisfying, unfettered railroading that the addition of a glorious summer's day on 11th July brought a person as close to Elysium as one could ever get wearing ear plugs, safety boots and gloves!

The narrative must now retreat from this idyllic high point to return to the Mail9 training programme. In a six-week period I had fourteen round trips and, perhaps in the eyes of my employer, very little to show for it. During that period I had passed tests to qualify on the Reading Line and to extend qualifications on the Harrisburg Line as far as CP-Phoenix, but Conrail may have considered that not enough. They may have thought that I was – to use slang occasionally heard in railroading – milking it. On 17th March 1995 I was taken off Mail 9.

In fact I had been quite industrious, though long hours working on three Maryland & Pennsylvania coal trains did not of course show up in Conrail's records. Much time had been spent at home preparing Conrail maps. Whilst still on Mail9 I had obtained permission for two round trips on the PICA. (By now, a separate Harrisburg-based job worked both the PICA and CAPI.) A few days after losing the Mail9 position I gained qualifications necessary to take trains not only to Morrisville but also to Camden. But these qualifications were of no use because I was without a position on Conrail.

# CHAPTER 14

# BUMPY RIDE

The following pages will reveal 1995 to be a year marked by uncertainty. Frequent dislocation meant I could never be sure of a future with Conrail, not even a medium-term future. On the day I lost the Mail9 position, Friday 17th March 1995, telephone conversations went something along the following lines.

"M.C. Deaver," said the crew dispatcher.

"Yes."

"I have to notify you that, with effect from one minute past midnight, you've been displaced," said the crew dispatcher, with perhaps just a touch of sympathy in his voice.

"What does that mean?" I asked.

"Well, it means you don't have an assignment," he said.

"So, what am I supposed to do?"

"I... I don't know. You'd better speak to your supervisor," said the crew dispatcher, beginning to feel the wretchedness of his task.

I telephoned the manager in charge of trainees.

"You see, Mr. Deaver," explained the supervisor, "it means you're not in the training programme any more."

"What happens now?"

"You've got to exercise your seniority."

"What seniority? I don't have any."

"You need to go to the computer," said the supervisor patiently, "and find a position that you can take."

I should be grateful. There was a time when newly hired Harrisburg men who had no place to go were forced to Oak Island Yard, a place where, owing to close proximity of New York's ravenous labour market, Conrail was always short of staff. Men spoke of fear of being banished there, of the possibility of having to live in a crime-ridden locality. Such stories conjured up images of knife-wielding marauding gangs in black leather jackets hiding behind every box car in Oak Island Yard waiting to pounce on unsuspecting brakeman recently seconded there against their will. Management had since abandoned a policy of forcing employees to Oak Island because too many had resigned, but if a position could not be found locally, Oak Island would be my fate. The risk was considered serious enough to warn my wife of the consequences: she would have to look after the house on her own whilst I moved to the Newark area.

I was never sure why I was taken off the training programme, my abysmally low status precluded demanding an explanation. Either my employer had grown impatient with lack of progress, or the training programme had run out of money. It was immaterial. I had no choice but to drive to Lancaster Dillerville Yard office and consult the computer, but not without first slipping in a shift on the Maryland and Pennsylvania coal train on Sunday 19th March. On the following Monday, I looked at computer listings for the nearest yards: Lancaster, Harrisburg, Enola and Shiremanstown. I found no vacancies, nor any employees with less seniority than I had. A number next to each person's name denoted seniority. In Reading, I came across someone whose number appeared to place him inferior to me, so I telephoned the crew dispatcher on duty and displaced the man.

On Tuesday a different crew dispatcher telephoned to say that the action was invalid because that man was in fact senior to me. I do not know how the mistake occurred, the previous crew dispatcher raised no questions. I was told I had five days to bump onto another position. The five-day period commenced at 12:53.

Whilst on British Railways I had encountered the term bump only twice. My regular mate at an adjacent signal box, Willesden New Station, had left to take a higher position in a modern power box. On finding it too demanding, he was allowed to return to his old position, and to bump the man who had taken his place. When my first signal box, Kensal Green Junction, was abolished, I could take any available open position at my level. I chose Acton Wells Junction, where a man was occupying a position but had not formally been awarded it. I bumped him.

Bumping was common on Conrail. In 1995 if a person were displaced he had five days to find a slot. The generous allowance dated back to times when the only way an employee could bump was to travel to a freight yard, personally enquire about vacancies, and make a bump on the spot. If there were no vacancy, he would have to travel in his own time and at his own expense to other yards. Five days was the period allowed for employees to roam the area in search of work. A computer in Lancaster listing all positions in the eastern portion of Conrail obviated the need for extensive travel. The five-day bump then became a gift of time. The nearest yard to me was actually York, but either it did not then have a computer, or I could not gain access.

I drove to Lancaster again, probably on Wednesday 22$^{nd}$ March, but still found nowhere to bump. Then, with just three hours of my 120-hour bump left, on Sunday morning 26$^{th}$ March I was able to make a successful bump, then promptly went to work on the Maryland & Pennsylvania coal train at 11:00 hours! The risk I took now seems inexplicable. Maybe it was a calculated gamble, I judged it to be extremely unlikely I would be called to work. I wonder if I told my wife not to answer the telephone. If I had been called, I would later have had to plead ignorance, but would suffer a blemish on my work record for a missed call.

\* \* \*

The man I bumped on 26$^{th}$ March obviously had less seniority than I had, another of the 1994 new intake. He had nowhere else to go. My understanding is that in such circumstances an employee is allowed to languish for a month without assignment, and is then furloughed. The only chance of reprieve would be if the carrier within that month called him to fill a vacancy.

It appears the man in question was furloughed and called back by Conrail at some point. About three years later we met in Enola. He told me of problems he had faced after I had ejected him onto the street in 1995.

"You know when we were at the initial interview," he continued, "what time was your physical?"

117

"Oh, I can't remember, maybe about one or two o'clock in the afternoon," I replied.

"That was roughly about the same time as mine. I must have been right behind you," he said, struggling to suppress bitterness in his voice.

I did not know how Conrail decided the order in which to interview applicants, but that order affected the time of medical examination the same day, which in turn determined seniority. In the case in point, a few minutes between the time of one man and another's physical meant the difference between keeping a job on Conrail and losing it. When the man spoke to me in Enola, my heart sank, though I concealed feelings. The discomfort was worsened by the fact that this man, in being an unassuming person, modestly built and a little slow off the mark, was very like an old signalman friend on the North London Line.

There was another parallel between Conrail and the North London Line. The voice quality of the crew dispatcher on early turn was startlingly similar to that of my best mate Dave Smith, though one spoke with the General American accent, the other with Cockney accent (more properly, dialects). I never met the American man, but when I told the story to an engineer who had met him, he revealed that the crew dispatcher, amazingly, had the same stocky appearance as my British friend. Since every person probably has a thousand clones across the globe, it should not be surprising to encounter a pair from time to time, even though it destabilizes our sense of uniqueness if we come across our own.

\* \* \*

The man I had elbowed off Conrail in 1995 and whose position I took had held the Extra Board in Hagerstown, Maryland State. The medium-sized yard had two names, Shomo and Vardo; I will simply call it Hagerstown Yard. Conrail's route from Harrisburg to Hagerstown comprised two parts, the first being former Reading Railroad metals as far as Shippensburg, a length of mainly single track railroad now known as the Lurgan Branch. The second part was former Pennsylvania Railroad metals from Shippensburg to Hagerstown, a segment now called the Hagerstown Secondary. A rival to Conrail, CSX Transportation, used former Western Maryland

Railway rails between Shippensburg and Hagerstown. A third railroad, Norfolk Southern Railway, came into Hagerstown from the south. The three railroads met and criss-crossed one another in the vicinity of Hagerstown Yard.

The distance from my York County home to Hagerstown Yard was a meandering eighty miles. The drive comprised sluggish travel on Route 30 as far as Gettysburg, a fast drive on Route 15 to Thurmont, a tortuous section over Catoctin Mountain, then a zigzag route to reach the southern end of Hagerstown where the yard was located. I should really not have taken the position because the journey took about two-and-a-quarter hours. With the normal two-hour call, I could not possibly arrive on time even if I jumped straight out of bed into the car. I asked the crew dispatch office to give me an extended call, with which they kindly obliged.

The telephone rang at about 17:00 hours on Monday 27th March for the position of utility man on duty at 19:59. Departure from home at 17:15 ought to have guaranteed timely arrival, but I got lost in back roads between Catoctin Mountain and the yard. When I did arrive, the reception was less than welcoming.

"Do you know this yard?" asked the yardmaster.

"Never been here before."

"You're just like the man they sent me a few days ago," the yardmaster said angrily. "He didn't know anything either. You new guys think you can just walk into any job in a yard you've never seen before. How the hell do you think you're gonna do the work if you don't know what the tracks are?"

I had no acceptable answer. Instead, I rummaged around the brain's store of stock responses and blurted out: "I'm just here to earn a buck."

This remarkably cavalier statement was totally out of character. It was about the only time I ever used the word buck in front of a stranger; it was as inappropriate as an American casually using the word quid in front of a British person. The bluster sounded as if I did not care about the job, nor about the yardmaster's concerns. The pitiful choice of words was a desperate effort to sound as if I had every confidence in retaining a position on Conrail no matter what the yardmaster thought. It was a hasty thing to say, partly the result of being agitated by an eighty-mile drive during which I had got lost.

Despite the yardmaster's anger, a brakeman position, which includes utility man, does not require that he be qualified. The yardmaster calmed down a little, found me a map of the yard, and told me that the first job was to take a crew to a train at the other end of the yard by driving them in the company truck, part of the utility man's duties at this yard. Off we went. Most vehicles in America have automatic gearboxes. I had had experience in driving them, but momentarily forgot, and once we were under way stamped on what I thought was the clutch to change from first to second gear and brought the vehicle to a sudden stop. Three burly men unexpectedly found themselves several inches further forward than they were a moment ago. They emitted guttural sounds, which suggested they were about to launch a stream of invective, but decided to swallow their words. I apologized; they regained their composure; we finished the journey. A ride in a yard jitney is usually quite rough; this ride was bumpier than normal. Why the men did not speak their minds I do not know, I deserved it. If a railroader makes a minor blunder – such as throwing a wrong switch - colleagues usually ignore it and allow him time to correct himself. That may have been the case here.

I remember nothing else about that night. My diary shows off duty at 07:59 hours, a twelve-hour shift. During that shift, at midnight to be precise, the number of men on the Hagerstown Extra List was cut, meaning I was once again without a position and on a five-day bump.

On Friday 31st March the computer displayed a vacancy on the Baltimore Extra List. The city of Baltimore was actually closer than Hagerstown, yet it seemed out of reach, over my head – it radiated all those kind of superior airs that discouraged outsiders. But it was the only option left, so despite the audacity of a junior employee claiming a job in the big city, I took the position. I was called to work that night, on duty at 23:59 for the midnight shifter.

I had just managed to hold onto employment with Conrail by hopping from one five-day bump to another. I then discovered stability in Baltimore. It was like precariously leaping from floating log to floating log, then landing on an island.

# CHAPTER 15

# BALTIMORE

Most people have no difficulty finding their way to work. Their shop, factory or office is in the same place every day. That was not the case for me in early Conrail days where place of employment changed frequently. So care had to be taken to drive off in the right direction, especially when a nocturnal telephone call suddenly wrenched one from deep sleep into a heart-pounding, disorientated semi-conscious state in which it was difficult to think. If called to Harrisburg or Enola, little mental effort was required to head north on Interstate Highway 83 and to contemplate later the correct exit. Any other yard required greater concentration. A call in the wee hours for either Hagerstown or Baltimore risked confusion because both were in the next state and both far away. From our driveway I had to make a left turn for Baltimore, right for Hagerstown; one night I drove twelve miles in the direction of Hagerstown before realizing I should be heading to Baltimore!

On the first call to Baltimore of 31ˢᵗ March 1995 no mistake was made. After taking a series of back roads from our home, I followed clear instructions in Conrail's booklet: Interstate Highway 83 southwards to the outskirts of Baltimore, then Interstate 695 - the Baltimore Beltway - in a clockwise direction to Interstate 95 leaving at exit number 59 to take city roads to Bayview Yard. Following quick introductions upon arrival, I was plunged straight into work. The YHBA68 conducted its business in the classification yard right outside the yard office.

Tracks were numbered with even numbers only, the highest being 82. Many had been removed, leaving a total of only twenty-six. Most of those twenty-six were paired, so that one switch on the ladder led to 46 and 48, the next switch to 50 and 52, and so on, an inside switch determining which one. A shallow hump near the yard office allowed cars to be dispersed by gravity. Despite working at night in an unknown yard, a mental picture of the paired but gappy sequence of tracks quickly formed.

A whole train, perhaps the inbound PIBA, was handled in one go. The usual procedure was to deal with, say, twelve cars at a time by closing the angle cock ahead of those twelve cars, and for a man at the hind end to hold the air hose firmly against his leg whilst swiftly opening the angle cock to dump the air. Gripping the air hose in this way prevented it flaying about and causing injury. Cars in emergency will not move, so air was released by pulling on a rod sticking out at the side of the cars, the release rod. The procedure was referred to as bleeding off cars. The train was slowly shoved over the hump and cars cut away in ones and twos to be drifted into different tracks. Cars without brakes will not stop, so the first few cars in each track had hand brakes applied before being cut away. In thus fashion we went to work.

At one stage in the night, radio exchanges went something along the following lines:

"Then it'll be one for 48, one for 46, one for 52," said the conductor.

"48, 46, 52. Roger," said I acknowledging the track numbers.

I lined up for 48, and after the first car had gone by threw the inside switch for 46, then walked down to line the 52 switch. The second car went into track 46. And so did the third car.

"Hey Steve," I said.

"Yes Mitch."

"I forgot to throw back 46/48 switch, the car for 52 went down the wrong hole."

"I'm going to come down there and kill you Mitch," said Steve unkindly.

Steve did not carry out his threat. The complete train was backed into 46 track for me to collect the misdirected car, re-align the switch and dispatch the vehicle properly.

The conductor worked close to the hump, the brakeman further down the yard. In the case of cars destined for the lower numbered tracks, those nearest the hump, the conductor made the cut whilst the brakeman merely lined switches. If cars for higher numbered tracks were cut by the conductor they would pick up too much speed on the long downhill run, so the whole train was sent to the brakeman to both make cuts and line up switches. In such case I separated cars on the ladder by the usual method of lifting the cut lever, a task usually undertaken in a stationery position. But the setting, the steady stream of cars coming over the hump, the fanning out of tracks, the worn path alongside switches - all brought back memories of watching shunters in Liverpool's Edge Hill Gridiron marshalling yard in the late 1960s. There, shunters used to run alongside rolling wagons applying brakes by means of a lever on the side of the vehicles. In honour of that memory, I began running alongside freight cars with one hand on the cut lever, the other on my radio to give the signal to stop when the cut was made. But that was not how it was supposed to be done. After a while the trainmaster, whose attention had been drawn to the irregular method of working, came and asked me to desist. (Incidentally, the Liverpool Gridiron was the first gravity yard in the world.)

Typical of midnight shifters, we continued working after 08:00, the timecard ultimately being closed to show a twelve-hour day. If the shift had left me hankering for more, I need not have fretted, for I was rewarded with a repeat performance the following night, again ringing up twelve hours.

A three-week stint in Baltimore included a night turn that traversed metals of a foreign railroad, the Mass Transit Administration, which used the former Northern Central route northwards out of Baltimore. Forays onto foreign rails required co-operation between both carriers. An obstacle to running on the Mass Transit Administration system was that they had their own Rule Book, Norac rules did not apply. They deftly overcame the problem by issuing *every* Conrail crew *every* night relevant extracts from their Rule Book, copies of the station pages and of course any bulletin information. An important departure from Norac rules was that an automatic signal showing red was STOP SIGNAL (as in Britain) not STOP AND PROCEED.

On another assignment, this time a daylight turn, the engineer took delight in pointing out the privilege of working on the best job in Baltimore! The travelling shifter journeyed thirty miles in a north-easterly direction on Amtrak's main line to reach customers.

Entering, exiting and travelling on the passenger network took up much of the day. At Amtrak's Oak interlocking, the shifter left the Northeast Corridor to use the Havre de Grace Yard Track, otherwise known as the Old Line, clearly a former alignment of the main line.

Certainly the most far-flung Baltimore assignment was a day in the city of Washington, District of Columbia, usually abbreviated to Washington DC, capital of the United States. (It is not always understood outside America that there are two Washingtons, the other being the State of Washington on the west coast.) As my wife slumbered, an early morning call initiated a sixty-mile drive from home to Bayview Yard, followed by a forty-mile deadhead trip to Benning Yard in the capital, where they must have run out of Extra Board men and had to rely on Baltimore. The day's work involved skimming the edge of Washington passenger station, which for the first time brought this wanderer face-to-face with Baltimore and Ohio Railroad signals, which are colour position light signals similar to those of the Pennsylvania Railroad except that signal message variants are achieved not by having a lower arm but by display of a marker light in one of six positions around the main signal head. A handful of such signal messages had to be included in Norac rules because crews met them in Washington. During this trip to the capital I recall servicing a scrap yard, and also seeing the brightly-coloured circus train of Ringling Bros. and Barnum & Bailey emblazoned "The Greatest Show on Earth". On returning home that night I surprised my wife with news I had been to work in Washington DC!

\* \* \*

Bayview Yard was like Harrisburg, Enola and Morrisville in being a long, oblong shaped affair with many tracks crossing at the centre. The upper end of Bayview (the northern tip operationally, eastern tip by the compass) gained access to Amtrak's Northeast Corridor via River interlocking. Also at this location the Sparrows Point Industrial Track led to a steel works. The middle of Bayview Yard was nipped into just five tracks, one of which was enigmatically named Jones's Lead.

The lower (southern or western) end of Bayview was the operational centre of Baltimore, and included the yard office, the hump, additional access to Amtrak via Bay interlocking and a clutch of mouth-watering track names: Old Wreck Train or Back Way, Next to the Cab and Lawn. This concatenation of railroad infrastructure veered away from Amtrak, turning ninety degrees to head due south and became the President Street Industrial Track. It marked the beginning of one of the most intriguing journeys on Conrail.

Industrial tracks are normally just a single track, but the President Street Industrial, effectively a continuation of Bayview Yard, boasted no less than *six* tracks at its widest point! West to east they read Trappe Road, South, North, Perryville, Bank and Incline. Incline was as much part of an adjoining intermodal terminal as the industrial track, but even without it, the President Street Industrial still had more tracks to its name than Amtrak's nearby main line! Lavish provision permitted simultaneous train movements.

After about a mile, at a location called Highland, the President Street Industrial became the Bear Creek Running Track comprising a measly three roads: Third, 1 and 2. The first trip along the Bear Creek Running fomented a rare experience: a completely new sensation in life! As the train rolled along, the nostrils were invaded by the most delightful aroma ever - fragrance from an adjacent spice factory. I had never smelt anything like it! The olfactory stimulation was so astonishingly and enjoyably new it had to be compared with other milestones, such as tasting curry for the first time, the first beer, adolescent experiences, that kind of thing, you know.

To return to the tour, after crossing Boston Street on the Bear Creek Running Track the railroad offered multiple routes. The most westerly was to continue on the same three tracks as before but under new guises: Main, Straight and Ladder. They ultimately led to a vast wind-swept desolate collection of under-used storage tracks where, to the delight of this railroader, a crew could work in utter freedom, much like USX Yard in Morrisville. The area took in the New Coal Yard and Empty Coal Yard (which together totalled twenty-three sidings) a wye and a track called West Baker which went off I have not the faintest idea where. In the middle of shifting this empty wilderness, I remember asking over the radio, "Which track do you want me to put this car on?"

"Oh, anywhere down there, it doesn't matter, wherever it's lined," said the conductor. In a time before every railroad track was allocated a computer number and every car had to be accounted for, nobody cared.

Adjacent to this neglected area, the Ladder Track served one of the most important rail customers in Baltimore, a huge coal exporting plant. Typically, six or seven 100-car coal trains daily, some run by Conrail, some run by CSX, converged on the site. The Ladder track branched into three approach roads where trains were taken right up to the unloading area and handed over to the exporting company, engines and all. Trains went round in a circle and came back to the Straight Track. Operations required considerable liaison to ensure supply of loaded trains corresponded to needs of the exporting company, which sometimes meant finding places to temporarily stable loaded trains. Since empty cars were much lighter, trains of outbound empty coal hoppers were often longer than trains of inbound loaded coal hoppers. This necessitated extensive re-marshalling of empty cars.

One place where this juggling of empty coal hoppers took place was a location known as Fifth Avenue, which comprised eight tracks. Fifth Avenue, adjacent to the coal plant, was spanned by a large gloomy overhead bridge which hampered visibility. Switching was further impaired by not knowing exactly where tracks ended. No stop blocks existed, rails just petered out in a most uncertain fashion.

South of Boston Street at the point where the Ladder Track continued southwards towards the coal plant, the Bear Creek Running Track proper, now reduced to a mere single track, branched off eastwards to skirt Fifth Avenue sidings. Shortly afterwards, the delightfully named Penn Mary Yard where Conrail and CSX interchanged cars fanned out north of the alignment. The running track then proceeded in a south-easterly direction to Dundalk Marine Terminal, the limit of my knowledge.

During the first few days in Baltimore I worked the YHBA64 from Bayview Yard to Dundalk Terminal, where we seemed to go round and round in circles serving waterfront sidings. At one stage I sauntered about twenty yards away from the track to peer over the dock side at the churning Patapsco River estuary. Four-foot waves crashed incessantly against stonework in a never-ending battle pitting ancient tidal forces against man's handiwork of more recent history. As I stood mesmerized by waves that slapped and sloshed and relentlessly rolled over one another, I thought – what was there to stop anyone walking straight off the quay into this cauldron? Nothing of course, except common sense. But whilst the terminal was sufficiently well-lit to avoid an accidental plunge, why were there no protective barriers? The obvious explanation is that any kind of fence would nullify the purpose of a quay, that of loading and unloading ocean-going vessels.

* * *

Baltimore conversations were lively. One engineer was actually born on Merseyside, England. He said that on the few occasions he had returned, women took a shine to him because he was from America. We swopped reminiscences about *Beano* and *Dandy* comic papers, Ribble buses, Yo-Yo biscuits, pickles and about the North of England dialect where the definite article was contracted to the letter t, as in "put t'kettle on." As the conversation ended, the engineer crumpled and said, "I'm a limey at heart."

Ed the jitney driver lolled about the traincrew room awaiting his next instruction. He had not shaved that morning and may have had a rough night for his clothes were bedraggled. John the engineer, who thought the jitney driver's degree of suavity could not pass without comment, looked down at him, took a deep breath, and with quivering lip, said, "Ed, you just fill every inch of my body with desire!" Ed blushed. I laughed heartily at this mock romantic encounter. Though a ridiculous lampoon, it was nevertheless one of many cases where the matter of relationships cropped up in Baltimore, both in this initial April 1995 period and on future occasions.

In 1995 it was well known in Bayview Yard that a certain man had left his wife for another woman. The new relationship tired the man so much, during lunch break he laid his arms on the table, put his head down and went to sleep. A year later when again working in Baltimore I was curious to know how the man was holding up in the gruelling new relationship. I could not remember his name so described him to a colleague as someone who had left his wife for a paramour. My colleague replied in a matter-of-fact way: "I've no idea which man it is, it could be anybody here."

On another occasion when describing to an engineer bachelor days in Liverpool's discotheques, I said that whilst my aim was simply to meet a nice girl, a minority of men viewed night clubs differently. One man boasted four conquests in one week. The engineer looked at me carefully to gauge my constitution before saying: "I had four in one day."

At a later date I told that story to another Baltimore man, who responded: "*Four*? Phew. I had three in one day, but *four*?" He shook his head in disbelief.

Despite the second man's amazement, it struck me there was little difference between the eccentricities of forming instant relationships with three different women in one day and forming instant relationships with four different women in one day. Either would have been impossible in circles I moved in; I could go to discotheques for weeks on end without even getting a date! I hasten to add both men had long left those days behind. Clearly we had lived in different worlds.

Did the fact that Baltimore was a port have any bearing on preoccupation with relationships? I say this because in moving around different parts of of my native country I was able to compare life in land-locked parts such as rural Yorkshire and the West Midlands with ports such as Liverpool and London. In ports the pastime of drinking alcohol added zest to life rather than encumbering it with sullen guilt. A man and woman meeting was cause for celebration, not condemnation. In short, ports expressed greater *joie de vivre*, the principal manifestation being robust pursuit of relationships.

In search of explanation for the Port Effect, it is tempting to quote Dorothy L Sayers when she has Lord Peter Wimsey say in *Gaudy Night*:

"One is always vulgar at watering-places."

However, this upper class 1930s usage refers more to an absence of refined conversation rather than to lasciviousness, so this hopeful line of enquiry has to be abandoned!

An alternative explanation may lurk in the dual outlook offered by a seaside location. The resident has a choice between turning towards land and facing all that civilization has to offer, including *mores* that constrain and restrict behaviour, or making an about turn and looking out to sea where nothing enslaves the mind, where soothing hypnotic lapping of waves might induce in the susceptible a letting go of inhibitions. Close proximity of a vast body of water melts circumscription and allows a person, if he or she so chooses, to turn one's back on land-based conventionalism.

Another thought is the exuberance that used to sweep through Liverpool each time a ship docked. Even if those elevated spirits were promulgated mainly by the fairer sex, it is not difficult to see how the whole tone of a city might be uplifted by invasion of large numbers of visitors, neither is it beyond comprehension to grasp that a city's ability to respond in such a way might imbue the population with more sparkle than elsewhere. Doubtless ports of London and Baltimore similarly rose to the occasion when a ship came in. Underwriting this firecracker response to maritime schedules was Liverpool's wealth of the The Beatles' legacy, London's capital status and Baltimore's fortuitous proximity to Washington DC.

I had no complaints about Baltimore's contribution to my own wealth, nor to the enrichment of railroading experience. The city provided respite from being bumped around, afforded a lively insight into urban life, and was an acceptable alternative to working east from Harrisburg. However, to me Baltimore remained a detached portion of Conrail, always a little out of reach. Despite its attributes, a lengthy commute was not in its favour. Phase One of the Baltimore engagement came to an end on Sunday 23rd April 1995 when I was bumped off the Extra List.

# CHAPTER 16

# MOUNTAIN CLIMBING

An hour after being bumped off the Baltimore List I bumped onto the Lancaster Extra Board, only to be kicked off eight hours later. Whilst relaxing on the five-day bump, I was surprisingly called to work in Hagerstown. On Wednesday 26th April 1995 I bumped onto the Enola Trainmen List, which provided two week's hectic work. The Enola Trainmen List covered work in Harrisburg Consolidated Terminal and, as such, saw a cross-section of yard work.

On three occasions I doubled back. On 28th April I worked on the Change Crew – a crew that shuffled locomotives around – from 07:00 to 15:00, then doubled-back to work as utility man from 23:00 to 07:45. That day, the 29th, I again worked a Change Crew from 22:31 to 06:31, doubling-back to a yard job in Shiremanstown 15:00 to 01:00. On 3rd May I worked utility man from 07:00 to 15:00, doubling-back to another utility man position 23:59 to 07:59.

On the face of it, doubling back asked a lot. But if a two-day period were considered where a man worked eight-hour shifts starting at 00:00, 16:00 and 08:00, he would be off duty just as much as he were on duty, a total of twenty-four hours in each case, which seems reasonable. What has to be taken into account however is that staff needed time to travel home, and that they were usually given a two-hour call to come back, both of which ate into rest time. The demands of doubling-back were recognized, in that employees were awarded an additional payment. In Britain I heard of some signalmen who continuously doubled-back on eight-hour shifts. I could not have done it.

I think it had long been a tradition in American railroading to work yard jobs as efficiently as possible in order to get a quit, as railroaders say. The drawback was that if expediency resulted in shifts lasting only five or six hours, it was very tempting for carriers to find the crew additional work. Over the years however it has become increasingly difficult for crews to undertake their work with dispatch owing to introduction of new rules, rules implemented across the United States for reasons of safety.

Probably the most important safety rule change concerned getting on and off moving equipment. The question would seem odd to a British student of railway practice, since guards and shunters never did ride on the side of rolling stock because there was nothing to grab hold of; they always had to walk along the ballast. But in America, switching used to be executed with rapidity as men rode on ladders fixed to the side of freight cars, hopping on and off whilst the train was in motion to position themselves for the next task. Rule books once said that such getting on and off always had to be done whilst the train moved at low speed; they now said it could not be done at all. I heard that having to change such an ingrained practice threw men out of their rhythm, and in some cases brought on accidents, the very thing the new rule was aimed at preventing. But that was transitional - the new rule introduced round about the time I started on Conrail had to be followed without question. If a crew were shifting with just a handful of cars, time lost was not great, but if a conductor were hanging on the rear of fifty cars and had to wait until the train came to a complete stop before alighting, work took so much longer.

A second new innovation was three-step protection. Each time a man on the ground had to foul equipment, that is, go between cars to couple, uncouple or do anything else, the procedure had to be as follows:

"Conductor Deaver to engine number 6025 give me three-step protection."

The engineer then had to apply brakes to prevent the train from moving, centre the reverser lever (like putting an automobile into neutral) and open the generator field switch which immobilized the locomotive. He then replied on the radio, "Three-step applied on 6025." Only then could the conductor reach in between cars. Yard crews were allowed to abbreviate radio communications somewhat, but that did not excuse them from the three-step routine, which was heard constantly on yard radios throughout the day.

Use of engine numbers to identify trains was an older rule. We were told the true story of two crews shifting in a yard, when one conductor said over the radio, "Okay John, bring 'em back twenty feet to couple." Unfortunately there were two engineers named John working in the yard, with tragic results. It could be argued that the train's name would be easier to remember, but when the PICA and CAPI passed each other on the road, as they did every night, a radio transmission from one could hastily be mistaken as coming from the other.

The rush of work on the Enola Trainmen List, though demanding at times, engendered a feeling of security, a feeling I was less dispensable, less likely to lose my job. The fear of being cast out to Oak Island Yard at last receded, though never fully disappeared. Peace reigned, but only briefly. At one minute past midday on 9th May I was taken off the Trainmen List and forced to sign an extra board known as the Enola Road Conductors List. When holding a position on an extra board, the employee was expected to work when called: the American expression was that the person must *protect* the extra board. If the extra board covered several routes, the employee had to know all routes before being allowed to work. (I understand that was also the case with train drivers at locomotive depots in Britain.) The Enola Road Conductors List was Pennsylvania equity. Originally, it probably covered routes fanning out from the eastern end of Enola Yard, that is, everything that could be reached from the Enola Branch, including the now lifted Low Grade route that cut across Lancaster County to reach such places as Philadelphia, Morrisville and North Jersey. I knew only Lancaster, Morrisville and Camden, plus the Reading Line as far as Alburtis interlocking, so had to mark off to learn the remainder – but managed to slip in a couple of Maryland & Pennsylvania coal trains along the way.

\* \* \*

The most important part of Conrail on which I had yet to qualify, and therefore the most urgent, was the Allentown area, which brings me to the lacuna in the chapter headed Names. Two stations on the route to North Jersey were skipped because the place-name common to both was so revered that its use for railroad purposes brought on such uneasiness I could not write the name and glibly move onto the next topic. The two stations were CP-Bethlehem and Bethlehem DED (dragging equipment detector). CP-Bethlehem was a complex interlocking on the Lehigh Line where both the Reading Line and Bethlehem Secondary came in. The detector was about two miles east of the interlocking on the Reading Line.

The railroad name Bethlehem was derived both from the town and from a steel works located there. Each time we passed the steel works, which was adjacent to the Lehigh Line, I stared at blast furnaces glowing with white-hot steel. The molten metal would ultimately be poured into railroad vehicles called torpedoes to be taken round the mill. A stone's throw from tracks, the liquid steel glowed so brightly that buildings, girders, support pillars and all else were silhouetted, save furnaces that glowed fiery red. A menacing wall of smouldering whites, reds and blacks dared trains to come any closer. How could this hellish place bear the name Bethlehem? How could the name so affectionately remembered from childhood in the Christmas carol "O Little Town of Bethlehem" - sung to the tune Forest Green in Britain – a name carried into adulthood with respect, be at the same time applied to a smoking, steaming, sweating, sweltering pagan inferno? To United States residents Bethlehem Steel is a household name, but to a foreigner, use of the hallowed name for a steel works and secondarily as title of a piece of railroad seemed, at first sight, an affront to Western culture.

The clash is reconciled by reference to the 1916 book *The Story of Bethlehem Steel* by Arundel Cotter. Its author reports that on 24th December 1741 a religious group known as the Moravians escaping persecution in Europe set up a new community in the Lehigh Valley, Pennsylvania. In honour of the birthday they would be celebrating the following day, they named their new home Bethlehem. It was not until a hundred years later that, quite separately, iron ore was discovered in nearby Saucon Valley. On 8th April 1857 the Saucon Iron Co. was set up to exploit the find. Two years later the name was changed to Bethlehem Rolling Mills and Iron Co. The book hints at lengthy deliberations over the company title. Between 1859 and 2003 the entity underwent several name changes, the last being Bethlehem

Steel Corporation. Thus the decision-making process of attaching the name Bethlehem to a steel works took a lengthy and roundabout route.

Throughout its existence the Bethlehem plant contributed tremendously to the United States economy, particularly when, in the early 1900s, it pioneered what was then described as the Bethlehem section, now referred to in the States as I-beam, in Britain as a girder. Also of inestimable importance was railroad rails production.

With the passage of time original indignation has faded, and I have come to accept that the birthplace Bethlehem and Bethlehem Steel are capable of being countenanced quite separately and their due significance acknowledged without detriment to one or the other. Sadly, Bethlehem Steel was dissolved in 2003, victim of overseas competition and a general decline in heavy industry.

* * *

In 1995 Harrisburg was part of Conrail's Harrisburg Division. Most eastbound destinations were in the Philadelphia Division, and men needing to qualify had to travel to that division to be examined. A division post just east of Alburtis placed Allentown and Bethlehem – my main priority - in the Philadelphia division. Officials periodically made themselves available in Allentown for qualifying purposes, the next opportunity was Friday19th May 1995. Numerous trains went to Allentown, only a few to Bethlehem. It was therefore imperative to master Bethlehem, so on Monday the 15th I asked the crew dispatchers to place me on the next PIBE, Conway to Bethlehem. I was duly called on Tuesday 16th, but on arrival at Harrisburg GI8 was informed PIBE was running late, and that the crew were therefore switched to a coal train UBB122 which, fortunately, was also bound for Bethlehem.

Unbelievably, the train had to call at Millards quarry on the Harrisburg Line to pick up yet more weight in the form of loaded stone cars. Whilst the conductor carried out the lengthy process of doing a full brake test, two things troubled me as I waited on the engine. First, how were we to climb a steep gradient that rose from CP-Bethlehem with loaded coal *and* loaded stone? I later expressed that concern earnestly to both engineer and conductor. Second, were we going to have enough time to do everything? Both were worrying, because if I missed the chance to qualify on 19th May, when would there be another?

After leaving Millards, the next stop train UBB122 made was at CP-Burn on the edge of Bethlehem Allentown Consolidated Terminal. An intermodal train overtook us. I was then pleased to learn that we were waiting arrival of two more locomotives to assist in making the gradient. Whether they had been provided owing to my remonstrances, or whether they had been laid on anyway, I did not know. Whatever the case, time was ticking away.

At last the engines arrived. The conductor and I set about making connections so that all locomotives could work together as multiple units. The task of hooking up those connections was described by railroaders as m.u.ing, pronounced emm-YOU-ing. The required four pairs of hoses, namely the train line, the sander, the locomotive independent brake and the independent brake operating line, were matched. Angle cocks were turned in each case. Short gangways between the two coupled engines were lowered and safety chains secured.

"There's no jumper cable!" exclaimed the conductor.

The jumper cable was something that looked like an elephant's trunk and which made electrical connections between two locomotives. Locomotives should have a jumper cable on each end, but often did not. Neither engine had one.

"There's probably a jumper on one of the other ends," I said helpfully. "You go to the front engine, I'll go to the hind engine."

Moments later we met again. "There's none on the back," I said.

"There's one on the front," said the conductor, "but it's fastened on."

At this point I wrested the initiative, because I had more at stake than the conductor: "Let's go and see if we can get it off."

We tried, but it was permanently fixed. Frustration set in. Following radio calls to the Lehigh Train Dispatcher, it was decided to take the train into Allentown Yard where we could pick up another jumper cable. Both the route through Allentown Yard and the straighter route via East Penn Junction met again at CP-Bethlehem where the Bethlehem Secondary began. As still more minutes ticked away, we collected and fitted a jumper cable, made the necessary tests, and left Allentown Yard. We then learnt that PIBE, the train we were originally called for, was now overtaking us via East Penn

Junction. Our train had to wait at CP-JU interlocking, just before CP-Bethlehem. Since PIBE had to get out of the way before we could move, chances of completing the journey retreated, along with my chances of qualifying in three day's time. Such was the daunting task ahead that stiff gradients beyond CP-Bethlehem now seemed to rise so fiercely we would have to break out crampons and safety ropes to scale them! As we sat at base camp, the prospect of failure weighed heavily: I would have to re-schedule a trip to Bethlehem and hope for a future qualifying session in Allentown.

"Lehigh Dispatcher to the UBB122, are you ready to copy Form D?" crackled the radio, making us all jump in our seats.

"Ready to copy," replied the conductor joyfully.

The conductor duly copied a Form D for the Bethlehem Secondary. Because the Secondary was only a mile long, special instructions stipulated that the Dispatcher's permission must simultaneously be obtained to occupy the Saucon Running Track that was a continuation of the Secondary. The signal cleared and we were off!

After departing CP-JU we crossed a girder bridge over the Lehigh River. The home signal for CP-Bethlehem was tucked away high in the bridge's ironmongery. Two diamond crossings took the train onto the Secondary, where four locomotives roared with gusto as they began the climb. We crossed a succession of grade crossings. Between each street were stretches of grass; it looked as if we were slicing through residents' front lawns! At station sign Hem, the Bethlehem Secondary became the Saucon Running Track. A little further, huge numbers of sidings branched off on either side. On the right lay former Saucon Yard, closed and abandoned only within the previous twelve months. On the left lay Iron Hill Yard containing thirty-nine tracks under the control of Iron Hill East yardmaster. A separate railroad, grandly named the Philadelphia, Bethlehem and New England, operated within the Bethlehem Steel complex, of which Iron Hill was part. We came to a stop at the next station, Lehigh, to back off stone cars into Iron Hill. To deliver the coal hoppers demanded one more climb, the steepest of the whole expedition, to a yard called PBNE Coal Field. This was reached by the appropriately named Number 1 Hill and Number 2 Hill Running Tracks. We took Number 1 Hill. On arrival we proceeded to split the train amongst six tracks in the Coal Field, tracks identified as

A, B, C, D, 3 and 4. The longest track held only thirty cars. Tracks branched out, then met again at the far end where there was room to manoeuvre before reaching a coal dumping area. With such a layout, the scheme was to run up one track with cars, cut them off, and come back another track for more, always making sure one track remained open to release the locomotives.

At one or two o'clock in the morning it was uncertain whether work could be completed before running out of time. Circumstances would make the outcome clear. When the engines travelled back to collect a second string of cars, it was found a coupling could not be made. A cut had been made on a curve and, once vehicles parted, couplers sprang to a straight alignment and would not meet. Despite our combined efforts neither coupler could be manoeuvred into position. In fairness, even in daylight, unless the man on the ground is very familiar with the territory, it is difficult to spot a curve when standing right on it; we were working in pitch black conditions. The problem was eventually solved by hooking up air hoses to charge the train without being coupled to it. In due course the brakes released from emergency, the train began to drift backwards till air hoses parted, at which point the cars made an emergency application on themselves and stopped moving, the short distance travelled being sufficient to allow a good coupling. Judicious use of hand brakes controlled the operation.

The coupling problem had cost much time, so much there was now no chance all work, including disposing of the locomotives, could be completed. A jitney arrived with a relief crew, the same jitney took us to the hotel.

On Wednesday the crew worked a train back to Harrisburg. On Thursday I caught another train to Allentown and remained there till Friday to qualify. Examinations were in the form of specific questions for each line. Designed primarily for Allentown based personnel, they included many questions on shifting local industries. I did not do particularly well, but the examiner, knowing qualifications were for road work only, was lenient and gave pass marks for all lines in the immediate Allentown area up to and including the route to PBNE Coal Field.

As months and years went by, vastness of the Bethlehem Steel layout gradually revealed itself. Though no more official qualifications were obtained, here and there I inched further into the complex to find disused parts as barren and empty as anywhere on Conrail. Iron ore jennies were unloaded at the Finger Yard, a collection of short sidings that divided like a hand. On one occasion I worked along the edge of the 700 Yard comprising thirty-seven tracks. Beyond the 700 Yard, apparently the 200, 300, 400, 500 and 600 Yards stretched far into the distance, so far they disappeared round the curvature of the earth.

On a cool blustery April day in 2015 my wife and I visited Bethlehem. We retraced on foot, as far as possible, the final assault of 16th May 1995, that between CP-Bethlehem and PBNE Coal Field. The first section was easy, as the Bethlehem Secondary Track had been lifted, replaced by a walking trail. The Saucon Running Track, for the most part, was also gone. We walked alongside its former alignment. The Finger Yard and Iron Hill Yard enjoyed new business, but the latter was fenced off from where the now lifted Hill Running Tracks used to lay. We followed the abandoned route, much overgrown.

The trek came to an abrupt halt. A bridge that evidently had spanned Route 412, a bridge of which I have no memory from that dark 1995 night, had been taken away to widen the highway. Its absence curtailed our 2015 expedition preventing us reaching the PBNE Coal Field. The outing was nevertheless a bracing and rewarding exercise in nostalgia. The Philadelphia, Bethlehem and New England Railroad, after a period of dormancy when steel making ceased, was back in operation handling new traffic. As for blast furnaces that once so troubled a Conrail trainee, they have been preserved, and now stand cold. Rusting. Bleak. Defiant.

* * *

The 16th May 1995 Bethlehem expedition was not the only mountain climb, the whole Conrail qualifying programme was a formidable rock face. Cramming to pass qualifying tests was the most difficult part, offset by the thoroughly enjoyable if time consuming exercise of preparing study maps. The test paper itself comprised eighteen questions covering physical characteristics, speeds, gradients, rules in effect and special instructions. My formula for passing tests was to reproduce painstakingly each page of my maps on the reverse of the test booklet, then answer questions by referring back to them.

Conrail gave trainees remarkable freedom. A telephone call to the crew dispatcher would lay on a trip wherever I needed to go. If I had to stay an extra day in a hotel to sit qualifying tests or to study a yard, no questions were asked. Jitneys ferried me here and there on request. I do not know to what extent supervisory staff monitored my efforts, if at all, but timecards recorded everything.

The learning profile when I started on British Railways comprised a steep two-month period studying rules and regulations and learning Kensal Green Junction signal box. It was followed by a less demanding slope lasting about a year when I was officially trained yet still encountered new aspects of a signalman's work. After that, I sailed along a plateau of being master of the job. On Conrail, the initial period of learning a multitude of yards and hundreds of route-miles took about a year. The easier slope of being qualified yet still learning took another year. The subsequent plateau of being completely trained did not match the care-free period on British Railways, because there was always one corner of a yard unexplored, always another set of peculiar operating arrangements to learn. A signalman's area of responsibility stretched a few miles: a road conductor's patch covered a sizable portion of the United States.

# CHAPTER 17

# PHILADELPHIA

Assignments such as the PICA returning as CAPI were described as regular jobs. Regular jobs usually had three crews, one called from home to work eastbound, a second called from the hotel to work westbound, a third resting at home: the job was said to have three sides. Another regular job, the Mail44 to North Jersey, had one of its three sides Pennsylvania equity, and was therefore covered by the Enola Road Conductors List in case of absence. It was the only North Jersey position allocated Pennsylvania equity. As part of the programme to qualify on the list, four learning trips were arranged on Mail44. It went to work at about midnight, returning the following evening as TV3. On the fourth trip I remained behind and reported to Oak Island Yard to sit qualifying tests for North Jersey territory and for the Lehigh Line.

There then arose the knotty problem of learning central Philadelphia, which comprised South Philadelphia Yard and a four-mile section connecting the yard to an interlocking named CP-Field at milepost zero on the Harrisburg Line. There was no daily train to Philadelphia. There used to be, men said, but in the mid-1990s Conway traffic for Philadelphia was included in the PIAL, then relayed on the ALPG Allentown to Philadelphia. At one time numerous coal and iron ore workings ran between Harrisburg and the city of brotherly love, but were now sporadic. If I had asked crew dispatchers to call me for the next Philadelphia train I could have waited a week. The answer was to catch any available train to the Philadelphia area, stay in the hotel, and subsequently cover outstanding territory on foot.

South Philadelphia Yard was the eastern end of the Harrisburg Line. In its heyday the yard had been extremely busy, but apparently much traffic had been lost to Baltimore. Its current status was a familiar picture of layer upon layer of mostly empty sidings. Endless waves of disused rusting tracks evoked in one trainee an irrational affection, but could not alter the fact that under-use of South Philadelphia Yard was a tremendous waste. Fortunately, efforts to revive and re-use it would come in the future.

On a glorious warm and sunny Saturday 3rd June 1995 I reported to South Philadelphia Yard office and told supervisory staff of my plan to walk to CP-Field and to catch a jitney back. They smiled a little, but raised no objection. Of note in this central part of the yard were the Old Greenwich Hump, a Car Shop track numbered 10½ and another track called the Southern Pocket. As I struck out westwards I had to give other employees met on the way an explanation for a traincrew member walking along the track without a train! One conductor could not believe I was undertaking such a hike.

Along the northern edge of the yard ran a collection of tracks, one named 4B&O. In this part of Philadelphia tracks of the former Pennsylvania and Baltimore and Ohio Railroads interwove. Next south stood the Departure Yard, then the Receiving Yard, then the Coal Receiving Yard. Between the latter two ran a key track named 4 Departure from which access could be gained to the seventeen-track Ore Yard. At the far end of the Ore Yard were two semi-circular tracks named In and Out. Between them an isolated section of narrow gauge track was home to a unique diesel locomotive. By bearing against small solid buffers incorporated in the design of iron ore jennies, the narrow gauge diesel engine pushed the jennies round the semi-circles. I do not know if the locomotive was still in use. The Ore Yard was next to Pier 122, the Ore Pier on the Delaware River.

All tracks converged to become just three at the western end of the yard in the vicinity of Broad Street overhead bridge. Beyond the bridge my march began in earnest along four tracks described as, from north to south, 4B&O, Number 1 Running, Number 2 Running, 3B&O. Later, a long right-hand bend brought CP-Penrose interlocking into view, a sprawling affair where four-track territory ended, where two tracks numbered 1 and 2 went straight ahead, where a single track branched off left to CSX and where sidings came in, also on the left. Fine old Pennsylvania Railroad position light signals lorded it over the site, which had seen busier times. Though the interlocking still saw active service for through traffic, the complicated layout could not beat back a pervasive air of redundancy. I paused to record signalling details, and to absorb the atmosphere of this quondam hot spot, then pressed onwards along the straight route.

A long viaduct built adjacent to Philadelphia's 25th Street carried Rule 261 double-track towards the next interlocking, CP-Gray. A disused switch off Track 1 pointed to a sheer drop down to street level; the building it served must have been demolished. Two mileposts were passed, HE2 and HE1. I suppose the prefixes, that stood for Harrisburg East, were necessary, otherwise the mileposts would have had to be numbered minus 1 and minus 2 from milepost zero at CP-Field. Below the railroad, row after row of city houses stretched into the distance. Each of their occupants, too, had lives as complicated as lives of railroaders whose trains occasionally rumbled overhead. Two disparate streams of existence never interacted, never exchanged the time of day. High on the viaduct, I speculated loftily how different their realities might be.

At CP-Gray the Arsenal Connection track branched off left, and the Harrisburg Line continued a short distance as single track to CP-Field. The two interlockings were only a tenth of a mile apart. Within CP-Gray a switch led to a small power station. One engineer told me they used to drop off coal hoppers there.

As the hot and thirsty journey reached its goal at the simple one-switch interlocking of CP-Field, I paused to savour the moment of consummation. The plan for returning to South Philadelphia Yard involved finding a way down to street level, locating a telephone, and waiting for a jitney, each of which was so fraught with difficulty that after a brief period of head-shaking mental re-adjustment, I changed my mind, turned round and walked all the way back again!

\* \* \*

It is an appropriate moment to relate an unhappy tale that unfolded in South Philadelphia Yard, but to do so a leap forward must be made to 1998 when I was a fully trained road conductor. Wednesday 25th November was the day before the national holiday of Thanksgiving, an occasion when Conrail, to their credit, made an effort to get men home for the celebration. On duty at 06:00, the engineer and I were called on this bright and sunny day to deadhead to Philadelphia and to bring back a gondola train loaded with steel, the train symbol being PMT19. On arrival at the yard I set about reading bulletins and studying paperwork in the locker room. The engineer went to speak to supervisory staff about the motive power. After a while he returned to tell me that a certain switch had been damaged by derailment, and that we were to pass over it with extreme caution as only temporary repairs had been effected. Identity of the switch was unclear. We both studied the map and concluded the switch in question must be where the Ore Yard Lead met Number 4 Departure, but agreed it would be better for me to speak again with supervisory staff before commencing work.

Whilst the engineer checked over the locomotives, I went to the yard office and met the trainmaster and two yardmasters who were in the middle of changing shifts. One of the three spoke to me. "Did the engineer tell you about the derailment?"

I nodded. The man described how the derailment had occurred, and continued: "Now, you've gotta really take it slow over the switch, 'cause we haven't been able to do a proper job on it, Thanksgiving coming up and all that. But we've gotta get your train out of here. So take it *real* easy!"

"Roger," I said. Then it occurred to me they had not confirmed which switch it was, so I added: "Now, it's 4 Departure and Ore Yard Lead?"

One of the men nodded the affirmative.

With that settled, I climbed the bank between the yard office and what was known as the Class Yard where the engines were stabled, threw my grip in the cab, and began work. Our motive power was Class SD60I number 5623 and Class SD50 number 6749. We travelled down 7 track to the west end of the Coal Receiving Yard, at which point we changed direction to traverse the ladder in order to reach 4 Departure. We had not gone very far when the engine began to ride roughly, bumping in fact, then the nose of the engine dropped with a bigger thump. We had derailed. I alighted, and discovered to my horror one rail laying over on its side, the switch frog smashed and all six wheels of the leading truck on the ground. (The frog is the central part of a switch where two rails cross, apparently so named because the component looks like a stretched-out amphibian.) A hasty call to the yardmaster brought a representative from the Maintenance of Way department running. "I told you to take it easy!" he yelled at us.

"I thought it was the Ore Yard switch!" I yelled back.

"NO, it's the number 8 switch!" said the man angrily.

We had travelled over the defective switch at a normal speed of a few miles an hour instead of creeping over it. An unpleasant meeting followed between supervisory staff and traincrew. It became apparent, though no one admitted it, that when I had said, "Now, it's 4 Departure and Ore Yard Lead?" officials thought I was requesting confirmation of the route to take, not asking identity of the defective switch, which was the true purpose of the question.

An air of resignation hung over all concerned; each of us had fallen short in communicating. Not one of the three officials had made it clear to me which switch was defective. This may be owing in part to the yardmasters' change of shift, whereby each had assumed the other had made the facts clear. The engineer had not grasped at the outset which switch it was. My economy of words had resulted in an ambiguity. I should have said: "Now, it's the 4 Departure and Ore Yard Lead switch that's defective?" A Maintenance of Way representative should have been at the site. Two weak links in the chain of communication were nods of the head. When I was asked if the engineer had told me about the derailment, I nodded because I knew of a problem, but not the details. I should have said, "Yes he did, but can you confirm which switch it is." When I spoke to the official about 4 Departure and Ore Yard Lead, he acknowledged with a nod because he was unsure what I was talking about. He should have said, "If you're talking about the route to take, yes, that is correct." Probably all of us allowed the upcoming public holiday to occupy too many of our thoughts at the expense of applying complete concentration to the job. The episode excelled as a textbook lesson in communication failure. As someone who took pride in communicative skills, I was particularly disappointed in myself. A tacit acknowledgement that all shared blame prevented the matter going further.

But the problem remained of the train. Because a crane would have to be called in to re-rail the locomotive, management decided to implement a seldom-used procedure, that of putting the crew in a hotel for a respite period of four hours. A respite period is within the hours of service law, in that it permits a crew to be on duty up to sixteen hours after first signing on, provided the total number of hours actually worked did not exceed twelve.

With the understanding that a jitney would return to pick us up at 14:30 to be back on duty at 15:00, the engineer and I settled into the hotel for a respite period, which could have been re-labelled a spite period. Shortly after having made myself comfortable, the telephone rang. It was the engineer. "Hey Mitch. I've gone and left my good glasses on the jitney. The ones I'm wearing are my sunglasses. I need my other glasses to take the train back, 'cause it'll be dark. They're prescription safety glasses, so I need them."

"Can't you manage without 'em, John?" I asked.

"No. Anyway, I phoned the Philadelphia crew dispatcher to tell him what happened, and he didn't believe me," continued John.

"All right. Leave it with me a while," I said.

I waited about fifteen minutes, then telephoned the crew dispatcher. "The engineer left his normal safety glasses on the jitney that deadheaded us here. He says he can't take the train back unless he has them. We're not supposed to wear tinted glasses when it's getting dark."

"Yeh, right!" said the crew dispatcher with bitter sarcasm.

"No, honest, he really did leave his glasses on the jitney," I insisted.

The crew dispatcher suspected the story had been invented so we could deadhead home early for Thanksgiving Eve. Nothing further happened till an hour or two later when a jitney arrived to take us back to Harrisburg. It seemed probable that enquiries were made of the taxi company that took us to Philadelphia, when it was discovered a pair of safety glasses had indeed been found in one of their vehicles. This Conrail assignment earned the distinction of being one of the most unproductive ever by virtue of deadheading both ways without coupling to a train, never mind moving one.

* * *

In the mid-1990s a couple of regular jobs ran to the Philadelphia area. Other trains to the region were unpredictable, but included coal traffic destined for power stations and more coal traffic interchanged with CSX in the Belmont locality. Trains to and from

145

South Philadelphia Yard itself were few and far between. Worthy of mention was one round trip to the yard on 29th September 1997 where we brought back train ZWW970 comprising 160 car-loads of iron ore. As usual, the ore was in pellet form, each granule about a half-inch in diameter. The beads habitually fell through small crevices in car bodies, resulting in South Philadelphia Yard being carpeted in the material; they were recovered magnetically from time to time. Motive power for the 8500 foot 19,023 ton train were Class SD80MAC 5000 horsepower locomotives 4122, 4120, 4118 and 4128, two at the head and two in the middle of the train. This class of locomotive was a departure from the usual design in that the prime mover was an alternating current engine rather than direct current. The lead locomotive was equipped with an additional panel to operate the central locomotives remotely, so that, for example, when the head end of the train was over a summit, power could be eased off on the lead locomotives but maintained on the other two. Locomotives in the middle of trains was common practice in some parts of North America; ZWW970 was the only instance I saw on Conrail.

The discontinuous nature of traffic flows between Harrisburg Consolidated Terminal and Philadelphia posed problems for crew dispatchers. If an eastbound train arrived in Harrisburg, it seldom sat around very long before being manned and taken to Philadelphia. The crew was then normally placed in the hotel in the hope of a return working. Sometimes there was no return working. When crews complained about rotting in the hotel, they were frequently told of a westbound empty coal hopper train in the offing, or phantom hopper train as crews derisively called it. Ultimately, when it was deemed undesirable to hold a crew any longer for a ghost train, they were deadheaded home. I heard the record for a crew stewing in a Philadelphia hotel before being sent home was thirty hours.

I speak scathingly of lengthy stopovers in Philadelphia hotels in order to reflect the way most men felt about them. I felt less strongly, for two reasons. First, I enjoyed relaxing, watching television and having no chores to do. Second, crews were paid for each hour spent in the hotel from the seventeenth hour through the twenty-fourth, eight hours pay for doing nothing. I said to others it seemed not a bad deal; they said it was blood money. This payment was often called cabin-track time, which I think dates from times when crews took rest in the train's caboose on a track specially reserved for that purpose. Once the twenty-fourth hour had passed and maximum cabin-track payment had been earned, I too would begin agitating to be deadheaded home.

Philadelphia did not escape the Port Effect. As an engineer and I sat in a hotel waiting for a jitney, I noticed every woman who walked by smiled at us. Some time elapsed before the explanation became apparent: the engineer was smiling at every woman, no matter her age, as she went by. Though he was a little older than I was, he had an infectious boyish smile women found irresistible.

The same hotel had a discotheque. About 21:00 hours, again whilst waiting for transport, music drew me in the manner of the Pied Piper. As I was in work clothes, I gave no impression of genuine interest, but sauntered casually towards the room. Records played may have been new, but the disco beat was unmistakable. Women on the dance floor boasted the same trim outline I remembered from Liverpool's 1970s night clubs. The similarity was uncanny, it was like stepping back in time. But as I drew closer the mirage shattered: the women were not quite as young as they appeared from a distance. Then I remembered I was wanting in youth too.

The hotel that Conrail used in Philadelphia changed from time to time. In another hotel, the usual time we were called to work of mid to late evening coincided with on duty time for dancers at a local establishment. They also stayed in the hotel. So whilst waiting in the lobby, we were entertained by a procession of young women hurrying to their labours - they always seemed to be running late. High heels of one diminutive young lady accounted for ten per cent of her height; she ran like an ostrich.

On more than one occasion in this hotel a somewhat mismatched couple signed in at the reception desk. We heard from hotel staff that they were regular customers, and that they were man and wife. It did not escape notice that the smartly-dressed woman possessed well-formed legs of such length they seemed to reach her armpits. A flimsy dress hardly contained an ample bosom that spilled from the top of the garment like porridge boiling over. Her partner by contrast was a somewhat untidily-dressed man of spare frame, with all the charisma of a car park attendant.

On a second appearance of the odd couple, an inquisitive nature compelled me to use the legitimate excuse of handing in my room key at the reception desk to take a closer look at the remarkable woman. As I leant against the counter, waiting, I saw a classically sculptured square face that nevertheless revealed a twenty-first birthday to be some way behind her. Looking the woman straight in the eye for a second revealed a surprising lack of warmth. It reminded me of an undersea natural history programme that featured divers (protected in cages) coming face to face with sharks. One diver spoke of looking into the shark's eyes hoping to see some glimmer of feeling, some sign that the creature had a soul and was not just an eating machine, but the diver saw only empty black discs devoid of all emotion. The striking woman in a Philadelphia hotel had eyes similarly bereft of sensitivity, as inert as doll's eyes, lifeless.

# CHAPTER 18

# FILTER BELLE

Growing up in Yorkshire County, England, inculcated upon a young mind a thrifty way of speaking whereby only that which was worthwhile saying was actually said - the fact that such laconicism might result in periods of silence did not matter. This economical form of communicating had to be sacrificed if a young man were to progress in life, especially in an urban setting, even more so in dealings with the opposite sex. Whilst changes were made over time to improve conversational language I nevertheless endeavoured to retain a critical ear, taking care to assess everything heard, to judge whether or not it had value. Eight years as a signalman afforded an opportunity to refine this skill as discourse with other people was limited, most of the working day being spent pulling levers and ringing bells. Moreover, the period provided opportunity to read newspapers in depth and acquire greater respect for language. I trained myself to hang on to every word.

Circumstances altered when I moved to America. During 1989 I began working in places surrounded by many others, and found myself in the middle or on the periphery of multiple simultaneous conversations. Particularly when I worked in a warehouse between assignments on the Maryland & Pennsylvania, the sheer volume of talk was so overwhelming each spoken word could no longer be scrutinized. A new, binary strategy had to be adopted. Plan A was a decision that subject matter was pertinent and that I would listen. Plan B was implemented for unimportant or irrelevant material, and where I would close the ears and allow words to drift off into the ether.

During early 1995 the latter circumstances arose in Harrisburg GI8 yard office whilst discussing with a colleague route knowledge necessary to become a qualified road conductor. As the conversation proceeded, another colleague stood at short distance listening. At one stage, he interjected, "Filter Belle." Since I had not the faintest idea what he was saying and since I was not directly in conversation with him, I chose to invoke Plan B, ignore the meaningless rubbish and continue talking with the first man.

A few weeks later in a similar conversation, I was startled when another colleague uttered the same balderdash, "Filter Belle."

"I don't understand you," I said.

"Filter Belle," he repeated.

What did those words mean? Was Filter Belle a lady from the southern United States who specialized in filtration systems? Observing my bewilderment, the colleague then enunciated clearly and slowly, "Phil to Bell, the interlockings on Amtrak. It's the part of the Northeast Corridor you need to know to be able to get to Edgemoor Yard. It begins with Phil Interlocking where the Harrisburg Line comes in and ends at Bell Interlocking where you leave Amtrak for Edgemoor. Phil to Bell."

\* \* \*

Thus next to be learnt was a twenty-mile stretch of the Northeast Corridor that passed through Philadelphia's outer districts, that took in site of the famous Baldwin locomotive works, that passed under the Commodore Barry Bridge linking Pennsylvania and New Jersey and that included in its lineside attractions a factory manufacturing iron chains of such unbelievably massive proportions that pilfering amongst the work force could hardly be a problem.

The first stage of mastering Phil to Bell was reconnaissance on a round trip with the PIED that went to Edgemoor, Delaware State. At Belmont in Philadelphia City, PIED continued straight on the Harrisburg Line, rather than turning left for Camden. The Harrisburg Line, now only single track, passed through the middle of Amtrak's expansive Zoo interlocking without making connection with it. At one time several switches did connect with Zoo – named after the nearby Philadelphia Zoological Gardens – when traincrews had to learn the whole spaghetti bowl-like layout in order to qualify. By the time the new batch of trainees arrived on Conrail we were saved that ordeal. Conrail's single track passed very close to Zoo tower itself, still open in the 1990s. It was manned by two grades of operators, those personnel who just operated the miniature lever frame and a director who made decisions.

After Zoo, trains ran along an elevated portion of track called the High Line which afforded a commanding view of central Philadelphia, spectacular at night. At CP-Field the Harrisburg Line proper made a sharp left turn along the route already covered on foot. PIED continued straight for about a mile to be greeted by an arresting display of no less than six Pennsylvania-style position light signals in a row mounted on a gantry, or signal bridge. These were home signals for Phil interlocking and marked the boundary between Conrail and Amtrak. Title of the Amtrak dispatcher who now took over was CETC-4, pronounced Seateck. Phil was an impressive layout containing no less than eleven crossovers within its boundary, movements being so complicated additional signals were erected within the interlocking to facilitate them. The additional signals were not called inner homes or startings as in Britain, but merely interlocking signals.

The next interlocking on this four-track section of Amtrak's Northeast Corridor was Baldwin, the next Hook. Hook boasted six tracks, the first being labelled the Naught, followed by 1, 2, 3, 4 and 5, though 5 was out of use. Holly interlocking followed, which featured a flyover that placed passenger lines 2 and 3 on the west, freight lines 1F and 2F on the east. This was because freight trains exited the Corridor on the eastern side at Bell interlocking. At Baldwin, Hook and Bell, towers that once controlled the interlockings were still standing.

Train PIED returned to Conrail territory after leaving Bell, first passing what was known as the Advance Yard, then arrived at Edgemoor Yard proper which was thirty tracks wide. One of them was called the Speedway. The track from Bell to the yard was named the Northbound. At one time it was called the Shellpot Running Track. It was regrettable such a florid name had become obsolete.

To return to the Amtrak portion of the journey, as a signalling enthusiast I would have no trouble memorizing interlocking layouts. Trickier were numerous speed restrictions for freight trains, mainly over bridges. Most difficult to remember were the route's fifteen passenger stations: Darby, Curtis Park, Sharon Hill, Folcroft, Glenolden, Norwood, Moore Prospect Park, Ridley Park, Crum Lynne, Eddystone, Chester, Lamokin Street, Highland Avenue, Marcus Hook and Claymont. Someone living in or near Philadelphia would know the places, a long time resident of Eastern Pennsylvania could well have heard of most. For someone new to America – never mind Philadelphia – the stations were just a random collection of names; the fact that a few were either British or British-sounding helped not a jot. Somehow or other they had to be memorized. The PIED and its return working the EDPI held out little hope because they saw everything in darkness. I therefore took the crew's advice and obtained a pass from Amtrak to see the railroad in daylight, the recommendation being that I ride local services operated by SEPTA rather than Amtrak's long distance trains.

On three separate days I arranged trips on SEPTA's Philadelphia to Wilmington service which included the Phil to Bell section. Upon showing a pass and explaining the purpose of the journey I was welcomed into the cab by each of the SEPTA engineers. From time to time the conductor would join us. Lively conversations ensued about such varied subjects as how much Conrail men liked running freight trains, Conrail itself, Amtrak, seniority and bumping, gardening and the price of houses. I was shocked by a typical Philadelphia house price of a quarter of a million dollars, though by the 2010s such prices had migrated to York County. And was again shocked when, after trundling along at modest speed between all the little stations, south of Bell interlocking SEPTA multiple unit trains accelerated to about ninety miles per hour.

So animated and interesting were conversations with SEPTA traincrews that they distracted from the task of studying. I could absorb nothing, so on the third day decided to walk part of the route, to become intimate with the infrastructure, to have time to stop and stare, to smell the creosote, to be a wide-eyed boy again, to enjoy the railroad.

To the disappointment of the crew concerned, I alighted at, I think, Curtis Park, and walked until I was weary, I cannot remember how far. Every station's architecture was different. I lightly sketched the appearance of each so that it could be recognized at a glance.

Every signal gantry was also studied, its design carefully noted. Whilst Phil home signals were neatly arranged in a row, such tidiness did not continue further down the line.

The plan did not work very well. Having to continuously watch my footing, I managed to walk right under a signal bridge without noticing, and had to retrace my steps. Sketching stations was not problematic, but certain premises off railroad property were far more interesting. Like the North London Line, some stations boasted welcoming hostelries next door. I had to suppress desires and plod on. When I reached a station – whose name I do not remember - that stood in a shallow cutting and had nearby a convenience store, I stopped. I was tired and thirsty on this fine June day, and needed an excuse to halt. The next northbound SEPTA train took me back to Philadelphia.

Amtrak accepted nothing less than complete proficiency before permitting on their property any person in charge of a train. It was therefore with some trepidation that on 20th June I arrived at their headquarters in sumptuous 30th Street Station to be examined on Phil to Bell. The examiner knew every last nook and cranny of the Northeast corridor and expected same of his students. Though the normal procedure was to ask a number of set questions, at the outset I asked if I might simply recite everything I knew, as the only way I could pass the test was to call up in the mind's eye pictures I had drawn and to describe everything. The examiner agreed. When sitting tests on Conrail, if I momentarily forgot something, I could go back and fill in the blank later. Such expediency was not available in an oral examination.

I had five pages to regurgitate, the first taken up entirely by Phil interlocking, which was almost impossible to translate into words. "Can I draw Phil?" I asked. The examiner agreed, and placed a sheet of paper on the desk. I drew it successfully.

The examiner seemed impressed, but said to me, "What's this called?" pointing to a length of track between two crossovers.

The brain panicked. I could not remember seeing any names of track sections *within* interlockings. "I... I don't know."

"It's a pocket," he said contentedly.

"Yes... yes," I spluttered. "Yes, I know it's a pocket." The official had used a term in general use for any shortish length of track between two connections on parallel tracks.

Regaining confidence, after giving speeds within Phil interlocking, I mentally turned to the next page. "Heading south from Phil, you've got Tracks 1 to 4 east to west, all 261 cab signals, fifty miles per hour on Tracks 3 and 4, forty miles per hour on Tracks 1 and 2 to milepost 5, then thirty miles per hour. Then just before milepost 6, there's the gantry with Phil's distant signals on it, and the switch off Number 1 going to Crystal X." Crystal X was the name of an industry the siding served. Who knows what it manufactured. Speeds I recited were for freight trains; Conrail crews were not expected to know passenger train speeds. I continued: "Then we've got Darby station, Curtis Park station and Sharon Hill station. That's where Number 1 and 2 Tracks go back to forty miles per hour. Then there's Folcroft station and..."

I could not remember. I had forgotten the name of the next station. In theatrical terms, I had dried up. With red face I looked down to the floor. The examiner widened his eyes and leant forward in the hope his actions would magically draw the name out of me. After what seemed a very long time but might have been three seconds, it came to me: "Glenolden. Then Norwood, Moore Prospect Park. From automatic signals number 95 – they're the distants for Baldwin – to Moor station it's forty miles per hour on Number 4 Track. Then we get Ridley Park station and Crum Lynne..."

And so, by picturing five pages of hand-drawn maps like a slide show, I was able to complete the performance without further hitch, bringing the curtain down at Bell Interlocking. Phil to Bell was the only part of Amtrak needed for the Enola Road Conductors List, and was the most difficult qualifying test I ever had to endure. I recall complaining at a later date to a Pennsylvania conductor - an older man who frequently protected the Enola List - of having to remember all the stations. "Ah yes," he said. "You mean Darby, Curtis Park, Sharon Hill, Folcroft, Glenolden, Norwood, Moore Prospect Park, Ridley Park, Crum Lynne, Eddystone, Chester, Lamokin Street, Highland Avenue, Marcus Hook and Claymont." He recited the entire list without rehearsal!

\* \* \*

When in due course I became a qualified road conductor I looked forward immensely to using the hard-earned qualifications from Phil to Bell, but in actuality was called very infrequently. By contrast a colleague somehow used to keep catching the PIED. Train dispatchers made a determined effort to get the outward PIED over the road to avoid crews running out of time on Amtrak. The inward EDPI had to work along the way and frequently did not make it back to Harrisburg. Assignments called Short Turns, sometimes known as Pull Ins, were called to re-man and complete the journey of stranded trains. I was conductor on a Short Turn crew that relieved the EDPI at a location, maybe, fifteen miles east of Harrisburg, when who stepped off the engine with his grip but the aforementioned colleague. I said to him, "How come you keep getting the PIED and I don't?"

His response was something facetious, like: "It's who you know!"

One trip down Phil to Bell stands out. Another middle of the night job, it was a coal train to be set off in the Advance Yard north of Edgemoor. The night progressed satisfactorily, and as we rumbled along the single track from Belmont to Phil at about 07:00 hours, we contemplated our fate: Amtrak did not like freight trains on the Northeast Corridor from 06:00 to 22:00. (As an aside, a rule was in place that mixed freights such as the PIED were not allowed at all within those hours unless running late, but how could a train be running late if there were no timetable to run to?) To return to the night in question, the Philadelphia Dispatcher radioed to say discussions were taking place about what to do with us. I do not know if tying the train down at Phil was an option. As we neared Phil, the Dispatcher called to say, much to our surprise, that Amtrak was going to run us.

Again, this is a practice that in another country would be unthinkable. To inconvenience passengers in order to accommodate a freight train would not normally have been countenanced on British Railways. But that is just one viewpoint. An alternative assessment is that the decision illustrates excellent co-operation between Conrail and Amtrak, a concession being made to avoid a train left standing at an awkward location.

The two centre tracks, 2 and 3, on this section of the Northeast Corridor were reserved for high-speed passenger trains. Station platforms for local services were therefore provided only on the two

155

outer tracks, 1 and 4, which were also used by occasional freights. We found ourselves heading southwards on Track 1, normally used for northbound services. If we had been routed down Track 4, it would have been necessary for our coal train to cross Track 3 at Holly to gain freight lines at Bell, which would have brought to a stand all southbound passenger trains in the rush hour whilst we did so.

Travelling on Track 1, the engineer and I noticed we were focus of attention amongst commuters crowding platforms on the far side of the railroad. As they waited for their Philadelphia train, each passenger looked daggers at our dirty, noisy, lengthy coal train grumbling along. Evidently the people had been advised to remove themselves from Track 1 to Track 4 in order to catch their usual train. This must have been no easy task when footbridges or underpasses were not provided. (At some stations fences had been erected down the middle of tracks to stop passengers walking across the lines.) Commuters could not understand why their daily routine had been interrupted, why the convenience of catching a train at the same place and time each morning had been forfeited for a load of coal. Maybe the mysterious Filter Belle had something to do with it!

# CHAPTER 19

# THE TRENTON LINE

When I first heard the name of an extra board known as the Enola Road Conductors List an assumption was immediately made that it was derived from Enola Road that ran alongside Enola Yard. In time I heard about another list called the Rutherford Road Conductors List (which, by the way, I understood to be Reading Railroad equity). I knew that Rutherford was some distance outside Harrisburg, and assumed that the Rutherford Road Conductors List was similarly named after a highway that linked the two places, although it did seem a bit of a coincidence that both lists were named after a street. A month or two may have elapsed before the unexpected discovery of yet another list that, astonishingly, was also named after a thoroughfare: the York Road Trainmen List. This was particularly worrisome because I regularly travelled from York to Harrisburg and never came across a York Road.

The idea that the Enola Road Conductors List owed its name to a highway became firmly lodged in the brain. This line of thought was exposed one day whilst shifting in Enola Yard. An employee, upon hearing a British accent, said over the radio anonymously, "Where are you from?"

In the middle of a move and not wanting to get into a conversation which properly should not have been taking place anyway, I replied, "Enola Road Conductors List," placing emphasis firmly on the word Conductors. Another person who heard the exchange later remarked that the way I said it made it sound illustrious. The truth is it only sounded impressive because I was saying it incorrectly, the cadence was wrong. Emphasis should have been placed on Enola, because I would eventually learn that it was a road conductors list based on Enola, not a conductors list based on Enola Road! The same applied to Rutherford and York lists.

Regardless of the misunderstanding, I had thought that being forced to sign the Enola List meant security at last, but it was not to be. Whilst busy qualifying Phil to Bell I was bumped off. There followed a twenty-day period during which I bumped onto and was removed from the Enola Yard Trainmen List three times. Yearning stability, I bumped onto the Rutherford Road Conductors List on 3rd July, even though I had not completed all road qualifications.

In the small hours of 4th July 1995 I was summoned to work the PIAL, the Pittsburgh to Allentown. On a date not normally associated with good fortune for the British, my first assignment as a road conductor would prove to be a splendid day! The engineer for this inaugural trip was a quiet, mild-mannered man, not an echinoid type of engineer difficult to converse with, as some were. The locomotive was of the comfortable wide cab variety, a Class SD60I number 5628. It was brand new, and had only been in service seven days. The second locomotive was Class SD60M 5527. With forty loads and thirty-seven empties weighing 5623 tons, the job was a straight shot. We sailed right through to Allentown without a stop and immediately deadheaded back. I was home after lunch, able to spend the rest of the public holiday with my wife!

It was the conductor's task to prepare timecards, and to enter the employee number of all crew members. Mine was 767377, a good omen some would say. The extra board meant working with a different engineer each time, so I began writing down all engineer employee numbers, the 4th July engineer being the first. A year or so later I saw the same man, and said to him jokingly, "You're number one in my books, John!" Unfortunately, when faced with that kind of flattery men become wary. Not remembering what had been for me a red letter day, John scowled. I tried again: "I mean, you were the first engineer I worked with as a road conductor, so you're first in my notebook." He still looked perplexed, so I dropped the matter. Another year passed and I saw him again. This time I held up the notebook, pointed to his name at the top of the list, and said with a grin, "You're number one in my books, John!" He got the joke this time and laughed.

I was able to hold the Rutherford Road Conductors List for two weeks. During that period a conversation took place with a senior member of the list about the territory covered. "To hold the Rutherford list," he said helpfully, "you should really know the Trenton Line, in case we get diverted that way."

He spoke the words in a matter-of-fact way demanded by such a humdrum statement. But what I heard was: "you should really know THE TRENTON LINE..." To me it was not just another line. When the man spoke, I pictured the route name like opening titles of an epic film, hewn from rock, staggeringly tall, complete with boisterous orchestral accompaniment! The route was elusive, unknown, remote as a distant planet. I had touched only its southern tip on the way to Camden. It beguiled like forbidden fruit. Its name even had a superior ring to it. Imagine a proud father saying, "Hi. This is my son Trenton. He's just been accepted at Harvard University." The Trenton Line was odd man out, in that it did not radiate eastwards from Harrisburg like other routes but ran perpendicular to them. Though a swift path to North Jersey, no Harrisburg train regularly went that way.

I was told the only sure way to see the entire Trenton Line was to ride a certain job out of Baltimore. Originating in Florida, it was a train consisting of nothing but box cars loaded with orange juice, presumably bottled, bound for North Jersey to quench the thirst of the greater New York City metropolitan area. The train was nicknamed The Juice; its official name was CSOJ. A crew was specially assigned to it, and took it all the way from Baltimore to North Jersey using the Trenton Line northwards from Philadelphia, then deadheaded back. There was no return working, presumably empty box cars made their way southwards amongst mixed freight. But it ran most irregularly, and would have been more troublesome to catch than a South Philadelphia train. As appealing as the idea was, I decided against riding The Juice. The Trenton Line would have to be covered by other means.

\* \* \*

When working the Morrisville Pool at a future date, we had been called out of the hotel as usual but were told of a change of plan concerning the train back to Harrisburg. Normally it would have been one of the intermodal trains or the MOPI, but that was not to be the case here. The engineer had details. "What it is, Mitch," he began, "We're not taking a train back, we're just taking light power."

"Oh," I said, half paying attention, half studying bulletins whilst standing.

"Now the problem is," he said with tension mounting in his voice, "there's a train on its way eastwards that needs the Morrisville Line." He paused, then said weightily, *"So we can't go that way."*

Paperwork fell through my hands to the floor. Wide-eyed and pale-faced, I spun round to face the engineer squarely, and said, "You don't mean..."

Violinists sawed vigorously at their instruments.

"Yes, I do mean..." said the engineer manfully.

Strings played again.

"No!"

"Yes!"

More strings.

"No, I don't believe it," said I tumbling backwards and falling into a chair.

"Yes, you'd better believe it," said the engineer. "We're going to have to go by..." The full orchestra came in thunderously. The camera zoomed in to a close-up of the engineer's firm countenance as he spoke those towering words: "...THE TRENTON LINE!"

"Trouble is, John," I said as I began searching elsewhere in the bulletins now that our routing had been changed, "I'm not qualified on the Trenton Line. I've been wanting to, but there just hasn't been the chance."

"It doesn't matter, you don't have to be," said John. "For light engines, I don't need a qualified conductor, just a brakeman." Aware that access to the route was a problem amongst new men, he could hardly suppress a smirk when he said, "So this'll be a chance for you to see the Trenton Line." At least I would see half of it, from Morrisville southwards.

Delighted at the news, I hurried to complete formalities and climb on board. We took the engines to the eastern end of Morrisville Yard where the two-mile long Fairless Branch linked the Morrisville Line's CP-MA to the Trenton Line's CP-Fairless Jct. Close by, the Trenton Line burrowed under the Morrisville Line. A connecting track between two levels, such as the Fairless Branch, would be called a chord on the British network. Once under way, I opened the Rule Book at the Trenton Line and tried to assimilate as much as possible.

As we headed south on the single track, we were accompanied on our right (west) as far as a station called Neshaminy by SEPTA's Tracks 1 and 2. After passing, amongst other features, an industrial siding called Theresa Friedman and a place called Bustleton, we approached CP-Cheltenham Jct. From there to CP-Newtown Jct., a distance of about four miles, Conrail and SEPTA shared double track through the passenger stations of Lawndale and Olney. The stretch came under the control of SEPTA "A" Dispatcher, but radio contact, in accordance with the standard two-tier arrangement, would be with the block operator at Wayne Tower. I recall a future occasion when, heading in the opposite direction, our train was held at CP-Newtown Jct whilst morning rush hour commuter trains scurried to and fro over the complicated layout. It reminded me of busy junctions in the southern half of London.

The most memorable part of this Trenton Line inaugural trip was between CP-Newtown Jct and the next interlocking, CP-Nice, where the railroad dug a trench through Philadelphia's central area. The cutting was lined with retaining walls. It appeared the route once accommodated two tracks, but increasing loading gauges now left room for only one. Two architectural oddities, presumably bridges, spanned the tracks. Their arched form reminded me of two things at once, canal bridges in Venice and supporting structures called flying buttresses. The latter in turn reminded me of a story from days in British public service when the government wished to raze one of their buildings but were prevented from doing so because flying buttresses hung in mid-air between that building and another. The structural and legal consequences of proposed demolition were unclear; I never did hear the outcome. But whenever I think of the Trenton Line, flying buttresses spring to mind!

CP-Nice was another interlocking that had seen better days. It boasted four tracks, 1 to 4, though Number 3 seemed to be in poor repair. Number 4 was relegated to a siding for a bakery making a well-known brand of tasty confectionery. I speculated the interlocking's name came about through association with such nice food, but was told its origin lay in the district of Nicetown where it was situated. I still preferred to think that Nicetown was named in recognition of the bakery. Track 1 took us to CP-Laurel Hill where we negotiated a sharp right-hand curve to join the Harrisburg Line at CP-Falls.

I qualified on the southern half of the Trenton Line on 7th September 1995. The occasion of the northbound train being held up at CP-Newtown Jct may have been the only other time I travelled over it, I cannot remember. Opportunities to ogle at the flying buttresses and admire the nice bakery alas were few.

\* \* \*

Gossip circulated that Conrail would soon begin running trains regularly over the Trenton Line, at least the northern half of it. It seemed unlikely that good fortune would again offer a ride over such distant territory, so a decision was made to undertake something I had vowed never to do, to qualify on paper without seeing the railroad. Therefore by blindly memorizing stations, speeds and all else with no idea what the line looked like, I qualified on 18th September 1995.

I have been unable to pinpoint date of the maiden trip over the northern half of the Trenton Line, but on the day in question I perched on the edge of the conductor's seat eager to see for the first time that which I was supposed to already know. We approached the Trenton Line from the Morrisville Line. At CP-West Lang located at the eastern end of Morrisville Yard we diverged left onto the Wood Connecting Track that led to the Trenton Line's CP-Wood. At CP-Wood four lines - the Wood Connecting Track, SEPTA's 1 and 2 and the single-track southern half of the Trenton Line - were re-arranged into two tracks heading north.

Once on the Trenton Line, Yardley station was passed, shortly followed by a bridge over the Delaware River that marked the boundary between Pennsylvania and New Jersey, followed in turn by West Trenton station. West Trenton was the terminus for passenger trains and marked the end of the territory remotely controlled by SEPTA Wind Tower. Immediately beyond the station stood Conrail's Trent tower, which controlled the interlocking in front of it that gave access to passenger stock storage sidings. Trent tower owed its survival, I am presuming, to circumstances similar to those surrounding the longevity of mechanical signal boxes at British seaside towns, such as Blackpool, Skegness and Littlehampton: it is useful for railway management to have a person on site to visually confirm arrivals and departures at passenger train termini. Trent's key role did not however guarantee immortality. It closed in 1997. (Of interest to a signalling enthusiast is that Trent tower, America, shared its name with a large electronic signal box in the British East Midlands, Trent power box. The British establishment closed in July 2013.) About three miles north of Trent tower the Trenton Line's double track became single at CP-Wing.

It will be recalled that in America any officially identified railroad location is considered a station. So far, stations listed in the Rule Book and shown on my maps had been easy to spot. On the remaining twenty miles of the Trenton Line, which was single track entirely to its junction with the Lehigh Line at CP-Port Reading Jct., stations were less obvious. After several trips I eventually concluded the first station, Pennington, could be pin-pointed by a distinctive hump-backed bridge. If there were doubt where Glenmore was supposed to be, a detector at almost the same site confirmed its location. Similar circumstances applied to Belle Meade further along. Welcome relief from uncertainty came in the form of Hopewell. The former station building, an architectural jewel, not only remained intact, but had been taken over and was in the process of being renovated. It is a pity the heritage value of such fine old buildings is not universally appreciated.

Skillman was identified by a doubled-ended siding, Harlingden by juxtaposition of another siding and an over-bridge. Now we arrive at the case of Hamilton. I did my best to determine the site of milepost 52.6, the purported location of Hamilton, but try as I might could find not a single trace of railroad business. It was just fields; no village could be seen. The abscondence was baffling. After many trips I came to the reluctant conclusion the only hint of Hamilton was a farm silo about a quarter-mile across fields. Finally, as we neared the end of the Trenton Line, Weston station was marked by an over-bridge.

Not forgetting the lecture I received in early days on the importance of knowing Landis on the Harrisburg Line, it troubled me that stations on this part of the Trenton Line were so spectral. When expressing this concern to an engineer, though he did not outright concede stations were difficult to spot, he said if it were necessary to identify his location he would use mileposts. Indeed, I may have overstated the issue, because I cannot recall the dispatcher ever enquiring after our progress on the Trenton Line. Probably once a train was given the road at one end of the twenty-mile single track section, nothing could be done till it reached the other end. Taking all matters into account, it seemed stations at the northern end of the Trenton Line were more or less irrelevant. At one time they were anything but. *A Railroad Atlas of the United States in 1946* confirms the list of active passenger stations on this stretch to be Pennington, Glen Moore, Hopewell, Skillman, Harlingden, Belle Meade, Hamilton and Weston.

The route that was now single line was once four-track Reading Railroad. Imagine the East Coast or West Coast Main Line being reduced to single track! The comparison is not fair, of course; the original Reading trackage never matched the status of a primary British route. But at some stage in history four tracks through northern New Jersey were justified. Where did all the traffic go?

Though radio contact with the dispatcher was not frequent on the Trenton Line, one exchange is worth mentioning. A mixed freight had been brought northwards that included a batch of cars to be set off in Manville Yard, located where the Trenton Line joined the Lehigh Line. As we secured the hind part of the train on the Trenton Line, I noticed youths trespassing in the yard. Later in the operation whilst riding the rear car through the lengthy yard, I said on the radio, "Okay to bring 'em back another ten cars for a stop while we wait for these scallywags to get out of the way."

It seems probable the dispatcher needed to run another train, because he was listening. On hearing my remark, he said over the radio rhetorically, "*What* did he say?" At the time I thought the dispatcher was amused by use of a dated British term, but the dictionary surprisingly reveals the word to be American in origin.

There would be times when I travelled on the Trenton Line frequently, other times when I saw it very little. In the latter case, whenever on a Morrisville job I would make a point of peering down onto the Trenton Line as we crossed over it on the approaches to Morrisville Yard. That way, I could say I had been over the Trenton Line that day and thus kept up-to-date my qualifications!

# CHAPTER 20

# THE PORT ROAD

By the summer of 1995 I had mopped up outstanding territory to qualify for the Enola Road Conductors List, and began to eye other lines. On 28th July I passed the test for the ten-mile long York Secondary, which was easy since I already knew half of the thirteen-track York Windsor Street Yard from Maryland & Pennsylvania days. Qualifying on the York Secondary resulted, on a handful of occasions, in conducting the Sunday coal train destined for my previous employer. For example, on 20th February 1999 two Class C40-8W locomotives 6235 and 6263, a Class SD60 6840 and a Class SD60M 5549 – a total of 15,600 horsepower – hauled 110 cars weighing 11,571 tons from Enola to York. Ascent of the York Secondary from the banks of the Susquehanna River was the steepest incline crews working east from Harrisburg encountered. When working Conrail coal trains into York, it was strange approaching the old stamping ground from a different direction. In one instance, when the coal train neared York Yard in the small hours of Sunday morning, a time I knew my former workmates would be waiting with their locomotives, I surprised them by switching channels and announcing our arrival!

Another job I caught occasionally was the daily round trip Enola to York, the WPEN62, otherwise known as the Yorkie.

Knowing the York Secondary invited consideration of the York Road Trainmen List. On 22nd November 1995 I bumped onto it, but lasted only three days. I bumped onto it for a second stint on 13th December, and surprisingly managed to hold the position for twenty-three days. I think the half-dozen gentlemen residing on the York

List were much more relaxed about their domain than those on other lists, and tolerated the interloper barely qualified on the extra board he was meant to protect.

The main qualification I lacked for the York List was the Port Road. The Port Road Branch ran alongside the Susquehanna River. In its original form it stretched from a location east of Columbia to Amtrak's Northeast Corridor at Perryville. The former Dumfries to Stranraer line in Scotland was also known as the Port Road, though only as a nickname. Used sparingly in both countries, it seems any use of the word *road* in connection with railways stirred emotions. Describing sidings as Middle Road or Back Road somehow inflated their importance. I was surprised to hear of the term "the Thirsk Road". If the title The Port Road does not convince you it ought to be a novel by Rudyard Kipling, consider the swashbuckling yarn that could be formed by stringing its station names together: "Down to Safe Harbour, me hearties, catch McCall's Ferry to Port Deposit. You take care of the Pilot Mr. Minnick. Then when we turn nor-east-by-east at West Rock, over the side we go, head for Star Rock then on to Wildcat Tunnel to pick up the booty!"

The complete list of stations on the original Port Road is Port, CP-Cres, Star Rock, Safe Harbor detector, CP-West Harbor, CP-Harbor, McCalls detector, Pequea, CP-McCalls, McCall's Ferry, CP-Holtwood, CP-Midway, Fishing Creek detector, Fishing Creek, Peach Bottom, unnamed detector, Williams Tunnel, MD-PA State Line, Frazier Tunnel, Wildcat Tunnel, CP-West Pilot, CP-Pilot, Conowingo, Conowingo detector, CP-West Rock, Rock, Port Deposit, CP-Tome, CP-Quarry, Minnick, unnamed detector, Aikin and Perryville. Harbor is the American spelling. Excluded from the official list of stations were three flumes, named Mann's, Fisherman's and Frey's, that crossed over the Port Road before they disembogued into the river. Another peculiarity of the Port Road was installation of slide detectors, wires strung at the foot of steep cuttings to detect rock falls and which, if triggered, would put signals back to red. Such signals were plated SP. In another parallel with Scottish railways, similar signals are installed in the Pass of Brander on the line to Oban. The Scottish versions are semaphore signals permanently in the "off" position automatically returned to danger if falling rocks break wire screens.

From Port to Perryville the line hugged the banks of the Susquehanna; in some parts just a few feet separated ballast and lapping waters of the expansive waterway. The Susquehanna River was as wide as the Mississippi, but not as deep. Tracks alternated from single to double the entire length. Single line sections carved narrow ledges, pierced short tunnels or sliced through spurs that would otherwise jut into the river. Straight sections were rare, an anguine course found the easiest path. At Safe Harbor, Holtwood and Conowingo, hydro-electric schemes threw massive dams across the Susquehanna transforming the river behind into artificial lakes.

Milepost zero on the Port Road was at Perryville, where Amtrak's triangular interlocking named Perry permitted Conrail's freights to either turn northwards towards Delaware or southwards to reach Baltimore. Two daily freights – regular jobs based in Enola - went in the Delaware direction. Most remaining traffic headed for Baltimore, typically including three trainloads of export coal a day. Since Amtrak discouraged freights on the Northeast Corridor between 22:00 and 06:00, Port Road trains usually did not begin leaving Enola till about 19:00 hours, resulting in predominately nocturnal activity. This did not dissuade railroad enthusiasts from gathering in late evening to admire Conrail's engines trundling lengthy trains round Perry interlocking. On summer nights waves of ghostly spider web threads floated over the railroad, each carrying a tiny arachnid hoping to ensnare prey. The strands accumulated on engine fronts in a sticky mess.

It was the train dispatcher of course who decided which trains to run over single-line sections and which trains to hold back. But that decision was dependent on good information. Confusing data concerning train lengths one night resulted in two very long trains coming to a stand at the passing siding at Pilot, both hanging out each end, unable to pass. Fortunately, the train dispatcher's nightmare was easily resolved. The lengthy eastbound train was one of the Delaware jobs, the second Delaware job was standing at the next interlocking back along the line, CP-Midway. The second Delaware traincrew therefore took their engines to the rear of the first Delaware train, pulled away the cars that were hanging out, and took them westwards to CP-Holtwood where they attached them to the rear of their own train, an ingenious solution.

Whether it was the hint of adventure in the title, or whether it was the route's unique physical characteristics, employees spoke of the Port Road in somewhat more respectful tones than when speaking of other routes. I qualified on the Port Road on 27th December 1995. As much as I wanted to work the line, opportunities were usually limited to Short Turns called out of Enola. Some were not so short, in one case we deadhead all the way to Minnick at milepost 2 to recover a train.

On a fine Sunday 13th October, 1996, I was called to be on duty in Enola at 07:00 hours for an assignment labelled CPAMER1, which meant I would be conductor-pilot with an on-track self-propelled crane belonging to the Maintenance of Way Department. Like traincrews, crane operators had to be qualified on territory, but, probably through union agreements, had to be escorted by a qualified conductor whenever possible. I would meet the crane at Peach Bottom. The brand name of the piece of machinery, as well as its origins, was American. (A class instructor once let us into the secret of his unfailing ability to recognize an American crane: the machine had one-foot high letters "AMERICAN" embossed on the rear!)

I drove to Lancaster Yard to pick up bulletins, as it was closer than Enola, then made my way over rolling Lancaster County landscape to drop down the Susquehanna valley side into the village of Peach Bottom wherein lay a short siding. In the siding was a crane, not of the brand name American, but a smaller type going by the name of Burro. It appeared a simple error had been made; the crane to be piloted was made by Burro, not American. After waiting from 08:30 to 10:30 with no sign of the crane operator, I concluded something was amiss. I found a public telephone and called the crew dispatcher to tell him of the circumstances. He put me through to the Port Road Train Dispatcher, who said, "You were supposed to 'phone me first."

"Oh, I didn't know that," I replied.

"All right," said the train dispatcher. "Anyway, it is in fact an American crane you're supposed to be piloting. It's at McCall's Ferry now, you can catch up with him there."

In the absence of a conductor-pilot, the crane operator had started work, which he was entitled to do, presumably picking up scrap metal. I drove the ten miles or so from Peach Bottom to Holtwood

Dam, parked the car, packed a limited amount of tackle into my grip and set off walking down the track to McCall's Ferry. It was the only way I knew how to get there. It was now early afternoon. On arrival at the short McCall's Ferry siding, the American crane was nowhere to be seen, so I called on the radio. "Conductor-pilot to the American crane. Over."

"American crane," came the reply.

"I was told you were at McCall's Ferry. I'm there right now but I don't see you. What's your location?"

"Milepost 28," said the crane operator. "Go to Safe Harbor, I'll meet you there later today. That's where I'll be tying up."

Milepost 28 was on a completely inaccessible stretch of the Port Road. The operator, aware we had been playing cat and mouse for several hours, made no further attempt at rendezvous, and concluded that meeting at Safe Harbor would be the best way to round off what had been, as far as co-ordinated teamwork was concerned, an unfruitful day. Looking back at the farce, if I had met the crane at Peach Bottom or McCall's Ferry and piloted it to Safe Harbor, how would I have got back to my car?

Port Road traffic between Harrisburg Consolidated Terminal and Baltimore was handled by a pool based in Baltimore, the C&PD Pool, the initials deriving from the original Columbia and Port Deposit Railroad. In February 1996 I returned to work the Baltimore Trainmen List. After a couple of weeks, the local trainmaster granted time off to qualify on Amtrak's Northeast Corridor from Baltimore Yard to Perryville, which would enable me to work the C&PD Pool.

I rode Amtrak several times between Philadelphia and Baltimore taking a seat in the leading cab alongside the engineer. Ten interlockings, Perry, Grace, Oak, Bush, Wood, Magnolia, Gunpow, River, Point and Bay, had to be mastered, plus all other infrastructure, which included four passenger stations. The number of tracks on this section of the Corridor varied from two to five.

The impressive bridge just south of Perry included a 280-foot swing span in the middle. It was opened only about six times a year, when a technician was sent to the site, as the train dispatcher, CETC-3, did not have direct control over the mechanism.

One night we had to turn power on the wye at Perry. Three locomotives were taken onto the bridge to clear Perry's northbound home signals. At that juncture I had to go to the other end of the consist to talk the engineer back through the interlocking. I walked back along the side of the locomotive then swung across the gangway between the first and second units. In the middle of the manoeuvre I froze to the spot at what I saw. Between the locomotives and surging waters of the Susquehanna River was nothing, thirty feet of nothing: beyond the edge of the track was a straight drop. Like many others, the bridge had neither walkway nor parapet. If a person stepped off the locomotive or slid off the walkway in icy conditions, nothing would save that person. Shaken, I tightened my grip on the handrails, and using short shuffling steps completed the move onto the second locomotive. I nervously transferred from second to third units in similar fashion, taking care not to look down. (At a later date railings were installed on the bridge, all will be pleased to hear.)

The C&PD Pool was highly prized; I could only sneak onto it when nobody else was watching. The first occasion was just before a booked week's vacation in October 1996. It was no surprise to find myself bumped off on return. I somehow managed a six-day stint in December of the same year, which might be explained by road conductors bumping onto yard jobs to take advantage of holiday pay over the festive season. Two fearless attempts to hold the pool in 1997 resulted in tenure lasting only a few hours before being flicked off like a piece of annoying dandruff. When I bumped onto it in May 1998 I hoped that improving seniority would lengthen a stay.

It was a curious state of affairs. I had a seventy-five minute drive to work, would then work from Baltimore to Enola or Harrisburg and be put in the hotel in Harrisburg, which was actually closer to home! This would have appealed to some men, who, with the aid of a spare vehicle left in Harrisburg, would drive home. Crew Dispatchers did not object to such an arrangement, they simply called the employee at home. Such scheming had no appeal for me; the last thing I wanted was more driving. (There was also a legitimate arrangement called reverse lodging, whereby a person stayed in a hotel at the home terminal and went home from the away-from-home terminal; I recall a Harrisburg man reverse lodging for a regular job based in North Jersey.) Crews on the C&PD Pool were put up in a luxury hotel in the centre of Harrisburg, but the paucity of eating places at that time spoiled the experience.

At the time in question, 1998, men on the pool were hungry for work, and had had the number of crews cut to a minimum causing the pool to turn fast. Only about ten hours would be allowed at home before being called out for the next turn. It was more work than I needed or could handle, so was grateful when, after six days, I was bumped off. I never tried for the C&PD Pool again, and was content with forays down the Port Road from the Enola end.

Sometimes when the C&PD pool was exhausted, Enola-based men would be called to take coal trains to Baltimore and to deadhead back. I think it was on the eve of a public holiday that I was called for one of two such assignments running one behind the other. Such work kept up one's qualifications and provided an opportunity to once again enjoy the extravagantly tracked President St. Industrial. Occasionally a special train had to be run if an autoparts just-in-time delivery might not make it just in time. I caught such a train once. Hauling only about six cars, we were kept moving all the way down the Port Road, the Northeast Corridor, the President St. Industrial and the Bear Creek Running Track to CSX's Penn Mary Yard, where we placed the urgent consignment just in time! One of the delights of being a qualified road conductor was the immense satisfaction of rising to the occasion when the carrier was in a difficult spot.

When the Enola Branch was open all the way to Parkesburg, the section between Port and Parkesburg was known as the Low Grade. At that time the Enola Branch was the prime river route, the Port Road Branch merely fed into it. Since demise of the Low Grade, most traffic leaving Enola travelled all the way down the Port Road. In the late 1990s the Enola Branch was absorbed into the Port Road Branch. Station pages for the Port Road Branch were then changed to extend not just to Enola Yard, but through it and out at the western end as far as CP-Banks. Thus the term Port Road now applies to trackage from Enola to Perryville.

The last train on the Low Grade ran on 19th December 1988, coincidentally the same date I arrived to take up residence in the United States. Thanks to public-spirited efforts, the abandoned trackbed from Port to Safe Harbor has been converted to a walking and cycling trail. In the 2010s my wife and I have been able to take advantage of the amenity to enjoy views of the Susquehanna River, to marvel at the three flumes adjacent to the trail, to gaze at the Port

Road Branch a few feet below and, if we are lucky, to catch sight of a passing train.

\* \* \*

The 1995 Fourth of July celebration - the inaugural trip as a road conductor - arguably marked the end of being a new guy, as we were labelled, and heralded a period of greater security. My portfolio of qualifications expanded, and, thanks to steady attrition of more senior employees who retired or gained promotion, seniority doggedly moved up a step or two.

That does not mean I escaped being bumped around like a steel ball in a pinball machine. Over a 267-day period from 3$^{rd}$ July 1995 to 27$^{th}$ March 1996 I spent three days on the Rutherford Road Trainmen List, six days on the Lancaster List, six days on the Reading List, fourteen days on the Rutherford Road Conductors List, twenty-six days on the York List, thirty-one days on the Enola Yard List, thirty-seven days on the Baltimore List and 124 days on the Enola Road Conductors List. An additional twenty days were spent in limbo, that is, on the displaced list. During that same 267-day period I managed to clock up no less than ten shifts on the Maryland & Pennsylvania Railroad.

During that nine-month period I was displaced eighteen times. On eighteen occasions I was told I had lost my job. On each of those occasions I had to either find another assignment or move to North Jersey or join the ranks of the unemployed. It seems a precarious way of earning a living, but I mostly enjoyed the uncertainty, because no position was the ideal job. The ideal job was the Morrisville Pool, but that was out of reach. So I was reasonably content to hold positions for a week or two, then to stay at home on a five-day bump to catch up with chores, or to steal away for a shift on the Maryland & Pennsylvania.

This stop-and-go pattern would come to an end. One reason is that conditions of employment changed whereby a five-day bump became available only to employees who were switching terminals. If, for example, a move were made from one position to another within the Harrisburg Consolidated Terminal, it now had to be done within forty-eight hours. If the move were from terminal to terminal, the crew dispatcher had to be told of the circumstances to secure a five-day bump. Another reason for a quickening pace of work was that the economy began to heat up. Roll into this mixture a steady climb up the seniority ladder and the result was a much more demanding work schedule. Leisurely days were over.

# CHAPTER 21

# ENOLA ROAD CONDUCTORS LIST

At one time extra lists were consistently well-stocked with employees in order to meet any unexpected needs. As a result men worked only a few days a week, and owing to consequent lower income, incumbents tended to be those with less seniority. With the passage of time, carriers pruned extra boards to the minimum to save costs, causing lists to turn faster which in turn generated higher levels of income. The extra boards then attracted men with higher seniority. The position in the 1990s was that extra board workers were amongst the highest earners. Those on the Rutherford Road Conductors List enjoyed the greatest income, thanks to more North Jersey work and its associated mileage payments.

To give it its full name, the Enola Road Conductors Extra List was poor relation to the Rutherford List in that earnings were less. The Enola List covered just one North Jersey turn. The other factor affecting earnings was Morrisville work, which was mainly Pennsylvania equity and which was therefore principally covered by the Enola List. Most Morrisville trips were just a basic eight-hour day, not very remunerative. Road conductors, apart from the handful of York List diehards, flocked to the Rutherford List for higher earnings. However, the very thing that drove others away from the Enola List, the high percentage of Morrisville work, attracted me to it.

For much of the time spent on the Enola Road Conductors List, only I and one other man were on it. He had plenty of seniority so, puzzled, I asked about his choice. "Well you see," he began, "over on the Reading side, you've got the problem of track numbering."

"You mean number one track being on the trip back, not on the journey out?" I asked.

"Yes, I have trouble with that sometimes," he said.

This senior conductor had probably spent most of his working life on former Pennsylvania Railroad metals where Track 1 was eastbound. When traffic switched to the Reading route, he had to cope with the reverse arrangement. It was surprising the man had difficulty, for he was the man previously mentioned who could recite without hesitation all passenger stations between Amtrak's Phil and Bell! When he and I were the only people on the list, it usually meant that when I arrived home from work I was next to be be called. Conrail set up a telephone number that employees could call to ascertain their standing, whether they were first out, second out, and so on. With only two of us on the Enola List, there was little point calling the number.

Protecting an extra board meant being available for work twenty-four hours a day, seven days a week, all year long, public holidays included. When an engineer first explained this to me, I said, "But I don't understand. You're saying that when you're on the extra board, you don't get a day off at all?"

"That's it," he replied.

"But don't you get a rest day, or something like that, when you know you won't get called out?"

"Nope. You have to be available all the time," was the reply.

"I don't see how anybody can do that," I said. "I mean, working continuously from one end of the year to the other, only being off for vacation."

"What a lot of guys do, when they need a break, they just mark off sick for a day or two," my interlocutor said.

"But doesn't that get you in trouble, marking off sick when everybody knows you're not sick, you just want a rest?" I said.

"No. The crew dispatchers know that. They let you do it. You won't get disciplined, provided you don't do something stupid like all the time marking off sick for a week."

Though this insight brought some comfort, there remained a nagging unsatisfactoriness that pretending to be sick had to be part of a normal work routine. Nevertheless, the escape hatch enabled me to cope with the Enola Road Conductors List.

I remember explaining to someone that I was on call all the time. He could not believe it. A tradesman, he was only on call something like one weekend in ten. Few other professions are permanently on call; doctors spring to mind. On British Railways, relief signalmen theoretically always had to be available. In practice, I think their work was planned the week before, short notice being the exception rather than the rule. My understanding of British train drivers' rosters was that, if a depot had thirty different assignments, men worked one week on each, the last couple of weeks being on-call status. But I was now in America where employers' demands on workers seemed greater than in Britain, but where, it could be argued, a higher rate of pay compensated.

Amongst all employees who worked extra boards, I would guess most marked off sick every couple of weeks or so to give themselves a break. A minority hardly ever marked off at all. It was they who were the big earners. It was they and their kind elsewhere in American industry whose astonishing productivity built an economy envied by the rest of the world, an economy that, at the start of a new millennium, resulted in America being the sole surviving global superpower. It was they who exposed that the work ethic instilled in me as a youngster, though excellent as far as it went, fell short. I had been taught to work diligently from the beginning of the working day to the end giving my very best. The gold ribbon American worker said that was not good enough: one must work at every opportunity to push income to its highest possible level.

Such hard workers were a model for us all. But if I worked on the Enola List at an intensive pace for five or six days, concentration began to suffer. That was unacceptable. When roaring along at speed, traincrews had constantly to keep in mind bulletin information digested at commencement of the shift - that a flagman was on duty at milepost so-and-so, that a block operator was on duty at such-and-such crossover. Nothing at the lineside gave advance warning of either eventuality. Crews had to remember to radio ahead for instructions in case the train had to stop. It was a shared duty, both engineer and conductor had to be on top of bulletin information. I considered it imperative to be constantly alert. It is my opinion that complexity of American railroading will always be too much for a one-man crew. Whilst one-man operation is commonplace in Britain, anything unusual is protected by signals, a better safeguard than memory.

The first time I actually worked the Enola List was on 17th July 1995. As the 1990s progressed, I was on and off the Enola Road Conductors List many times. In busy times, which most were, a pattern developed whereby I would work five or six days, then mark off sick for about thirty hours. The carrier usually had difficulty manning trains at weekends, so I endeavoured to work through till at least Sunday evening before marking off. On the road, Mondays were usually slow because many trains began their eastward march from such places as Pittsburgh earlier in the day, not reaching Harrisburg till evening. It is quite possible I could have had a rest without marking off, but did not take the risk.

The intensity and variety of working the Enola List is illustrated by a period commencing Tuesday 7th May 1996. I was called to be on duty at 18:30 at Annville on the Harrisburg Line to work train UAP82 to Camden, after which we were put in the Philadelphia hotel. The crew worked ENS35 light engines back home, off duty at 00:15 on Thursday. I did not sleep long, for at 08:00 the telephone called me to be on duty at 10:00 to work UFM96 coal train to Allentown and deadhead back, off duty at 19:00. Hopefully a good night's sleep intervened, because the telephone rang again at about 06:30 Friday for ENG103 *cum* BAL149 which took up most of Friday till 19:55. On Saturday morning at 05:00 I deadheaded to Allentown to immediately turn round and work back ALHB1A, off duty at 14:15. Later on Saturday, I worked the York coal train USG24 to my old firm from 23:00 to 10:00. I was back again on Sunday night at 21:30 to deadhead to Philadelphia and immediately work back ZWW964 iron ore train, off duty at 09:45. Monday 13th May at 21:30 took me from Enola to Allentown on the HBAL3B, deadheading straight back to finish at 12:15 Tuesday. Tuesday evening demanded that I be on duty at 22:40 for the Mail44 and TV3 North Jersey hotel job, back in Harrisburg at 01:25 Thursday. At 10:00 on Thursday I had to deadhead to Lancaster to be brakeman on the WHLA80, the New Holland travelling shifter on which I first began training on Conrail, finishing at 23:30. Friday saw my working an MXW101 in Enola from 10:45 to 21:15; in Britain it would have been called a ballast train, in America it was known as a work train. A test train labelled

TES101 kept the kettle boiling on Saturday from 06:30 to 19:20. From 07:30 to 13:45 Sunday I worked a UFY234 coal train from Enola to the power station at Brunner Island, about twenty miles away.

To take a closer look at Friday 10th May, from memory, we took light engines to a quarry near Reading to pick up a train loaded with ballast. The day lasted from 08:25 to 19:55, a total of eleven-and-a-half hours. Suppose I immediately went to bed after getting home and fell asleep straight away at about 21:00, I could only have slept for six hours before the telephone rang at 03:00 for duty at 05:00. This was quite legitimate. The telephone could have rung as early as 01:55, because a working day of less than twelve hours meant an employee could be required to be back on duty eight hours later. This stipulation remained in effect till the hours of service law changed on 16th July 2009. From that date, demands on traincrews eased, for they were required to have a minimum of ten hours uninterrupted rest – no telephone calls - between assignments. Additional limitations on hours traincrews could work were also imposed from that date.

Whilst working the Enola Road Conductors List in the 1990s, I was tethered to home. The telephone could ring any time. Only two hours were allowed to get to work, which was usually Harrisburg or Enola, both a little under an hour away. In those times, before widespread use of mobile telephones – or cellular telephones as they are referred to in the States – some Conrail men, in agreement with the crew dispatching office, carried bleepers. Such devices were of no use to me. I could not be out shopping or in a restaurant, because I needed every minute of that two-hour call. Immediately after I had been called to work, a few moments were spent contemplating the destination, whether it be North Jersey, Philadelphia, Morrisville or Allentown. Next, I had to pack a lunch and change of clothing for the hotel. Whilst changing into my usual work clothes (that used to be called in England dungarees but which in America were called bib overalls) I attempted to give an indication to my wife when I would be back. Finally, I would kiss goodbye and speed off.

As with New Year's Eve described in an earlier chapter, it appeared accumulative fatigue especially piled up amongst traincrews just before a public holiday, so that the employer was often hard-pressed to run trains. One Christmas Eve the telephone rang. I had been at work earlier that day, and my wife snatched up the receiver to avoid my being awakened. "M.C. Deaver?" asked the usual deep gravelly voice.

"He's sick!" shouted my wife down the telephone.

"Oh he's sick is he," said the crew dispatcher with a chuckle.

The crew dispatcher knew his request was a forlorn hope. My wife marked me off sick and got away with it.

Even before considering unpredictable and unsociable hours, being repeatedly separated from a loved one strained marriages. An extra board engineer told me the story of his arriving home one morning after working through the night, and being confronted by his wife. She wanted him, there and then, to take care of their four children in order to give her a break. She complained he was not doing his fair share in raising their progeny. He said he could not do it, because he had been up all night. It was a case of neither spouse realizing how difficult the other's life was. The man did not grasp the demands of raising four young children. The woman did not comprehend how draining working continuously was.

Railways and railroads have a history of breaking up marriages. Some men were more vulnerable than others to the temptations of secondment to a far-off motel room. That said, I do not know if the divorce rate amongst American railroaders was any worse than prevailing high levels in the general population. By contrast, several marriages were marked by extraordinary stability. One engineer said that his wife had remarked how grateful she was for his faithfulness.

Incessant, untimely calls to work whilst on the Enola Road Conductors List however created tension between me and my wife. At one stage I had to plead with her to mow the lawn because I did not have time to do it. I could never go to family functions because I always had to stay by the telephone. I had to go to work regardless of anything my wife wanted me to do.

The lowest point in this respect came one day when, just as I was about to leave, I heard a scratching noise coming from the vicinity of our oil-burning furnace. Something was obviously amiss. But slavish obedience to the call of Conrail overrode the concern, and I pretended not to hear the noise, completed the farewell, and left. Upon return from the round trip, I was told a bird had been trapped in the furnace flue. My wife who, though fond of watching wild birds, hated close contact with them, had to dismantle the flue and somehow remove the bird to the outdoors. A better husband would have put his wife's distress first and not left home till the problem had been solved. It would have risked being disciplined for being late for work, but with a good work record I would have survived. I owe my wife an apology for the incident, which I do now in print. I am sorry.

\* \* \*

The picture so far painted may raise the question why, with so many disadvantages, anyone would want to protect the Enola Road Conductors List. The answer is that despite its drawbacks, the list had much to offer. Uncertainty prevailed, but that uncertainty translated into an anticipatory thrill each time the telephone rang. I never knew to which part of the eastern United States I would be flung. A destination of North Jersey or Philadelphia was particularly uplifting. Even if the call to work was in the middle of the night, embedded in the irritation of having to get out of bed was a modicum of glee at prospect of yet another Conrail adventure. Sometimes the train symbol, such as XBS13, gave no clue of destination. At first I simply reported to wherever I had been told to report and asked where the train was going when I got there. Such blind servility was inadvisable, I might not have been qualified on the route. I eventually began to ask the destination before leaving home.

Variety was not lacking. Morrisville and Allentown featured regularly, the Philadelphia area and Hagerstown less so. The solitary North Jersey assignment cropped up oftener than expected because the regular conductor unfortunately did not enjoy the best of health. The Enola Road Conductors List was provider of last resort: when all other extra lists had expired, crew dispatchers turned to it, such desperate measures being referred to as digging deep.

Each time I was called to substitute at another terminal it enhanced one's self esteem - it acknowledged a man's value. Hagerstown ran out of road conductors on a fairly regular basis. I was routinely asked to deadhead myself there directly from home, and as a sweetener, told to start the timecard straight away. Strictly speaking, I should have reported to Harrisburg where a jitney to Hagerstown should have been provided, but that would take extra time. A typical run was the NSAL, Norfolk Southern to Allentown, bringing back the ALNS after taking rest in the hotel. An extreme case cropped up for one man when he was asked to deadhead to North Jersey and immediately conduct a train all the way back to Hagerstown. He probably ran out of time before completing the trip.

An amusing byproduct of life on the extra board was waking up in a hotel and not knowing where on earth I was! Especially if I had been dreaming about England, the state of bewilderment could only be tamed by rapidly playing back in the mind's eye history of recent years to eliminate where I was *not* in order to find where I *was*. The first fact that had to be mentally re-established was that I married my American friend, then that we moved to America, and then that I worked for the Maryland & Pennsylvania. Finally, only by racing through Conrail employment history could I determine the current assignment and pin-point the hotel!

Undoubtedly, working the Enola Road Conductors List was the zenith of an entire American railroading career. It generated a tremendous feeling of self-worth. Crew dispatchers knew I was qualified on most routes and knew I was willing to work, even on weekends. USG coal train to York? Yes! I'm qualified to York. Hot cars to Baltimore Penn Mary Yard? Yes! I know Penn Mary Yard. TV2M to Morrisville? Yessir, that's my favourite! Coal hoppers to Camden? Good old Camden, I'll take it! Mail44 for Jersey? Delighted! Brakeman for WHLA80 in Lancaster? *Brakeman for WHLA80?* You *are* digging deep, yes, I can do it!

In any Conrail position, not just on the Enola List, spirits ran highest at the beginning of each shift. Since most starting times were at night, I would usually arrive at the signing-on point bolstered with a large convenience-store coffee to ensure I was fully charged! The moment of departure was particularly exhilarating when on quick footboard relief service at Harrisburg Fuel Pad. When we were ready to go, the engineer would radio the Harrisburg Terminal Dispatcher, "PICA4 to the Harrisburg Terminal Dispatcher. Over."

"Terminal Dispatcher. Over," came the reply.

"Why, Sir, PICA4 ready to leave the Pad. Over."

"PICA okay down to Harris. Dispatcher out."

Some engineers embellished an initial radio message by prefixing it with the word "why". Another facet of engineer and dispatcher exchanges was a propensity for each to address the other as Sir. It was a refreshing formality, one that reminded me of the shipping forecast

(Cromarty, Forth, Tyne, Dogger, etcetera) that used to broadcast early morning on BBC radio where the announcer would conclude his report with "Good morning Gentlemen." Once radio exchanges had been completed at Harrisburg Fuel Pad, there came the glorious moment of actually getting under way. The elation was like a cowboy on horseback bidding farewell by waving his hat in the air, his mount rising up on its hind legs, and the pair galloping off into the sunset!

This elevated mood was also enjoyed on return journeys after emerging from a hotel. Again primed with strong coffee, with supreme confidence I would storm into the local yard office and demand to be told what our instructions were! Each yard had local arrangements concerning whom to contact before boarding the train, crucial information that I kept in a notebook with black cover that I called my black book. High spirits overflowed in one North Jersey crew room when I decided, mischievously, to employ a best British accent to make the preliminary enquiry, which in this case was by telephone. "Yes Sir, this is TV213, engineer J.J. Smith, conductor M.C. Deaver, with engines..."

The enunciation turned a few heads. Whilst I was still on the telephone, a supervisor, presumably trainmaster, came from round a corner where he had evidently been listening. A broad grin splashed across his face. After conclusion of the telephone conversation, the man, still grinning, said to me, "Are you from Brooklyn?"

Quick as a flash I came back, "South Side."

This exchange must have resonated around the terminal, for about eighteen months later a man in Harrisburg GI8, pointing to me, said to his colleague, "He's from Brooklyn."

His colleague added drily, "South Side."

An advertisement used to run on American television where two British businessmen in Rolls Royces pulled up alongside one another. One opened a window and said to the other, "I say old chap, do you have any Grey Poupon?" On the Rule 261 double-track at CP-Capital interlocking just outside Harrisburg, another westbound train pulled alongside the one I was conducting, so that both were neck and neck. The engineer, having heard my voice on the radio answering detectors, opened the window and said, "I say old chap, do you have any Grey Poupon?" I was so stunned I was unable to compliment the man on his brilliant, opportunist lampoon of the advertisement.

One of the best speakers of British English in his time, several decades ago, was BBC radio newsreader Alvar Liddell. In a later period I always felt the relaxed manner of ITN newsreaders was the best spoken English of the day. Somewhere between was the suave cultured accent of actor Sean Connery who originally played James Bond. In another bout of playfulness, I thought I would emulate his way of speaking after we boarded a home-bound train at Belmont, Philadelphia. Once we were ready to move, I called the dispatcher on the radio. I deepened my voice, cleared the throat and spoke from the back of the throat rather than from the palate: "XCG72W to the Philadelphia Dispatcher. Over."

The female dispatcher responded in this fashion: "Oooh what a sexy voice!"

Now, let it be known my voice is anything but sexy. I was once described as having a "chirpy" voice. It is too high for my liking, has remnants of Liverpool's twang, has strains of the Cockney way of speaking and still shows traces of Yorkshire's flat vowels which are impossible to eradicate. But I did put it on, and radios deepen the voice even more. For the remainder of the radio conversation with the dispatcher, I moderated the accent a little in the view of the reaction. Another Harrisburg crew was in the vicinity and overheard the exchange, so word spread of a brief excursion from proper radio procedure.

A natural high point that also encouraged levity was finally going off duty at the home terminal. Engineers' parting remarks could include, "Sleep fast!" as a reminder that the list was turning rapidly, "Straight home now!" to discourage straying, and "Tell your wife I still love her."

# CHAPTER 22

# POOLS

At this stage a new term needs to be introduced: the thirty-day bump. This was not a generous allowance of thirty days to find a new home after being displaced, but a provision whereby a person who had held an assignment for thirty days could switch to another. In the first twelve months on Conrail I was grateful to hold a position for thirty minutes, never mind thirty days - anything to avoid being furloughed. Matters slowly improved however. By January 1996 I had managed to complete thirty days on the Enola Trainmen List which allowed for the first time a thirty-day bump. I moved to the York Road List.

On 2nd June of the same year, after a month-long busy spell on the Enola Road Conductors List, I was glad to be able to employ the thirty-day bump to take a vacancy on the long-coveted Morrisville Pool. As anticipated, the change resulted in working usually two days out of three instead of every day. However it transpired that actual trains worked varied somewhat from the norm. On Tuesday 4th June 1996 train Mail8Y, rather than Mail8M, took the crew from Harrisburg at 23:00, into the hotel and back at 19:00 on TV1, off duty back home at 01:30. On Thursday the crew was oddly called for a North Jersey job, TV4E, at 18:15, and deadheaded straight back to be off duty at 06:05. Friday saw PIMO7 starting at 17:25 from Harrisburg and deadheading straight back finishing at 05:00. On Sunday we were again called for the PIMO but took rest, and on Monday brought back light engines ENS102, off duty at 20:00. (This could well have been the Trenton Line diversion described in an earlier chapter.) The Mail8M called us to work at 03:45 on Wednesday, to come back on the Mail9 on Thursday 13<sup>th</sup> June finishing at 09:35. A very satisfying Morrisville episode came to an abrupt end when I was displaced five minutes after signing off duty. (Was I spotted in GI8 yard office and bumped immediately the moment I walked out of the door?)

On a further five occasions in the years 1996 to 1998 the Morrisville Pool availed itself to me (for varying lengths of time) and I was able to enjoy the stability, the comfortable breaks between assignments, and the stimulating walks and riparian delights of nearby Bristol. But as the economy gave up some of its earlier energy the pool became harder to hold. On the last of those five occasions, when I bumped onto it on 21<sup>st</sup> November 1998, I lasted only fifty-five minutes. Again, did someone overhear? However, in due course character of the Morrisville Pool changed and it lost its appeal, as will be described later.

One advantage of pool work was that it *usually* gave a little more time at home between assignments. Another is that territory was limited, so there was less of a mental strain, even though on the extra board being dispatched to all points of the compass did have its appeal. The Morrisville Pool worked only between Harrisburg Consolidated Terminal and Morrisville. The C&PD Pool, dealt with in the chapter on the Port Road, worked only between Harrisburg Consolidated Terminal and Baltimore. There remained one other pool, its geographical spread was greater.

\* \* \*

The RU Pool worked out of Harrisburg to Bethlehem Allentown Consolidated Terminal, to the Philadelphia area and to Hagerstown. Presumably the RU stood for Rutherford. The first attempt to bump onto the RU Pool was on 10<sup>th</sup> February 1997, when I lasted from 09:15 to 13:45 without working. On 5<sup>th</sup> July the same year I lasted eight days managing two round trips to Allentown before being expelled. I then bumped onto Baltimore's C&PD Pool which I held for only a few hours as previously mentioned. After being thrown out of that terminal I elected to take a five-day bump during which I happily exercised my seniority on the Maryland and Pennsylvania working two shifts before condescending to go back to Conrail before the five-day bump expired.

Two five-day sessions on the RU Pool in August and early October 1997 were followed by a session lasting from 16th to 31st October 1997. A 135-day period on the RU Pool from 5th September 1998 to 18th January 1999 was the longest stint on any Conrail assignment – if one discounts the abortive bump onto the Morrisville Pool of 21st November. The extract below was typical of that period.

On Wednesday 25th November the crew deadheaded to Philadelphia to bring back PMT19 in combined service, that is to say, we were paid mileage, which in this case was 246 miles round trip; we were paid nearly two day's pay for working from 06:00 to 16:00. The traffic itself was new, imported steel slabs about one foot thick, two to a gondola. The colossal weight meant these trains, called slab trains, were usually limited to seventy cars. After two full days at home, I was called for BUAL5 (Buffalo to Allentown) which worked from 00:30 to 08:50, after which we were put into the hotel. ALPI8F (Allentown to Pittsburgh) was brought back later that Sunday, the day lasting from 21:30 to 07:10. At 10:35 on Monday 30th November the crew worked eastwards with PIAL9 till 22:25, and after taking rest, brought back OIEL0 from 06:25 to 14:45. EL stood for Elkhart, Indiana State. On both the following Thursday and Friday, a crew deadheaded to Allentown to bring back in combined service the ALPI, hours being 01:30 to 10:50 and 19:15 to 05:00 respectively. On Sunday 6th December 1998 I worked from 02:00 to 11:50 on an empty slab train to Philadelphia, MTP22, and deadheaded back. On Monday MTP24 was similarly worked to Philadelphia from 18:05 to 03:30, but the crew was put in the hotel. It appears the carrier could find no work for us, so we deadheaded back to Harrisburg from 15:15 to 19:25 on Tuesday. At 04:00 on Thursday 10th December, a UEP60 coal train was taken from Harrisburg to the Philadelphia area where we finished at 14:55 and were put into the hotel. Later the same day, XAN87 was brought from Camden to Harrisburg, the shift lasting from 23:00 to 08:20.

On Saturday 12th December coal train UPS494 was taken from Enola to Allentown from 08:50 to 20:49, after which we were put into the hotel. The timecard thus showed eleven hours and fifty-nine minutes on duty, doubtless at the insistence of the engineer to ensure, if there were need, that we could be called out for a return trip after only eight hour's rest. If I had had my way, the shift would have been recorded as twelve hours long, which would have guaranteed ten hour's rest. However, it was all a moot point, because, after baking in the hotel till 13:45 hours Sunday, we were deadheaded back to Enola through lack of work in Allentown, off duty at 15:50.

Instances of deadheading out of hotels highlighted problems the railroad faced in matching supply of crews with demand of trains. The Harrisburg based RU Pool was single-ended. (Allentown men would have been within their rights in insisting on a moiety of the work, but I think they gave it away.) One would have thought that given an equal number of trains in each direction – and there is no reason to think that that was not the case – if all crews went to the hotel there would be a train for each to bring back in due course. But for whatever reasons it did not work out that way, as witnessed by the large amount of one-way deadheading described above. One obvious factor was that whilst such as the ALPI and ALHB might run daily, coal trains running in spurts upset the balance. Another point was that Philadelphia and Hagerstown trips could pull too many men away, forcing crew dispatchers to deadhead RU crews back and forth to keep Allentown traffic moving.

The nineteen-day November 1998 period described above was typical in that it showed a respectable amount of time at home before again being called out. A look at the entire 135-day period from which those nineteen days were extracted would show that trips were not only made to other RU Pool destinations of Bethlehem and Hagerstown, but to unexpected places too. In an excellent example of digging deep, on Tuesday 29th September I was seconded from the RU Pool to work an intermodal train, TV22, from Harrisburg to Baltimore. I probably had the option of declining, but did not dream of doing so. Four days later my crew took PIOI (Pittsburgh to Oak Island) as far as Port Reading Jct on the Lehigh Line and deadheaded back. This RU Pool employee was used on 23rd October on a Morrisville round trip including staying in the hotel. On 27th October and 11th November crew dispatchers were not above using me on intermodal trains to North Jersey; the crew deadheading back on both occasions. By 1998 I had qualified on one of the Delaware jobs. That qualification was not wasted as, on 16th December, I made a round trip to Delaware including staying in the hotel. "Join the RU Pool and see the world!" one man quipped.

A trip to Bethlehem is worthy of note. On reporting for duty at Harrisburg GI8, we picked up train PIBE from either 3 Relay or 4 Relay in the yard. The first car was a specially designed insulated car containing molten steel. It had been collected from a branch of Bethlehem Steel near Harrisburg by a local crew, and placed at the head of our train for delivery to the parent company in Bethlehem. I do not pretend to understand the laws of physics whereby hot molten steel can be stored for twelve hours without it and its container becoming one solid mass of cold useless metal. The steel remained liquid till we reached Bethlehem's Iron Hill Yard, where the local crew took it away. The transfer of molten steel on PIBE was a regular occurrence, at least for a while. Eventually, Bethlehem steel works and its numerous yards became more and more run down, but not yet to the point of extinction.

In the case of the Morrisville and C&PD Pools, conductors and engineers were permanently paired - insofar as any railroad staffing arrangement could be considered permanent. The RU Pool was quite different. An engineers pool existed solely for Allentown work and an engineers pool existed solely for Philadelphia area work. Hagerstown work was covered by an engineers extra list. Thus when working the RU Pool, a conductor never knew who his next engineer would be.

Whilst holding one of the RU positions a peculiar thing happened. A man from elsewhere in the pool bumped me and took my slot. A couple of vacancies existed in the pool at the time, which made his move even more perplexing. It was of no consequence, I simply took one of the vacancies, whether it was his or another was similarly of no consequence. Next time I saw the man I asked him about his inexplicable exercise of seniority. His reply went something like this: "You see, the slot you held was Lackawanna equity. I was in a Reading equity slot. When it comes to choosing vacation dates, Lackawanna is ahead of Reading in the pool. That's why I bumped you." In other words, he executed the bump just to have a better pick of vacation time.

The RU Pool was a mixture of equity, a mixture that changed occasionally. For example on 5th September 1998 the equity breakdown was eight Pennsylvania, four Reading, two Leigh Valley, one Lackawanna and one marked ERNY which I did not understand, a total of sixteen positions. This did not mean that the eight Pennsylvania men were called just for trains running over former Pennsylvania territory, for the pool was worked as all other pools, in strict rotation. It meant that eight places on the pool were set aside for former Pennsylvania employees, four places for former Reading men, and so on. If all Pennsylvania positions were filled and another Pennsylvania man wanted to work the RU pool, he could take, say, a Reading slot if nobody else wanted it.

Allocation of RU Pool equity was puzzling. The whole route from Harrisburg to Allentown was former Reading metals, a strong argument for giving most of the pool over to Reading equity. But the distribution of equity was such that Reading played only a poor second to Pennsylvania. To look at area history, *A Railroad Atlas of the United States in 1946* shows four railroads descending on Allentown: Central Railroad Company of New Jersey, Lehigh & New England, Lehigh Valley and the Reading, two of which were not represented in the September 1998 breakdown.

To return to work undertaken by the RU Pool, Allentown Yard, the most common destination, was divided into three distinct parts, the six-track Hump Yard where inbound trains arrived, the twenty-nine-track Classification Yard or Field into which inbound traffic was classified, and the Departure Yard, better known as The Park, comprising nine tracks where complete outbound trains were stored. Inbound cars were pushed from the Hump Yard over the hump itself to be dispersed in ones and twos into tracks that would become outbound trains. Close to the hump, the high-pitched scream of power-operated retarders pressing against car wheels to slow them down felt like a knife being twisted into the side of one's head; ear protection was vital. The motive power that usually pushed cars over the hump comprised a normal locomotive coupled to a cut-down version of a locomotive, the combination being known as mother and slug.

The most intriguing aspect of Allentown work was Burn time, not how long to stay in the sun to acquire sunburn, but the time at which eastbound trains passed CP-Burn. If train PIAL, the Pittsburgh to Allentown, left Harrisburg for Allentown followed by a loaded coal train for the same destination, it would be reasonable to expect that they would remain in that order all the way to Bethlehem Allentown Consolidated Terminal. Thus PIAL would pass CP-Burn at the western approaches to Allentown Yard, proceed through CP-Allen and along the single track Lehigh Line to change tracks at CP-Canal in order to reach the Hump Yard. PIAL trains were invariably lengthy, and usually had to be split between two tracks in the Hump Yard, all of which took time. Meanwhile the coal train immediately following would have passed CP-Burn a few minutes after PIAL, turned right at that interlocking to proceed on the Reading Line single track, through CP-Bethlehem, and probably enjoyed footboard relief on the Bethlehem Layoff track east of CP-Bethlehem. If both crews were staying in Allentown, the coal train crew would arrive in the hotel first, having effectively leap-frogged over the PIAL, and it would be reasonable to expect that they would be called out ahead of them for a return trip.

Not so. The deciding factor in calling order was time a crew passed CP-Burn. A note had to be made, and when telephoning the crew dispatcher to sign off duty, both the off-duty time and Burn time were given. Thus in the above example the PIAL crew would be called from the hotel first. Incidentally, CP-Burn was not just important from traincrews' perspective, it was also a location where rail enthusiasts gathered to admire and record Conrail's thundering freight trains.

Interesting circumstances arose on Friday 20th November 1998 when two crews were off duty in the hotel at the same time. The other crew had a better Burn time but had worked twelve hours so needed ten hour's rest. Our crew with inferior Burn time needed only eight hour's rest. In the event the other crew was called first. Our crew was left to vegetate in the hotel till the following Saturday when, at 15:00 hours, we were deadheaded home through lack of work. Because we had been held in the hotel a total of twenty-one-and-a-quarter hours, we earned a total of five-and-a-quarter hours cabin track time. I did not mind the sojourn, the Allentown motel was pleasant with good television channel selection. Fortunately the engineer also took a relaxed view of the enforced confinement.

The next time I was called out it was with the same engineer as the previous trip to Allentown and, once again, machinations of Burn time reared up. We were on duty at 07:20 for the PIBE, Pittsburgh to Bethlehem, hauled by locomotives Class C40-8W 6268 and Class SD40-2 6467. Despite the train symbol, we had no traffic at all for

Bethlehem, the entire train consist being destined for Reading. Once the eighty-seven cars had been set off in Reading Spring Street Yard, we headed towards Allentown but got no further than CP-West Laurel, a couple of miles north of Reading, where the home signal displayed STOP SIGNAL. To record what happened next, I can do no better than quote the timecard for that date, 23rd November 1998: "At 11.35am Harrisburg East Train Dispatcher instructed that this crew, formerly of PIBE2 light power, couple up to train ENAL3 which was immediately behind us on Track 2 at West Laurel. This was done and train went forward in that formation."

Thus one train with two RU crews now on board proceeded easterly, mindful of the vexed question of Burn time looming in the very near future. "Hey Steve, I've got an idea," I said to the other conductor. "If you wanted to have a better Burn time, why don't you go out and stand on the front of the engine just before we get there, so that you'll actually pass CP-Burn before we do?" He smiled at the suggestion. After a brief discussion, my affable engineer and I allowed the other crew to record an earlier Burn time, both crews being off duty at 17:30. In contrast to the previous trip, our crew was called out after only eight hours rest, on duty at 01:30 hours to work the ALBU Allentown to Buffalo, New York State, relieved as usual at Harrisburg.

# CHAPTER 23

# REGULAR JOBS

Conrail employed small armies of employees to protect extra boards and other small armies to man pools, neither groups knowing for sure when next they would work. Did *anyone* have fixed hours? one may ask. Yes they did, and those positions, called regular jobs, were typically filled by senior employees. Yard jobs, including utility personnel, nearly always had a specified start time, as did travelling shifters. Such assignments could be put back an hour or two, or even cancelled completely, but that was exceptional.

Though most road work was covered by pools or extra boards, a small number of regular road jobs existed, such as PICA-plus-CAPI and Mail44-plus-TV3, but their crews fared little better than others as they too were on call. There were no fixed start times, but they did know which *day* the telephone would ring. My understanding is that such jobs had to be called within a certain window – the PICA window may have been from 22:00 to 02:00 hours – otherwise crew members could, if they chose, refuse. It seemed unlikely men would turn down the PICA at, say, 04:00, because they would lose income and because they had already anticipated a shift of night work. Though regular road jobs were much coveted, the fact remained *all* road work was on call.

The obvious reason for all road jobs being on call was that there was no timetable; it was not known when a train would leave Harrisburg or anywhere else. Contrast this state of affairs with British operations where a specified path was nearly always allotted, which not only kept freights clear of passenger trains but which determined a start time for the crew. From my experience British freights usually ran within about thirty minutes of their booked time. Certainly in the 1980s, it appeared most freight train crews enjoyed fixed hours, even if each week saw a different job and different start time. In the 2010s, a timetabled path was still the order of the day for British freight, though with privatization and a bustling economy, it is likely timetable changes were more frequent.

Conrail endeavoured to run intermodal trains to a tight schedule even though timings were kept from traincrews. At the other extreme, most coal trains appeared to run subject to supply and demand, on the supply side whenever the mine finished loading them, on the demand side when power stations needed stocks replenished – which in turn was governed by weather. Coal trains suffered low priority, and would sometimes be allowed to sit around places like the Enola Old Line till needed, or till a crew could be put together. Such capriciousness would make nonsense of any fixed schedule.

The principal obstacles to drawing up a schedule for American freights were dimensional. Many trains covered hundreds of miles. Even if a punctual start were made every day at Oak Island, New Jersey, chances of a long heavy freight train keeping time all the way to Elkhart, Indiana, were slim. In the coldest part of winter, a hundred-car train may take twenty minutes longer to charge the air brake system, twenty minutes that is lost even before the train departed. To assemble an eighty-car train from two tracks could take an hour. The same train the following day comprising 125 cars from three tracks could take twice as long. How could such inconsistencies be built into a timetable? The chances of something going wrong with an American 100-car train are three times greater than something going wrong with a thirty-wagon British train. Thus for multiple reasons, a timetable or schedule for American freight trains is not realistic, and predictable start times for traincrews equally impractical.

\* \* \*

Despite the jockeying for regular road jobs amongst senior employees, time would come when I could hold one. The first was in May 1997 when, before being bumped, I made three round trips on the TV12 to North Jersey, returning as TV11. Two surprising facts surround this venture, the first being that I could hold any Jersey job at all, the second being that I remember very little about it! The only clear memory is that the destination was E-Rail (derived from the town of Elizabeth) which was reached via Oak, Pike, a location called PN and yard limits of the Chemical Coast Secondary.

The next regular job was a little less surprising in that, amongst all regular eastbound road jobs based in Harrisburg Consolidated Terminal, this was the least appealing. It was one of the Delaware jobs, ML420 outwards, ML411 returning. ML referred to multi-level automobile carriers, commonly called autoracks, equivalent of British cartics. ML420's lack of appeal was probably explained by its 120-mile trips always being slow and plodding, and by typically spending twelve hours in the hotel. Each round trip was a marathon. Nevertheless, I usually leapt onto a vacancy on "the Delaware job" - which is how I described it to my wife - whenever it popped up, the first occasion being in July 1997. Subsequent opportunities arose periodically. I will describe the job as it was in 1999.

The Delaware job was always on duty at Enola, usually at 19:00 hours. After letting the yardmaster know the crew was present and after grabbing paperwork and reading it, engineer and conductor were conveyed by yard jitney to Enola Diesel House to pick up motive power. With first the Diesel House's permission then the yardmaster's, the power travelled via the Diesel Outbound, 23B, Westbound, East Hump then backed into one of the Eastbound Receiving tracks to couple to the train. The required initial terminal brake test had already been conducted by car inspectors using a ground air line. Once permission to leave was given, a car inspector checked an application and release of brakes on the hind end and would watch the train roll by. Departure would be via Track 44 and either 4P or 5P to pass station sign Day, and to pass into the area controlled by the Port Road Dispatcher.

Progress down the Port Road was usually uninterrupted, perhaps an occasional short wait at one of the interlockings whilst a westbound train cleared the single track ahead. On the double-track Rule 261 section between CP-Quarry and Amtrak's Perry interlocking, eastbound trains always took the British (left-hand) side because a car inspector was positioned on that side, near Minnick. Speed had to be reduced for the car inspector who, by checking with a high intensity light, ensured each train destined for Amtrak was sound. ML420 turned left at Perry by means of the ten mile per hour curve to climb a steep gradient on Track 4 to Prince interlocking where four tracks became two. An equally steep down gradient took the train to Bacon interlocking where we crossed over to the easternmost track, number 1, as far as Iron interlocking. At Iron we crossed over to a track even more easterly, identified as A, not as 0 or -1. A track named naught did actually exist, and was alongside us when the train came to a stand at Davis interlocking in order to work in Chrysler Yard, Newark. This Newark was in Delaware, Oak Island Newark was in New Jersey.

Davis interlocking comprised four tracks, 1, 2, 3 and A. At the interlocking's northern limit Conrail's Delmarva Secondary came in from the east. On the west was found an out-of-use stub track, Track 5. Branching off Track 5 was another abandoned track rejoicing in one of those magically-sounding names one felt ought to have more significance than it actually did, Pomeroy. Davis Tower still stood, in reasonable but disused condition.

The bulk of ML420's cars were set off in Chrysler Yard. I would alight where a cut was to be made, and would possibly line switches if they were handy. "Okay ML420, take 'em ahead forty-three cars for a cut," I would say over the radio. Once the cut was made, I would give the instruction to proceed ahead. At that point, the head-end had already passed beyond the northern limits of Davis interlocking, so the whole train had to clear that location before a reverse move could be made, a distance of at least half a mile. In most cases the dispatcher, CETC-3, must have been watching track indications carefully, because quite soon after coming to a stand clear of the interlocking, the southbound home signal changed. "We've got Restricting in the signal, okay to bring 'em back ML420, fifty cars to a switch," I would say. The movement proceeded with my giving a countdown: twenty-five cars, twelve, six, three, two, one, half, far enough ML420. Sharp eyes will note that I cheated, twelve being less than half of twenty-five. Strictly speaking, the engineer should have halted at twelve-and-a-half cars lengths!

Sometimes the set-off was made on two or three tracks where one could clearly see cars would fit in the space available, other times the whole set-off had to go on one track, in which case the conductor, as a precaution, had to ride the hind end all the way back. A long return walk ensued, contributing to a drawn-out operation, unavoidable when dealing with lengthy moves. When coupled again to the remaining cars on the main line, a hind-end brake test was conducted and, at some hour in the middle of the night, we left Newark.

We continued about ten miles northward to Ragan interlocking, where we left Amtrak's Northeast Corridor to enter Conrail's New Castle Secondary, not without first obtaining a Form D of course. Speed had to be sharply reduced for the ten mile per hour restriction over Ward Moveable Bridge, and kept down as we entered Yard Limits at station sign Castle. We trundled along flanked by estuary marshland, as we were close to the Delaware River. At about milepost 4.5, we disposed of the train on various sidings, usually near another automobile facility, Honda. Our locomotives would be used for the return trip, and were normally secured on Brandywine Siding.

When finished, we radioed for a jitney, rode in it and booked off duty in the hotel, clocking up at least twelve hours. I was soon fast asleep. Rising in the afternoon, I would watch television briefly, then go for a walk. I can no longer pinpoint on a map where the hotel was, but I remember very clearly the surrounding mix of residential and commercial property because I eventually reconnoitred the entire district in search of new places to stroll. As we would not normally be called back to work till 18:00 hours, time was a friend.

Signing-on point for the return journey was Edgemoor Yard, destination of the PIED. There we gathered paperwork, collected a telemetry marker and were driven back to the location in New Castle where we had finished earlier that day. The jitney stopped at the rear of about a dozen autorack cars to allow me to hang the cumbersome marker, then took us to the engines. After the engineer inspected them, we coupled up, and whilst he charged up the train I walked to the hind end to begin the initial terminal brake test. "Okay ML411, you've got ninety pounds on the hind end, okay to make your reduction." A gauge on the telemetry marker showed brake pipe pressure duly reduced to seventy-five pounds, whereupon I proceeded to walk up one side of the train then down the other to ensure each brake piston had come out and to inspect the cars overall. On most cars, brake cylinders can be seen from the opposite side, but not on these autoracks, so after the application I had to walk up and down both sides *again* to check the release. "That's a good release ML411.

Good brake test." For the sixth time I walked the train's entire length to reach the head end. After necessary exchanges with the dispatcher, we proceeded via Amtrak to Chrysler Yard, Newark.

We came to a stand on Track A at switches referred to as 40, because they were at milepost 40. We left the autoracks on Track A and followed the yardmaster's instructions to pick up the rest of our train. At the time, there was unbalanced train working, in that the PIED took mixed traffic eastwards to Edgemoor Yard and ML411 returned it westwards from Chrysler Yard, other assignments obviously transferring it between the two. A timecard for 20ᵗʰ April 1999 showed that, with Class C40-8W engines numbered 6056 and 6212, ninety cars were picked up at Chrysler Yard. With so many cars it took time to get moving, and when backing up with that length of train the engineer had to exercise great caution to avoid slamming at the moment of coupling. Once a hind-end test had been done, a jitney took me a few miles down the line to rendezvous with the locomotives, somewhere near the town of Elkton. (It was always pitch black, I could not now identify the place.) From arrival at milepost 40 to departure from Elkton, the whole operation took two hours and forty minutes.

There was one bright spot as we laboured in the dark. During summer months at both Chrysler Yard and Elkton we were entertained by frequent short whistles, which were the mating call of a frog species, colloquially known as peeps, that made its home on Amtrak.

I recall once being held up on Amtrak on a sharp left-hand bend, so sharp the track was considerably tilted so passenger trains could take it at speed, but which was uncomfortable for a stationary freight train crew slumped to one side. "I'm going to radio the dispatcher and complain about this," I grumbled.

"Yeh, you do that," said the engineer with a grin.

"ML411 to CETC-3," I said in jest. "Yes sir, you'd better get the track guys out to look at this curve. The track's leaning over badly, it needs packing up under the one rail."

"And make it snappy!" added the engineer.

When back on the Port Road, the engineer and I would speculate how far we would get before those in charge determined we were not going to make it all the way to Enola. "Probably the Stone House," I would say, that landmark being a private house next to a handy access point. The occupants eventually complained about parked locomotives constantly drumming outside their home, so the location could no longer be used as a relief point.

"I'm going to say Wago," the engineer would say.

Three times out of four we never made it to Enola, resulting in thirteen-hour timecards owing to deadheading. Timecards had to be endorsed: "Concerning hours of service, no work was undertaken beyond twelve hours." Off duty at about 09:00, I drove home exhausted, slumped into bed, slept like concrete for several hours, arose unsteadily, perhaps mowed the lawn, drank beer, then tumbled back into bed to sleep for twelve hours. The next day I was as bright as a locomotive headlight, ready to do it again! Appeal of a rigid three-day cycle that included about thirty hours at home, if not a very productive thirty hours, ensured the Delaware job kept calling me back, despite its interminable shifts.

In October 1997 I bumped onto the PICA, but lasted just one trip. In 1998, the Camden job was spliced with a new intermodal service to South Philadelphia Yard to produce two new regular jobs. In August 1998 I was able to hold one of the positions for a couple of weeks, the PICA eastwards coupled with TV21 westwards.

The PICA had changed. The Shore Secondary became part of the Delair Branch that ran almost to Camden. In addition to Frankford Junction, the PICA now worked in West Falls Yard setting off traffic for Philadelphia. Philadelphia cars were now tagged onto the PICA rather being routed via Allentown. Like nearby Belmont, West Falls was a gloomy place at night owing to close proximity of Fairmount Park that provided no artificial light. An over-bridge slicing through the yard limited visibility further. On 23rd August 1998 PICA had a massive 169-car train, but adequately handled by combined 7300 horsepower of Class C40-8W 6243 and Class SD50 6832. We set off ninety-three cars in West Falls and picked up twelve cars on which an initial terminal test had to be performed, a monstrous nocturnal operation lasting almost four hours. We worked on Harrisburg Line Track 1 towards CP-Laurel Hill on the Trenton Line, as was usual practice. On the night in question the engineer had to ask for a signal at CP-Laurel Hill because the move took him well on the way to the next interlocking, CP-Nice. Riding ninety-three cars back through West Falls was a tediously slow operation as one could see no more than a few car lengths at a time. When West Falls work was complete, we moved on to Frankford Junction to set off thirty-eight cars, then ran out of time, deadheading the rest of the way.

Three days earlier when the workload had not been so heavy, we made it all the way to Camden. At about 10:00 hours PICA0 approached the towering Delair Moveable Bridge to find, as usual, the high signal protecting the bridge reading APPROACH SLOW. As we rumbled over the structure at the mandatory ten miles per hour, I said to the engineer, "Where's the pot signal?"

"Dunno. Meant to be somewhere here isn't it, at the end of the bridge?" he said, slowing the train to a crawl.

"I don't understand this," I said. "There's nothing in the bulletin about taking the signal away. Wait a minute, there's something at the side of the bridge."

The engineer brought the train to a stand. I went outside, climbed off the locomotive and looked at a flattish, triangular object laying on the edge of the bridge superstructure. With a foot firmly planted on each of two girders and nothing between the girders and the Delaware River flowing menacingly thirty feet below, I grabbed hold of the object and pulled it upright. It was the dwarf signal correctly displaying SLOW APPROACH. Something hanging from a westbound train must have knocked it over onto its face. Wires were still connected of course, so after making sure the signal was seated correctly on its concrete base, I climbed on board and off we went. A minor incident, but poignant to a signalling enthusiast: I had never heard of train personnel righting a signal that had fallen over!

\* \* \*

The next regular job was one trip on the WPLA75, a travelling shifter out of Lancaster that served Parkesburg and industries *en route*. Later in 1998 I worked for one day as brakeman on the diurnal Shiremanstown to Carlisle travelling shifter, WPST03, before being spotted.

In 1999 a new regular job was advertised: PIOI eastwards to North Jersey and bringing back ML401 westwards. However, the lumbering mixed freight always ran late and men would not have enough rest to bring back the autoracks train, so the crew usually deadheaded to Jersey and went straight to the hotel. This peculiar arrangement had little appeal to others, but the train being routed via the Trenton Line drew me like a prospector to a gold rush! I was unchallenged in the conductor's position; the engineer's slot was frequently filled off the extra board.

On duty time in North Jersey Consolidated Terminal after vacating the hotel could be anything from 23:00 to 05:00 hours. The train was assembled in the Garden Yard located in the southern part of the terminal. One night we had to take the middle eight cars out of a track containing twenty cars. After coupling the engines, I walked back to cut behind our cars, the intention being to set them aside and then ride back to re-couple. In the middle of the move there came a radio transmission: "Yardmaster to the ML401. Over."

"ML401," I replied.

"Hold what you're doing, I'm coming out there to see you," he said.

The next transmission was from the engineer who said the yardmaster requested I come to the head end. On reaching the engines, I met the yardmaster, a stocky man who, as he was the same height as me, was able, through our two pairs of safety glasses, to look me squarely in the eye. "You're screwing me!" he said.

"I'm not screwing you. I don't know what you mean," I replied indignantly.

"You're screwing me!" he insisted. "All you need to do here is pull the track, make a cut, set out, re-couple and shove back in. There's no need to walk all the way back to make a cut. You're wasting time."

"Then I'd be shoving back blind," I protested. "It's as dark as hell, I can't see back there. And it's an open-ended track. Someone could be coming in the other end for all I know."

"Look. *I'm* the yardmaster. I've made sure nobody will go in at the other end. Now get on with your job as I told you, and don't waste any more time." With that, he leapt back into his vehicle and sped back to the office. I finished moves as expediently as possible, and after the necessary brake test we departed, picking our way through Garden, Pike, Oak and CP-Valley.

The engineer sympathized with me, but I neither expected sympathy nor deserved it. Shoving into an empty track is a contentious issue. The rules say the person in charge of the movement should ensure it is safe to do so. When shoving into a short empty track in daylight, most would agree that by simply looking down the track a conductor could determine it was clear. But if a trespasser then ran out of bushes in front of moving cars and was injured, it is not clear what the conductor's position would be even though he had taken all reasonable steps.

In the other extreme of shoving large numbers of cars into a very long track, as sometimes happened in Enola, it was usual to provide an additional employee, a utility man, near the track end. In intermediate conditions, a conductor would be wise to ride cars at least so far back, dismount, then complete the move by directing it from the ground.

In the North Jersey incident, resentment at being corrected had to give way to servility. I could have been clever and invoked the dictum that, when in doubt, the safest course must be followed, but that would have just inflamed the confrontation further and could have resulted in my being taken out of service on the spot. Even if I had been entirely correct and the yardmaster entirely wrong – neither of which was the case – the yardmaster was still my superior. It is possible there were set routines in North Jersey I did not know of. Or other men could have been guilty of "screwing" the yardmaster. From this set to, pride and ego emerged in smithereens, but self-restraint and confidence stood firm. Railroading can be emotional.

* * *

"What the hell are you doing over here? Why don't you sod off back to England where you belong."

These were the ungracious first words I heard from engineer Big John, the exchange taking place in Lancaster Yard Office. Big John shared with some Irish-Americans an intense dislike for the British, inflamed by tremendously complicated events in Northern Ireland, affairs the British media chose to refer to as "The Troubles". The man took exception to sharing the same ground with a Briton.

"I'm here because I married a girl from Lancaster, Pennsylvania," I replied politely and accurately. I then moved away to another part of the office.

Big John was about six feet six inches tall, had broad shoulders, a muscular body and hands like shovels. As is the case with many big people, his size reinforced his self-confidence. It were as if he believed that being twenty per cent larger than anybody else entitled him to twenty per cent more of everything, not only food and space, which most would not dispute, but also opinion, about which there was less of a consensus. Big John was so overpowering many conductors avoided working with him. The vacancies so created and my appetence for better jobs tended to throw us together, a circumstance we both had to reconcile ourselves with. For a period we both held the ML401 job.

On one trip Big John found he could not suppress the question of Northern Ireland. I gave him a straightforward reply. "To be honest with you, concerning everything that went on in Northern Ireland, when I lived in Britain I was just like most people over there, I was fed up hearing about it. I shut my ears to it. And history is not my strongest point, I can't comment on what went on before because I don't know enough about it." Big John did not bring up the sensitive issue again.

Big John was under doctor's orders to take exercise, and he needed moral support. After the deadhead journey to a hotel in Linden, New Jersey, he persuaded me to join him walking for half an hour or so. Most streets around the hotel were crowded with traffic, so we took to nearby cemetery grounds, which were certainly peaceful if lacking in cheer. After the hike I would go to a nearby take-away restaurant, buy General Tso's fried chicken, eat it in the hotel, then sleep.

Locked together as we were on the ML401, relations steadily warmed between the Irish-American and myself to the extent that humorous interludes found their way into the locomotive cab, samples of which are given below.

I mentioned I had seen in an American television series Mr. French, an English butler.

"*He* was a gentleman's gentleman," said Big John.

"Not like me, eh?" I said.

"No. You're a hobo's hobo," said Big John.

"Talking of television, I suppose English programmes are too boring for Americans."

"When you read back a Form D with your accent, it makes me want to fall asleep," said Big John.

"Does your wife work?" he asked on another occasion.

"She works night shift at the slaughter house."

"Is that the British idea of a joke?"

"Not a very good one."

"What's more boring than two Englishmen at a party?" asked Big John.

"Dunno."

"Three. You know, there's a new English bar in Morrisville."

"Oh yes?" said I naively.

"It's called the Bore-a-Lot."

Good relations that eventually developed between us were such that in Harrisburg GI8 after he had said something foolish, I said to him, "I'm going to smack you!"

A yard conductor heard me and said to his colleague, "We'd better watch ourselves around this Deaver fellah here, he just said to Big John he was going to smack him!"

The friendship developed to such an extent he invited my wife and me to dinner – an offer I never did take up. Yet, his Irish pride would not allow the matter of his ancestry to disappear entirely from conversation. "Did you ever go to Ireland?" he asked.

"No. I didn't really have any reason to."

"So you wouldn't go and visit Ireland when you lived right next door to it," he said with some dismay.

"Never was much of a traveller. Hardly ever went to Wales or Scotland, and they're much closer." Then after a moment's thought, I added, "Hang on a minute, have *you* ever been to Ireland?"

Big John did not answer. His head hung low. His eyes moistened. He may have eased off the throttle a notch. It had not been the intention to embarrass or humiliate the big man, my question just seemed the logical thing to say. After a while I changed the subject, and the uncomfortable colloquy was forgotten. Despite some tense moments, cordial relations continued to prevail during the many trips Big John and I made together.

# CHAPTER 24

# SLOW TRAINS

The Delaware job - the ML420 and ML411 - needed a full twelve-hour day to complete its work; on many occasions that was not enough, a Short Turn crew had to take the train into Enola. On paper, this seems a poor show. Twelve hours to cover a distance of 113 miles, an average of about ten miles per hour, sets no record, but I hope I adequately explained the time-consuming nature of the train's duties. Contributing to slow progress of ML420 and of any other train on the lower part of the Port Road was the route's relatively low speeds, and the fact that it alternated from single to double track which restricted traffic flow. The other Enola to Delaware regular assignment, Conway to Eastern Shore, PIES, fared even worse. Its destination was Harrington, Delaware, about sixty miles further than the ML420's. Since it, too, had to work at Newark, it was no surprise the crew invariably ran out of time. Neither did they complete the journey back.

Employer and employee alike accepted that some regular jobs took a long time. Length of the working day on non-regular jobs varied enormously. On the RU Pool, some straight shot Harrisburg to Allentown trains quickly covered the ninety-odd miles; those scheduled to work along the way took longer and occasionally had to be relieved. Philadelphia jobs similarly varied.

On duty at 22:00 hours on 18th July 1996, coal train UEP80S left Enola for the Harrisburg Line via Rockville Bridge, its destination a power station in the Philadelphia area. Our instructions were that the head thirty cars were to be detached at Cromby, about thirty miles west of Philadelphia, and placed in the power station there situated on what remained of a Pennsylvania Railroad route. Access to the power station was a facing move from our Track 2, so cars had to be run round. This would not normally be a problem as two double-ended tracks ran alongside Track 2 at Cromby. However, on arrival I scouted the locality in the dark and found both sidings full of cars. Holding the hand radio above my head for better reception, I spoke on the radio to the dispatcher. "UEP80S to the Main Line Dispatcher. Over."

"Main Line."

"Yes, sir. We have to spot our head thirty cars in the plant here at Cromby, but we can't run round them because both Sidings 1 and 2 are completely full of cars. The only way we're going to be able to get our cars into the power station is to first shove one of these tracks out onto the main, towards Phoenix, and leave them there. Then we can use that track to run round, put the cars in the plant, then drag the other cars back in. We won't be going as far as Phoenix, but we'll be heading that way. Are we okay to do that?"

"That's a Roger UEP. Okay to work," replied the dispatcher.

"It's gonna take us a while though," I added.

"Understand UEP. Dispatcher out."

"UEP out."

Having to ride the point of every movement in darkness with only a hand lamp for illumination made distances difficult to gauge, so work proceeded at a low-geared pace, especially when approaching switches. With any run-round move, conductors had to be especially vigilant that switches were correctly lined. On this night I calculate I walked thirty car lengths no less than five times, plus another seventy cars to do the brake test. After much effort, thirty cars were eventually spotted in the power plant, and we resumed our journey eastwards. Spent, I was grateful to be relieved at West Falls Yard, off duty at 08:35.

Another drawn-out operation ensued when, on 14th December 1996, a crew on duty at 15:00 hours deadheaded to Millards Quarry twenty-two miles from Harrisburg to pick up a fifty-car train. The jitney ride took from 15:20 to 15:52. No less than nine locomotives of different classes, or models as they are described in America, were waiting there to haul the train back: GP38s 7727 and 7881, GP38-2s 8042, 8048 and 8049 and SW1500s 9522, 9534, 9535 and 9582. All had to be inspected by the engineer. It is possible a light engine movement had been abandoned at Millards, and rather than run another crew just to collect the power, it was decided to combine the operation with a trainload of stone. Once coupled to the train, an initial terminal brake test had to be conducted by walking first the application then the release. We may have been ready to move by about 18:00 hours, but had to wait for other traffic to clear before we could head west on the Harrisburg Line at 19:30.

We were held up by signals in the Hershey area for forty-seven minutes. At CP-Capital we had to tie down and cut away from the train in order to proceed a short distance to the beginning of the Lurgan Branch to cab signal testing equipment because the lead engine did not have the valid documentation for cab signals which commenced at CP-Harris. The test did not take very long, but the train stood at Capital from 21:26 to 23:07 as other trains took priority over a load of stone. When finally under way, we stubbed our foot again by going into emergency crossing Rockville Bridge between Harrisburg and Enola, resulting in my walking the train and another half-hour delay. The train was eventually put away in Enola and we deadheaded back to Harrisburg. It took twelve hours to move a train thirty miles - nothing to be proud of to be sure, but events were beyond the crew's control.

In many cases, the battle to get trains over the road became grimmer as the 1990s advanced. A good example is the PICA. My earliest experiences on the road witnessed this train always reaching its destination, with only a simple set-off at Frankford Junction *en route*. By the time I was able to hold the conductor's position a couple of years later, the train additionally worked at West Falls Yard making timely arrival at Camden extremely doubtful. This additional work was an example of the carrier's policy of attempting to get the most out of each train. Other factors reducing train speeds were greater overall volume of freight and greater emphasis on safety that caused employees to work just a bit more cautiously than before.

Another train that suffered retardation was the ALHB, Allentown to Harrisburg Consolidated Terminal. At one time it was nicknamed the Valley Sweeper, a reference to the Harrisburg Line following the shallow Lebanon Valley and to the train's charge of sweeping up cars along the way. After leaving Allentown it typically set off and picked up in Reading Spring Street Yard, dropped off cars at

Avon, east of Lebanon, then shifted cars for the chocolate factory at Hershey. (Its opposite number, the HBAL, worked similarly in the eastbound direction.) In the mid-1990s the ALHB usually managed to get over the road, and in many cases was able to put away its train on multiple tracks in Enola. However, as time passed the train seemed to get slower and slower. Its departure from Allentown grew less sprightly and shifting at different locations took longer. By the late 1990s, ALHB's workload became so burdensome it hardly ever reached Enola with just one crew. Its former nickname was replaced by, a shade over-dramatically, the Train from Hell!

Mechanical failure occasionally caused delays. Train TV1, usually a fast train, fared poorly on the night of 10th January 1997. Locomotives rostered on this occasion were SD60I 5616 and C40-8Ws 6128 and 6181. After leaving Morrisville, the trail-van train usually did not stop, so it did not bode well for it to be held up nine minutes at Norristown whilst SEPTA ran one of their passenger trains. Worse still, the train went into emergency in Pottstown on the Harrisburg Line. It fell to me as conductor to walk the train. Air hoses had come apart between two ill-matched cars, the eighth and ninth. Both had long coupler assemblies, and standard hoses could not bridge the gap when the train became stretched out, as it had on the slight uphill gradient in Pottstown. I had to walk back to the engines, get a run-round hose, return, attach the hose, do a hind-end brake test and again walk back to the locomotives, which took from 22:13 till 23:46. A run-round hose looks like a fire hose and is supplied with hooks so that it may be secured to car sides in order to bypass one car and directly connect air brake lines on cars cither side.

Not far from Harrisburg the run-round hose burst. In view of the downhill run into Harrisburg when cars would not be stretched out, I decided to re-couple using original air hoses, and proceed. When they came apart again a few miles later, I managed to find on one of the engines a short cast-iron bridging hose and used it between the cars. This useful railroader's aid was once called a Dutchman, but the term is now out of favour. Thus one of Conrail's star intermodal trains had an extremely unsatisfactory, irritating start to its journey west; a segment that normally took six or seven hours lasting eight hours forty minutes.

Train PIBE1 made a promising start at the civilized hour of 07:00 on 12th July 1997, but was held up at CP-Harris for forty-eight minutes. Two tracks became one between CP-Harris and CP-Capital. The single track was an appalling bottleneck as it would not permit trains to depart and arrive simultaneously at the east end of Harrisburg. Some years later the single track was doubled. We were again held for thirty-five minutes west of Lebanon as shifting was in progress in that town. Via the Pottsville Branch, we arrived at the north end of Reading Spring Street Yard at 12:30 and set off sixty-four cars, completing the operation at 13:40. So far, progress was unspectacular but typical for a train that had to work on the way.

The Harrisburg East Dispatcher then radioed to say that we had to break off from shifting and take our engines, SD60I 5579, C40-8 6048 and SD60 6844 to assist a westbound train, UXC40A, that had stalled at Wyomissing, about five miles away. We did as we were told and pushed the failed train as far as Sheridan - about twelve miles - an operation requiring careful co-ordination between crews and one that took two hours and forty minutes. On completion we returned to Reading and finished our work by picking up 100 cars.

Seven hours had already been rung up before we were called away. After making the pick up, we had less than one hour left before being outlawed. Needless to say, the crew was relieved in Reading and transported to the hotel in Allentown. Though there were very good reasons for lack of progress, the net result was nevertheless that in eleven hours the train travelled no more than sixty miles.

\* \* \*

So, whilst many trains such as intermodals and footboard relief coal trains could sprint over the road with haste, others became bogged down with switching along the way, or were simply victims of unfavourable circumstances such as congestion or failure. Infrastructure contributed to sluggishness in that there simply were not enough tracks to handle all trains, or interlocking design constricted traffic. It could also be argued - though not very convincingly - that absence of a timetable took away any incentive to get trains moving! The fact remained many trains ran slowly because nothing could be done to speed them up. Given this resignation, consider then the effect of a blanket of snow.

I am told Pennsylvania always used to experience several heavy snowfalls each winter, but times have changed. Twenty-seven year's residence in America has seen many mild winters with only a few inches of snow in total. Lest anyone forget how it used to be, harsh winters return every few years; 1995 into1996 was one of them. A snowstorm that began on 7th January 1996 lasted thirty-six hours, dumping so much snow it completely blocked many roads including the thoroughfare on which I lived. I had to mark off inclement weather, until the local highway authority cleared a canyon through the lane alongside our house, after which I marked back up. I was called for WHST01 on January 9th.

WHST01, a travelling shifter based in Shiremanstown, even in good weather was one of the more taxing assignments on the Enola Road Conductors List. With an on-duty time of 22:00 hours, it was a laborious operation just to get out of Shiremanstown Yard. Permission to work had to be sought from three different authorities. The train had to be shoved for the first couple of miles, which involved throwing numerous manual switches and flagging a grade crossing. Normal forward movement was resumed on the Lurgan Branch, where the train serviced a number of industries scattered along a distance of thirty-five miles.

On the night in question, there was so much snow on, around, between and underneath the train's cars it was impossible to pull ahead for a brake test. I had to push my way back through thigh-high drifted snow towards the hind end. When necessary to cross over between cars to reach an easier route, accumulation of snow was so great I had to use hands and feet to suspend myself between car ends, like a mountaineer using a rock face chimney, hardly in accordance with the Rule Book I know. The only way an initial terminal brake test could be carried out was by my walking first the application and then the release on three cars at a time, the train being then moved back for the next three. Normally two hours would see WHST01 leave the yard. On this night it was five hours. Two feet of snow hampered every simple task, such as unlocking and lining switches and flagging Gettysburg Road located on the Camp Connection which led to the Lurgan Branch.

Once on the Lurgan Branch, the train struggled twenty miles to CP-Carl interlocking, which was found to be iced up. Signal technicians toiled at length to free switches. The train was eventually backed from the interlocking into a glass factory with the intention of spotting desperately needed cars, but a truck busy unloading blocked our way. It was now 10:00 hours; we ran out of time. So close and yet so far. As we hung around waiting for transport to take us back to Shiremanstown, the trainmaster arrived and for a measurable amount of time stood opposite me and glared. The staring match did not last. I looked away, having successfully been made to feel guilty for failing to spot the urgent cars, even though I had fought all night long in miserable conditions of mountainous snow and perishing cold. By the time the taxi had ploughed its way back to Shiremanstown and we had marked off duty, the timecard showed fifteen hours thirty minutes.

Two days later I was called to Enola as brakeman on a special Yorkie, WHHB62X. Enola Yard was dreadfully snarled up; the crew had to wait five hours for the train to be ready. To combat the arctic conditions, Conrail had secured use of an aircraft engine mounted on a self-propelled on-track machine which, when fired up, directed a jet of hot air at switches sending snow and ice flying. It worked astonishingly well, leaving switches clear and bone dry. Unfortunately temperatures were so frigid, material the machine scattered instantly refroze to form a ring of solid ice around each switch. If it were then desired to throw the switch the other way, the jet blower had to be brought back because all moving parts of the switch had again frozen solid, even though they were free of snow and ice. Getting out of Enola and reaching York must have taken about seven hours for, once again, cars that urgently needed to be spotted were not spotted because we ran out of time. After waiting for a jitney in York and riding back to Enola to be off duty, the timecard meter had rung up fifteen hours and forty-five minutes.

Friday 12th January 1996 found me as conductor in Enola at 20:45 for an HBAL2A, Harrisburg Terminal to Allentown. It had been the intention to pull out of the western or northern end of Enola Yard on Track A, cross over at CP-Hip onto Track B, then proceed to Track 0 on the Rockville Bridge. However CP-Hip switches were frozen, so we were told to proceed in the direction the interlocking was currently lined, which was to Marysville, about a mile away. At Marysville we were to pick up signal technicians and bring them back to free the switches. (CP-Hip was so called because an adjacent rock formation had the shape of a human hip.) Switches were eventually freed, and after we had collected the train and carried out the necessary brake test, we proceeded onto Rockville Bridge.

For some reason which I cannot remember, the engine consist had to be turned; we had to spin the power, as railroaders say. The train was therefore secured on the bridge, and we cut away to make the turning move at CP-Wye on the opposite bank of the Susquehanna River. To expect the engines to whip round the triangular formation without a hitch would have been as realistic as expecting the sun to shine and immediately melt all snow. A track circuit showing occupied when it should have been showing clear brought the manoeuvre to a stand. We had to ferry technicians back and forth to cure the problem.

With the turning move finally completed, it was necessary for me to transfer myself to the hind engine to make a coupling. Before I left, the engineer reminded me of safety risks wintry conditions posed. If walkways running length of the engine were covered with snow and ice there was grave risk of slipping off. The most treacherous areas were the near-vertical steps at locomotive ends where a man could end up tobogganing down all five steps if he were not careful. The engineer spliced sound advice with humour: "When you get back there to make the couple, take your time. When you get down off the engine, if you're not careful you could easily slip off and you'd by right into the river. I won't be able to rescue you. I mean, I like you Mitch, but not that much."

In due course a coupling was safely made and the train was ready to move, but had to take its turn behind more important trains. As hours slipped by, it became apparent we were going to run out of time standing on Rockville Bridge. Short of a helicopter lift or floating a rescue raft on the river, little could be done. For a jitney to reach us, an excavator would have to dig a trench through snow. Word then came down that we had been instructed to work beyond twelve hours. The hours of service law provided that in exceptional circumstances a senior manager may direct a crew to work more than the normal legal limit of twelve hours - and these were truly exceptional circumstances. An eventual off-duty time of 12:05 meant we had worked fifteen hours and twenty minutes, close to the absolute limit of sixteen hours.

211

One may scoff at the resulting average speed of a third of a mile per hour to take a train five miles from Enola to Harrisburg, but another train that winter was even slower. We had been given the peculiar symbol of HBAL2A because a previous crew had been called as HBAL2 to work the same train. That previous crew had not even made it out of Enola Yard. They may have advanced one mile putting the train together, giving a speed that was just one twelfth of a mile per hour!

This chapter has described tardiness in trains owing to both the expected, in the form of sheer volume of work, and the unexpected, in the form of mechanical failure or foul weather. Such trains were a small percentage. By contrast the majority of trains moved across Conrail at good speed and delivered products to the intended customer in timely fashion.

# CHAPTER 25

# ENGINEER

"It's an absolutely *fascinating* subject," were the words one Conrail instructor used to describe the air brake. By way of introduction to train braking systems, let the clock be turned back to childhood days in Britain. At that time, the 1950s, most British freight vehicles had no brakes at all, apart from hand levers that had to be individually applied by guard or shunter. Slowing or stopping a train comprised of such vehicles relied solely on the locomotive's steam brake, greatly assisted by the locomotive's weight. A hand brake in the guard's van contributed to braking effort. All passenger stock and those freight vehicles that *were* equipped with train brakes used exclusively the vacuum brake system worked from the locomotive. Vacuum pipes connected between engine and rolling stock essentially sucked brake shoes away from wheels. If the train driver reduced the vacuum or if the train broke in two, brakes applied.

The vacuum brake was relatively simple, but was inferior to the air brake system, which had long been standard in America. The air brake system used compressed air. Again, if the train driver reduced the air pressure or if a train broke in two, brakes applied. By the time I started work on British Railways in 1980, the air brake had become the predominant design, though many freight wagons and therefore many freight trains were still operating with the vacuum brake. A number of diesel locomotives, of necessity, were dual braked. By the time I left in 1988, vacuum stock was limited to civil engineers' trains. Later, they were withdrawn completely.

A person new to railroad practices would be forgiven for thinking that a brake system relying on compressed air would simply use that

213

compressed air to push brake shoes away from wheels, and that if pressure were reduced for any reason brakes would clamp back on to wheels. In reality, the air brake is far more complicated. A simplified account of the American freight car air brake system is given below.

To begin, it is always assumed a freight car is devoid of any compressed air. In such condition brake shoes are held away from wheel contact by a strong spring, which means without compressed air the vehicle has no brakes (unless a hand brake is applied). The starting point therefore is to put compressed air into a car via the air hoses. Freight cars are normally charged to a pressure shown on instrumentation as ninety pounds per square inch. This measurement is the pressure *in excess of* atmospheric pressure, which is 14.7 pounds per square inch. (So the true working brake pressure is 104.7 pounds, but the nicety is generally ignored.)

Once charging begins, it takes a minimum of seven minutes to charge a car completely devoid of compressed air. It takes so long because air has to pass through a restricted orifice. However, that restricted orifice enables as many as fifty cars to be charged simultaneously in the same amount of time, seven minutes, owing to the high rate at which a locomotive shoots air back. Air pipes that run beneath cars and hoses that connect them may together be referred to as the train line. The train line, certain reservoirs and a maze of cavities within a device on each car called the control valve must be filled with compressed air. A reading of ninety pounds on a gauge attached to the rear of the train asserts the train is fully charged, at which point all car brakes will be released.

To apply brakes to the train, the engineer reduces train line air pressure by means of the brake handle in the cab. Imbalance between this lower train line pressure and ninety pounds pressure within the control valve causes a piston in the control valve (called the service piston) to move upwards. Such movement directs compressed air, by means of a slide valve, from a reservoir (called the auxiliary reservoir) into the brake cylinder. Build up of compressed air in the brake cylinder forces a piston to push brake shoes against wheels. The flow of compressed air continues until pressure within the control valve drops below the train line pressure, at which point the service piston moves back somewhat and halts the flow. With brakes now applied, the braking system is said to be in lap position.

A further reduction of air can then be made to apply the brakes harder. Four or five increments of brake application may be made, ranging from minimum to full service. Or brakes may be released. When the engineer operates the brake handle to release brakes, pressure in the train line once again rises to ninety pounds. This increased pressure bears against the service piston forcing it to move back down to its original position, which exposes channels for air pressure in the control valve and auxiliary reservoir to build back up to the same as the train line, ninety pounds. A channel is also exposed to empty the brake cylinder of compressed air so that brakes release.

Application of brakes as described above is called a service application. An emergency application of brakes may be initiated by the engineer if, say, he suddenly encounters an obstruction on the line. The train breaking in two will similarly cause brakes to apply in emergency. Every time the conductor cuts away from and leaves the angle cock open on cars, the exhaust of compressed air from those cars places them in emergency. Emergency application is effected by a second piston in the control valve called the emergency piston.

The emergency piston is so engineered it responds only to a sudden and rapid decrease in train line pressure. Such immediate evacuation of air causes the emergency piston to move upwards, which triggers two actions. First, a route is lined up for all train line and control valve compressed air to exhaust to the atmosphere in an instant. A rapid dumping of air by one car prompts all other cars in the train to go into emergency. (An observer standing alongside a hundred cars that were placed in emergency will hear a succession of explosive exhausts travel from front to rear of the train in about one second.) The second effect of this emergency piston movement is to permit compressed air from a second reservoir called the emergency reservoir to move into the brake cylinder. In emergency, combined volumes of auxiliary and emergency reservoirs apply the strongest possible brake pressure on wheels.

On the face of it, the engineer, through operation of the brake handle in the locomotive cab, is in sole control of a train's braking system. Or is he? A conductor must take care when opening an angle cock to feed air into a car to which he has just coupled that he does not do so too quickly, because control valves read a rapid drop in air pressure as a signal to go into emergency. The conductor must also ensure angle cocks are fully turned through ninety degrees when opened or closed. These are obvious steps a conductor must take to safeguard integrity of the air brake system.

Less obvious is the hypothetical case of his coupling locomotives to a string of thirty loaded coal hoppers sitting on a siding. Assuming that the cars have already been inspected, as soon as the conductor has put the air in and released three hand brakes, which might take the seven minutes needed to charge the cars, arguably he would be perfectly in order to instruct the engineer to go ahead. However, too many factors, such as cold weather or leaking air hoses may hinder proper build up of air pressure. A wise conductor would be in no rush, and would couch his instruction more carefully: "When you've got your air, okay ahead."

* * *

It appears guidance given to engineers concerning the air brake has varied over the years. At one time a formula existed, based on cars that were being hauled in the train. But it is difficult to imagine how a formula could have worked. It is of no concern, as the formula method has fallen by the wayside. A dictum that used to be slavishly followed was that the train must always be stretched out. When climbing a gradient, the train naturally stretched itself out. Otherwise, the couple of inches of play between two coupler knuckles should, it was argued, always be eliminated by maintaining a brake application, which inevitably resulted in the train being dragged along. When descending a gradient, a sufficient reduction in brake pressure had to be made to keep couplings stretched. On level track a minimum application was made, with sufficient throttle being employed to overcome the brakes. Using throttle whilst simultaneously applying brakes is known as power braking (or stretch braking) and though pitting one part of the locomotive's capabilities against another, it gives the engineer greatest control over his train. Power braking is still widely respected in many circles.

A need to keep a train constantly stretched out may have been borne out of an overriding desire to avoid jerking the hind end owing to a caboose containing the conductor and others being positioned there. Sudden deceleration or acceleration would throw men about the caboose. Cabooses eventually became redundant for most trains. During my time on Conrail, an engineer would apologize if he occasionally misjudged and the train ran-in on a down gradient causing locomotives to briefly lurch forward. I used to respond that the very minor discomfort did not matter, it made no difference to me. My assuagement ignored the fact old habits die hard, and that engineers took pride in their job.

The keep-the-train-stretched-out school was replaced by cycle braking. On a long downhill gradient sufficient reduction in train line air pressure has to be made to keep the train within speed limits. If no change were made to that level of braking, contrary to natural thinking, the train would in fact gradually slow itself down and come to a complete stop. The explanation is this: at the initial moment of applying brakes nothing happens, but very soon afterwards brake shoes begin to bite, and as the train slows down the task of decelerating it further grows progressively easier, so it will eventually stop altogether. Since that is not the desire, brakes must be released, allowed to recharge and applied again further down the hill. Cycle braking involves making an initial application, then releasing brakes only when speed is low enough to allow time for charging and re-application before the speed limit is breached. The procedure may be repeated several times during a descent.

At all costs the engineer must avoid over-use of the air brake. If it is constantly used without allowing enough time to recharge, it will not function, resulting in total loss of braking power. In railroading circles such misuse is dismissively referred to as urinating away the air, though the verb is replaced by one less polite.

So far in this dissertation no mention has been made of the dynamic brake. When the dynamic brake is set up, electric traction motors that turn engine wheels become generators. In such conditions the electric motor magnetic field makes it harder for wheels to turn, which then slows down the train. The engineer adjusts engine output to increase the strength of the magnetic field in order to reach the desired level of dynamic braking. Power produced by traction motors functioning as generators when in dynamic mode is dissipated as heat through grids on the roof of the locomotive.

The air brake can be applied in stages or it can be released altogether. The freight air brake cannot be decreased gradually. The dynamic brake can be adjusted incrementally to increase or decrease retardation, and for that reason is a far superior method of braking on a long down gradient. The disadvantage of dynamic brake is that braking takes longer to take effect, and for that reason a train must be run slower. Power braking is not possible with the dynamic brake. The dynamic brake will not completely halt a train on its own, the air brake has to be used for the final stage. Nevertheless, authorities encourage use of dynamic brake over the air brake as it saves money on brake shoes and avoids risk of inadvertent emergency application. Some railroads go so far as to discipline engineers for using the air when the dynamic brake could have been used.

The engineer has at his disposal the air brake, the dynamic brake and a brake for his locomotives only, called the independent brake. An additional way of slowing down trains on a rising gradient is by throttle modulation, which is simply reducing the locomotive's output.

One of the most difficult tasks an engineer faces is starting a heavy train on an uphill gradient. One approach, when the stop is made, is to allow the train to run-in and become bunched before applying the air brake. When time to move, the air brake may be released straight away and the engines throttled up so that the train begins to move one car at a time, which lightens the load considerably. Another approach is to come to a stand with the train stretched out. When ready to move, the engineer could apply the air brake, put the engine in reverse to bunch up the train, then proceed as previously described. Alternatively, a start could be attempted from a stretched-out condition.

In some cases it will not be possible for the locomotives to gain enough momentum to move the train. To start from a dead stop a long heavy train on a steep rising gradient may be asking the impossible, in which case an additional engine should be requested, or the train taken in two halves. The better course is to avoid stopping a heavy train on a hill, which all concerned endeavour to do.

Whenever possible, stopping on a rising gradient that is located on a curve should be avoided. Starting a train in such territory could result in stringlining, which is the eventuality of wheels popping over the rail on the inside of the curve owing to excessive draught forces. The risk is heightened when lightweight cars, such as empty flat cars, are sandwiched between heavier cars.

The throttle is more straightforward than braking systems, with settings of idle and notches 1 to 8. The received wisdom is to move the throttle, either to increase power or to reduce it, just one notch at a time.

To produce a person thoroughly able to handle any train presented to him – or her – a training programme must include, in addition to knowing how to start, slow and stop a train, all other aspects of locomotive operation. Though engineer training may take a year, it covers only basic competence. I was once told that it takes an engineer *four years* to completely master just the Harrisburg to Allentown route. That is not to say the engineer could not run trains elsewhere reasonably well, it is just a statement how complicated gradients are, and how much train handling varies from train to train on just one route. No amount of classroom training nor expert guidance on the job can alone manufacture a first class engineer. The finer points of running a locomotive – the American engineer *runs* a locomotive, not drives it - is a skill impossible to translate into technical language, and can only be developed with time and experience.

I worked with at least ninety different engineers on Conrail. In the manner in which they operated controls, I could tell no difference amongst them. In truth, a railroad engineer has no room for flair - stop signals have to be stopped at, speed limits observed, and there is little flexibility in the rate at which a long heavy train can speed up or slow down.

Over time, a grasp of the engineer's perception of his job migrated from his side of the locomotive cab to me on the conductor's side. To be in complete control of the train the engineer must be able to think simultaneously in three areas. He must foresee what lies a mile or two ahead so that he can plan - whether there is a change in gradient or speed limit, whether there might be a flagman on duty, and so on. He must be cognizant of that immediately in front of him, the message a signal displays, a grade crossing for which the horn needs to be sounded, that the track is free from obstruction. He must bear in mind that the tail end of the train may be a mile or two behind where the prevailing speed limit and gradient may be quite different. (By 2015 such information, plus suggested throttle positions, could be shown on computer screens installed in locomotive cabs, but the technology was not available in the 1990s.)

I recall being home-bound on the Delaware job rounding the sharp curve at Amtrak's Perry interlocking when the engineer said to me, "You've got to be careful here, there's a little hump back there that can catch you out." He meant that a release of the air brake at that point could possibly result in a run-out in the hind part of the train with risk of breaking a knuckle. When delivering the Maryland and Pennsylvania coal train one Saturday night, the train topped the summit on the York Secondary and began its descent to York. The locomotives were clearly still in eighth notch, so I said to the engineer, "At what point do you start easing off the throttle?"

"Ease off one notch when maybe ten or twelve cars are over the hill, then gradually throttle back," he replied. When cresting a summit most of a train is still climbing a gradient so power is maintained. By the time a train is in equilibrium with an equal number of cars either side of the hill, the engineer will probably have already begun to brake.

The above two cases are the only instances I can recall of discourse with engineers on specific circumstances. Apart from deducing that a roaring engine going downhill meant dynamic brake was in use, I was for the most part unaware of train handling techniques being employed. Much of what an experienced engineer does is by instinct. The automatic brake handle is not graduated, apart from a notch for minimum service, so it just slides to whatever position the engineer places it. It is located at waist level where the engineer operates it by feel rather than by looking at it.

But as far as disposition is concerned, each engineer struck up an identical demeanour of evenness. It is crucial for the man or woman in the seat to avoid fluctuations in mood that may interrupt concentration on the railroad to come, the railroad here, the railroad a mile back. In early days I recall getting excited over something unimportant, a peculiar load on a passing train, say. The engineer jumped in his seat at my exclamation. "I thought you were trying to tell me there was something wrong," he said. I apologized, and in future voiced remarks in more restrained tones. Eventually I trained myself to speak in monotone, even when mentioning something crucial, such as an upcoming block operator in attendance. A two-man traincrew was a joint operation. On the road it was my duty to assist the engineer in keeping abreast of bulletin information and all else that mattered.

As for the engineers as people, their personalities were as mixed as any random selection of the population, ranging from the placid man with whom I worked on the first road conductor job to the bristly echinoderm. One engineer used to say of me, disarmingly, "He thinks it's for real!"

I generally got on well with engineers. Safe conversational topics with men were beer and women. An engineer confided that in times gone by they enjoyed greater prestige and higher relative rates of pay. A result of this enhanced social standing was greater appeal to the opposite sex, the engineer told me with a twinkle in his eye. "We used to attract bimbos," he said. "Do you know what I mean by bimbos?" I replied that he need not fear as I understood the term.

\* \* \*

In these pages I have given only an outline of Norac signals. In order to pass the test to be an engineer each student had to be able to identify all twenty-four different Norac signal messages in each of its multiple forms, a total of 159 different aspects. No similar requirement was made of qualified conductors, perhaps it should have been. In time I grew familiar with most aspects, position light signals being easier to learn than colour lights. One Norac colour light signal message was unique in that it gave information on not only the interlocking immediately ahead but also on the next one down the line. MEDIUM APPROACH MEDIUM, red-over-yellow-over green, said medium speed through interlocking switches directly beyond the signal and medium speed through switches at the next interlocking.

Dwarf colour light signals were the most difficult. One of the high versions of MEDIUM CLEAR was red-over-green; the dwarf version was green-over-flashing red. One of the high versions of MEDIUM APPROACH was red-over-flashing yellow; the dwarf version was yellow-over-flashing red.

It is not clear why these illogicalities arose. As a signalling enthusiast one would have thought that I would have rejoiced in such complexities; I did not. Each time one of these topsyturvy aspects was met, I was able to remember what it meant, but only after staring at it for a moment. It worried me that if I were ever forced to attend Engineers' School that the brain would panic and not be able to answer the signal quiz correctly, and that I would fail to qualify as an engineer.

# CHAPTER 26

# REVELATION

"I head north on Route 501, then at Schaefferstown keep going straight west on 419, you know, don't turn right for 501. And that takes you straight to it."

"I usually take Route 72 north, then hang a right at Quentin, and it's just a couple of miles down the road."

American men love to talk about route planning: the British instantly grab a road map. Americans celebrate their pioneer spirit by doing without maps: the British view maps as a work of art. Furthermore, the British take enormous pride in cartography, witness the superb Ordnance Survey series. Regrettably, global positioning systems have to an extent usurped both the American and British approaches to navigation, though enthusiasm for that new technology seems greater amongst women.

The author's love of maps and penchant for drawing them found expression in an eventual total of no less than twenty-three pamphlets of Norac railroad, that ranged from two to eighteen pages of illustrations per pamphlet. The maps, invaluable for coping with uncertainties of the extra board, were well received. I would happily run off copies on Conrail's photocopiers for any new employee who asked. Some artwork was particularly creative, such as the area around Harrisburg's Rockville Bridge and lines approaching South Philadelphia Yard. Passing such landmarks as the extant but derelict passenger station at Royersford always brought a ping of delight as I compared the structure with my sketch of it.

When on duty I would select the relevant map, fold it neatly, tuck it, for protection, inside a laminated copy of Norac signal aspects, and place it handily in my rear overalls pocket. I would occasionally be taunted about the importance I attached to maps and about a constant reference to them. Some men took the matter further. "Why don't you try working without your maps, Mitch?" said one engineer a year or two after I had started on Conrail.

"I've tried a couple of times," I replied, "and whilst I didn't goof up, I just somehow need that re-assurance that the switch I'm throwing is the right one."

"Yeh, but it's a bit like a man recovering from a leg injury," he continued. "He'll keep using the crutches until they're taken away, and then he's forced to walk without them. Maps are your crutches."

"I know what you mean, John, but I still like to keep them handy in case my mind goes blank and I can't remember."

On a later date the same engineer and I took a train to Allentown Yard. After disposing of it in the Hump Yard we were instructed to take the light power from the west end of the yard to the east end and stable it somewhere. "What I normally do," said John, "is I stay at the same end and let the conductor give me radio signals back through the yard. But if I'm not sure about the conductor, I change ends."

"Oh, I'll be all right. I've always got my maps with me," I said breezily, wafting a map of Allentown Yard in front of the engineer. The engineer changed ends. The expression of no confidence felt like a punch in the abdomen. I concealed my dismay, and said nothing.

Again in Allentown Yard, but with another engineer, after diverging off the single-track Lehigh Line at CP-Canal. we came to a stand close to the hump tower where six tracks of the Hump Yard fanned out. The yardmaster had told us on which tracks the train was to be put away. I stood up, slipped my radio into one overalls back pocket and clipped the microphone to my jacket lapel. "I'll go out and get lined up then." As I spoke to the engineer I refolded my Reading Line pamphlet to show the layout of Allentown Yard and placed it in my other back pocket.

The engineer watched, and said, "Don't you know Allentown Yard *yet*?"

Stung by the acerbic criticism, I could not muster an adequate response. "Oh, I know the Hump Yard," I blustered. "It's just that in the dark I can't tell which switch goes where." I climbed off the engine and began walking ahead lining up switches, surreptitiously consulting the map in the hope of not being seen.

The truth was that even in daylight I would have had to consult the map because, typical of asymmetry found in most yard layouts, eight switches at the east end of the Hump Yard led off one another irregularly like branches of a tree rather than in numerical sequence. I found it impossible to remember such random formations. It would have been the equivalent of a musician having to memorize every note, a cook every recipe.

The engineer's pointed remarks struck home. Even though using maps seemed perfectly acceptable to me, after about two year's service on Conrail I should have known Allentown Yard, but did not. I had long been aware of poor memory, but it was only after this reproach that I began to think deeply about severity of the handicap, and consequences of it. I wondered if other 1994 men experienced similar problems, and said to one, "I can't remember all these different yards we go to, I have to use maps when I'm lining up switches. How do you get on?"

"What I normally do," he said, "is when we arrive at a yard, before I get off the engine, I just glance at the map then put it back in my grip. After that I'm usually okay."

Another 1994 man casually mentioned he was going to qualify on about fifty miles of Amtrak territory, an expanse that would have taken me at least two separate sessions to memorize and pass the oral test. Yet another man could remember numbers of every automatic signal he saw; I could hardly remember one.

Till this time I had always had confidence in my own ability. I had been successful in all previous positions, but they were different. In each case I was guided by something tangible rather than memory. When in public service, legal precedents for documentation were always referred to. When in manufacturing sales, the actual customer's paper order was always to hand. In the signal box, track diagram and lever identification plates were permanent fixtures. But on Conrail I was expected to carry all information in the head. Absence of such discipline in previous posts did not excuse me from compliance now. The troubling inability to retain facts forced a review of all that had gone before.

At the age of five years I must have been able to bluff my way through first class at infants' school, because I emerged from it without knowing the ABC. We were supposed to be able to recite the alphabet - without benefit of the American children's alphabet song. I could only remember the first part, up to about N, but got away with it because I was considered so bright teachers *assumed* I knew the full alphabet. The impression of great intellect at a young age is again illustrated by a story my mother told me, although I have no recollection of it. I must have uttered something profound – profound for a six-year old – because a visitor remarked, "You're going to be Prime Minister!" These facts plus good report cards all through school days suggested above average mental ability. That elevated opinion was never questioned until I discovered it took me far longer than compeers to memorize material for General Certificate of Education Ordinary Level examinations. The struggle to cram was so painful I turned my back on academic life and left school at age sixteen. Despite the shortcoming, accomplished careers followed in several fields. Mental self-esteem was not threatened again until the inability to remember Conrail's track layouts rose up to slap me in the face at age fifty-two forcing an unhappy conclusion that most of life had been lived under a misapprehension of being cleverer than I actually was.

* * *

Something else happened in Allentown Yard. An eastbound train had been put away in the Hump Yard, probably by splitting it between two tracks, in which case I would have radioed the yardmaster with the last car placed on one track and the first car going into the other, as was my usual practice. The yardmaster then radioed an instruction something like, "Bring your engines back through Track Two in the Hump and tie 'em down on the east end of Four in The Park, and the jitney'll come along and take you to the hotel." "The Park" was the term commonly used for the Departure Yard. This we proceeded to do by my giving the engineer over the radio a countdown in car lengths to shove back through the Hump Yard into the beginning of the Departure Yard. I then told the engineer to halt the engines when they were in the clear. I helped apply hand brakes, and we placed our belongings on the ground to await the jitney. Social chatter between conductor and engineer was usually greatest at the beginning of a journey, but by the end of the shift men had run out of conversation. So the engineer and I stood around, somewhat apart, he gazing in one direction, I another.

I looked across the adjacent Classification Yard where endless tracks seemed like a wasted asset because there was nothing on them. The reality was all traffic was bunched at the west end where it had rolled by gravity from the hump. A box car then suddenly rumbled by a few tracks over, throwing out any suggestion of redundancy. Humping operations had re-started after a brief hiatus. Abrupt appearance of the box car was a provocative reminder how dangerous railroads could be: a trespasser or careless employee attempting to cross empty tracks would have been mowed down by the free-wheeling vehicle. The jolt focussed thoughts, which in turn begot a realization I had just lived through a *deja vu*. Some time, somewhere, I had had an identical experience. *Deja Vus* are not uncommon, and as the jitney arrived to whisk us off to the motel I gave the experience little thought.

After checking into the room I switched on the television, flicked through channels as was my wont, and switched it off again. As I sprawled on the bed gazing at an uninteresting ceiling, thoughts returned to the rolling box car. This *deja vu* seemed more real than others, as if I had stood in the same spot and witnessed exactly the same thing, but I knew that not to be the case because it was rare to stable locomotives on the east end of the Departure Yard. As I thought about it more, the previous experience steadily grew in lucidity and began to reach further back in time, a long way back in time, until at last it arrived at its origins: it was a dream I had when a boy.

In the year 1953, when I was eight years old, my family moved from a town to a nearby village. A busy double-track railway line ran through the village. Friendships formed with men working in the local signal box, friendships that began a lifetime's interest in railway signalling and set the stage for an eventual career as a British Railways signalman. In time I explored neighbouring stations and made friends with railway workers there, in particular a porter at one station. He was in his late teens, the modest generation gap fostering a friendship more relaxed than those with older railway workers.

Part of the porter's duties was to travel by British Railways bicycle every Friday to the village station where I lived in order to service paraffin lamps in semaphore signals. In a dingy room underneath the signal box, amongst piles of slimy paraffin-impregnated signalling logs called train register books, a conversation took place one day. "I 'ad this dream last night, John," I said.

"What did yer dream about?" he asked.

"I dreamt I was in America, 'n these trucks were going along by theirsens. They were going along t'line on their own, with no engine pulling 'em." Trucks was the 1950s term for freight vehicles, theirsens was dialect for themselves.

"Well, that means yer gonna go to America and invent trucks that go by themselves."

"Eh?"

"Dreams always come true, yer know," said the porter. "So that means when yer grow up yer gonna go to America and invent trucks that move on their own." The porter spoke evenly, without the dramatic heaviness that should have been attached to words that turned out to be remarkably prophetic. The interpretation about inventing self-propelled freight vehicles was of course wrong, but the dream's prediction of placing me alongside free-rolling freight vehicles somewhere in America was flawless. The dream foretold the future with astonishing accuracy, it was a premonition.

* * *

What is to be made of this? The dream's American location and freight vehicles moving by themselves are the only two elements I remember. I have no idea what placed the dream in America, but that was indisputably the case. The drifting freight vehicle is a little problematic. In Allentown Yard I saw a fifty-foot box car float by, doubtless followed by other cars on other tracks. As an eight-year old I am sure I did not dream of fifty-foot vehicles, because I would have said to the porter, "And the trucks were really long." I did not say that. The 1950s dream would have had to have been of British Railways stock, about fifteen feet long. Nevertheless, at the moment in the Allentown motel when I connected the childhood dream with what had taken place an hour earlier, it was clear beyond doubt one foretold the other. Owing to the discrepancy in vehicle design, the dream was not a *vision* of the future but a representation of it, a message about things to come.

The topic of premonitions is little discussed. I have experienced several minor premonitions in the past, mainly about relationships, but never gave the phenomenon much thought. How do premonitions work? One explanation is they do not exist, they are merely coincidence. I could not accept that, certainly not for the boyhood dream. Premonitions are about seeing into the future, about acquiring information on matters which have not yet happened, about juggling with time. In the case in point, a child fast asleep in rural Yorkshire, England, during 1954 saw what was going to happen in Pennsylvania, United States, during the 1990s. How?

In an effort to keep feet firmly on the ground concerning a subject that is anything but down to earth, it would be wise to begin by not paying too much attention to science fiction treatment of time. Productions such as *Back to the Future*, *Peggy Sue Got Married* and the perennial BBC show *Dr. Who* may be marvellous entertainment but offer no serious explanation of the ability to skip time. Travelling into the future may be achieved on a small scale by permanently moving from the east to west coast of America thus slowing the passage of time by three hours of time zone change. Or by taking better care of oneself and extending life a little. Suspended animation, whenever it is invented, would offer a longer trip into the future. Einstein's theories of relativity look more promising. In his book *Discovering Relativity for yourself* Sam Lilley tells us that an astronaut on a round trip, for example, lasting two years and nine months travelling at sixty per cent of the speed of light, on returning to earth would find three years had elapsed: the astronaut had thus moved three months into the future. All these examples of time travel offer only a one-way ticket to the future; they supply no means to report back. To explain premonitions time needs to be much more liquid, in order to permit simultaneity of past, present and future, to allow co-existence of now and will be.

In the 2010s a new speculation emerged that may be pertinent to the conundrum of premonitions, a postulation that only the present time exists and that past and future are mere illusions. Alas, the suggestion that the moment of one minute ago when I was stung by a wasp did not really exist, despite throbbing pain as evidence to the contrary, is difficult to accept.

Serious arguments are put forward supporting the idea of travelling back in time. Einstein's general theory of relativity permits it. In recent years interest has grown in concept of the "wormhole", a cosmic tunnel able to connect different points in time and space. Though such ideas circulate in the respected scientific community, I find them worrisome.

Picture a prospective time traveller, whom we shall call Fred. At a little before 12:00 hours, Fred aims at himself a video camera, then at midday precisely he sits down in a chair. For good measure, an invited audience watches. Fred sits comfortably for five minutes, then, at 12:05, he somehow or other is able to travel back in time just five minutes to the moment he first sat down in the chair. There is only one possible outcome, at 12:00 hours Fred and only one Fred sits down in a chair. Time travelling Fred is either annihilated or he becomes his earlier self (it does not matter which) because it has already been recorded beyond doubt that from 12:00 to 12:05 all that happened was that singular Fred sat in a chair. If he became his former self, when it was again 12:05, he would have to repeat his time-travel act and disappear, because that too has irrefutably been established. The best that can be hoped for Fred is that he would be locked for eternity in a cycle of advancing five minutes and repeatedly going back to do the same thing again.

It is asking a lot to believe seriously that travelling back in time is possible. Stephen Hawking in his book *A Brief History of Time* puts forward the chronology protection conjecture that argues some as yet unknown law of physics prohibits travelling back in time.

I tend to think of my dream from the boy's perspective – as a peek into the future. But what about the point of view of me as a fifty-year old man? When I watched the box car drift by, that idea of a freight car moving by itself was transmitted back in time from the 1990s to the 1950s. Such conveyance of brain impulses required the co-existence of me at two different stages in life, and communication passing from one to the other. Though I did not bodily go back in time to confront my younger self, there nevertheless was a handing back of information from an older me to a younger me, which comes uncomfortably close to travelling back in time, the impossibility of which I endeavoured to prove earlier, and which Stephen Hawking's conjecture argues against.

How could time be manipulated to link events separated by 3000 miles and forty-some years – a boy fast asleep in bed and the same person working on a railroad as an adult? An alternative explanation could be that the dream was planted and subsequent events made to happen to ensure it came true. Either line of reasoning is beyond human experience, beyond human knowledge, beyond human comprehension. Nothing on earth can satisfactorily explain such command of events. I believe we must look beyond this realm to a much higher place for an answer, and the only answer there can be is that it was His plan.

Sometimes I find it difficult to resist asking myself why, but such wonders are not for me nor anyone else to question.

\* \* \*

The above assessment was not formulated in haste, but took a long time to coalesce. In 2012, some years after the conclusion had been reached, one of the most remarkable books ever, *Proof of Heaven* by Eben Alexander MD, was published. It describes a spiritual journey, including visiting empyrean, whilst in a coma. The neurosurgeon reveals that in the celestial kingdom time does not behave as it does in our world, in that it is nonlinear. Eben Alexander also states that from those higher worlds one could access any time or place on earth.

To accept the idea of a plan is to accept the idea of predestination, and implications of predestination are enormous.

At age nineteen I worked in public service. I had recently purchased on credit a brand new Ford Anglia Super, and though I usually cycled the eight miles to work I sometimes used the car. Along the route I began to notice a fashionably-dressed young lady evidently waiting for a prearranged lift to the same place of work. I cannot remember the details, but somehow, on an occasion when I drove the car, I was able to ask if she would like a lift home that night. She gladly accepted.

When two people meet, intense desire in one party is common, intense desire in both rare. When we met at the work day's end, two people grinned from ear to ear, overjoyed at the prospect of a relationship showing every promise of mutual happiness even though we had very little knowledge of one another. We made our way to my parked car exchanging small talk – probably about which departments we worked in.

On reaching the car, I put the key in the lock, but it would not turn. I took it out and tried again, with the same result. My face reddened. What had been an ecstatic tryst suddenly turned sour. After several unsuccessful attempts at opening the door, I had to locate and beg my office supervisor to give two people a ride home - he lived close to where we lived. We dropped off the now fuming teenager. She and I never spoke again. The next day I caught the bus to work, and found the car door unlocked without a hitch at first attempt. It is impossible to say for sure of course, but had the mechanical problem not scuppered the romance, I may well have settled down and remained in Yorkshire for the rest of my life.

In a Liverpool discotheque during the 1970s I danced with a young woman on three consecutive weeks, each dance advancing the friendship to a point where a date became the natural progression. When we sat down for a first drink together, I accidentally knocked over a partially consumed pint of beer drenching a smart tan-coloured suit I was wearing. The date was over. But it was measure of the strength of feelings we had for each other that the relationship survived the ordeal. I saw her twice more, then she told me over the telephone her mother had forbidden her seeing me again, at which point the courtship abruptly ended.

The mother's disapproval was probably owing to a combination of my age – I was about eight years older than her daughter – and the view that I was not good enough for her. But had the beery blunder not occurred, I would have asked to speak with her mother and explain my intentions were nothing less than honourable. It is highly likely a marriage would have taken place a couple of years later. As it was, the dreadful *faux pas* had dashed male confidence, had broken the spirit, had undermined the will to fight, even though I feel sure the young woman would have stood by me.

Throughout the 1970s I visited Liverpool's discotheques on average twice a week, usually in company of similarly driven young men, one of whom was a mite more perceptive than others. He felt I should have enjoyed greater success with the opposite sex than I did. One evening we had met two young ladies. He had happily arranged to see his partner again (he had copped off was the Liverpool slang) whereas mine had spurned every advance.

When the night was over he said to me, "I just don't get it. You're a decent enough bloke, you dress well and yer can dance. But you just don't cop off. I don't know what it is. I don't get it." When he had finished speaking I politely acknowledged his words, but offered no response. His analysis was spot on, but pride prevented me from conceding so and from admitting that it troubled me more than it did him. When meeting women, particularly in the second half of the 1970s, it felt as if a suit of armour prevented emotional contact. Promising romances floundered for one reason or another. Things were not as they ought to be, but I put it down to getting older or being cloyed with repeated nights out. Resilience and adaptability fortunately see most people through trying times, and whilst there may have been periods of self-pity, for the most part I begrudgingly accepted that being without a permanent partner was just how it was.

Now, from the comfort of contented marriage and soothing retirement, I can look back to see how each stage of life, satisfactory and not so satisfactory, had to be strung together - like patterned beads each dependent on the previous. Those connections were not apparent at the time because they were too drawn out, and because I was too busy living them. The exceptional circumstance of a village signal box open to the public permitted a boy to be immersed in railways without falling foul of authority, a juvenile adventure that set the stage for a later signalman's career. The option of remaining in native Yorkshire was thwarted by a jammed car door lock. I had to be drawn to Liverpool. The city's beautiful women did that admirably, but I was denied marriage that would have rooted me firmly in Britain. I had to be free to follow a series of steps – a model railway shop, contacting fellow signalling enthusiasts, Merseyside's signal boxes – that would catapult me to being a signalman in London. Early years in the capital saw relations with the opposite sex go through an unrewarding phase, which left me free to meet and marry an American woman. An ensuing railroad career in the United States positioned me in Allentown Yard where I was able to live out the boyhood dream. Hence this long, elaborate and abstruse story is about railways and affairs of the heart being inextricably entwined to ensure a dream came true.

It was only after ruminations spanning many years that I came to realize certain episodes in life that were previously thought to be chance happenings were not random at all, but were deliberately placed to ensure I followed a predetermined path. It is a sentiment possible only by accepting there will always be some things we simply do not understand, which in turn is contingent upon recognizing our inadequacy and accepting we are not masters of our own fate. Humility is a long time coming, but ultimately is the only path to a door that will open to peace.

# CHAPTER 27

# NORFOLK SOUTHERN

Whilst the history of American railroading is in part expansion of short lines as a result of larger railroads shedding unprofitable sections of their systems – the Maryland & Pennsylvania's line to Hanover is a good example - of greater significance are mergers and takeovers that periodically re-draw the entire railroad map of America. One such tectonic shift was about to take place on Conrail.

In the mid-1990s both CSX Transportation, Inc and Norfolk Southern Railway Company jealously eyed Conrail and its access to lucrative New York markets. Envy turned to desire in what has been described as the bitterest takeover battle of the century when CSX and Norfolk Southern in turn outbid one another for Conrail's shares. It was a fight to the death; whichever won, it would not be long before the victor swallowed up the loser. But it was a battle neither side could win. The share price climbed so high the two giants eventually had to agree a truce and share the spoils between them. Shareholders in Conrail, including some employees, benefited enormously from the tussle.

Details gradually emerged of the agreement to cleave Conrail. Of relevance to me was that all lines radiating from Harrisburg, including those in the easterly direction I worked, went to Norfolk Southern. CSX took the Trenton Line. Owing to the difficulty of carving up equitably the hubs of North Jersey, Philadelphia and Detroit, they were designated shared assets. Operations in those areas would be carried on neither in the name of Norfolk Southern nor CSX, but Conrail. Not only was the name retained in those conurbations but also the blue locomotive livery. Shared asset employees, as all other

Conrail employees, were given a three-way choice: they could join Norfolk Southern or CSX or they could remain with Conrail. Shared asset demarcation lines were drawn up, but road jobs operated by Norfolk Southern and CSX were still permitted to terminate and start their trains within those boundaries.

On 8th June 1998 the National Surface Transportation Board announced approval of the split. By 22nd August 1998 principal agreements between Norfolk Southern and CSX must have been drawn up because that day was deemed to be the control date, the date new owners took financial control, though employees continued to work and be paid as usual. Later in 1998, Norfolk Southern's black liveried locomotives began to make occasional appearances in Harrisburg. As the year drew to a close, Norfolk Southern was said to be "ready to go".

By early 1999 seniority had advanced so much I rejoiced in holding a series of regular jobs, notably the deadhead-one-way ML401 and the ML420 Delaware job. During those halcyon days, it was announced Norfolk Southern would take over completely on 1st June 1999. Every single job was put up for bid, employees would take up their new positions on 1st June. My first choice was conductor or brakeman on the York Yard job which started work at 06:30, but which was just ten miles from home. The York Yard job was one of the most highly prized, a seniority of thirty-five years being the minimum qualification. So the application was laughable. My next two choices were North Jersey regular jobs Mail44 and TV12. But it was the following pick, the Morrisville Pool, in which I was successful, being told on 21st May that I had been awarded slot HMHM07CO.

Some jobs advertized were for work from Harrisburg to Hagerstown and beyond onto Norfolk Southern's metals. These high mileage positions attracted some men willing to learn new territory, but they had to mark off to qualify prior to the effective date. Their absence made worse an existing shortage of crews, and added to a general restlessness in the final days, an unsettled time reflected in my pocket diary failing to show exactly which position I held!

I looked forward to the change. How different would it be? The new employer had a reputation for being disciplinarian, but as a careful employee I felt no threat. There was some resentment about a southern entity taking over a northern operation. The north and south divide in England was socio-economic - and I wonder in the 2010s, given a globalization that links everyone to everything, how much of that divide remains. The north and south divide in America is rooted in the Civil War and its antecedents. On the one hand the rift is smoothed over by a highly mobile population, yet on the other hand is vigorously maintained by those who cling to the past. It is not surprising a few Conrail men were contemptuous about encroachment from the south.

As the takeover date loomed information began to circulate about the change from Conrail's computer systems to Norfolk Southern's. On 24th May all notice boards in Harrisburg GI8 were changed in readiness for the new employer. On the 26th a trainmaster handed out new timetables, safety books, hats and pins, and informed all that safety was a condition of employment.

The Conrail emblem comprised two heavy parallel horizontal lines terminating at the right-hand end in two letter Cs. The Norfolk Southern emblem was a stallion rampant. An emblem from a CSX constituent was a sleeping cat, the Chessie cat. Unofficial artwork appeared in yard offices showing the Conrail emblem overlaid with stallion and cat emblems, and endorsed Gone Rail.

My last timecard under Conrail, of Sunday 30th May 1999, was complicated. Called as Short Turn STAMR3, the crew deadheaded to Brunner Island, and under the guise of UFY536, undertook work within the plant using locomotives C40-8W 6260 and SD60M 5507. We then took that power over to the adjacent main line and coupled to engines SD40-2 6522 and C40-8W 707 at the head of ESPI9, Eastern Shore to Pittsburgh, and took the whole ensemble into Enola. (The 700 series C40-8W power, though painted in Conrail blue, were leased from Locomotive Management Services. The engines were marked boldly LMS, which shocked a British enthusiast who associated those initials with the London, Midland & Scottish Railway!) Finally, UFY528 involved a trip to Brunner Island and back with engines SD60I 5629 and C40-8W 6103, completing a twelve-hour day. The employer arranged for everyone to be at home on the evening of 31st May so they could take up newly awarded positions on day one. I did not work at all on that Monday, which happened to be a public holiday. I was able to enjoy Memorial Day with my wife, so that I was completely relaxed, rested and ready to spring into action on the dawn of a new era.

\* \* \*

Despite high hopes, weeks that followed were one of the most uncomfortable times in recent American railroading history. I will not dwell on the period. One reason for not doing so is respect for a former employer. Another reason is that this book sets out to record accurately what is after all a very successful industry, an irreplaceable support beam of the American economy. To give too much coverage to a disquieting but temporary state of affairs prevailing in the summer of 1999 would distort the picture. Conversely, without mention the record would be incomplete.

The 1st of June 1999 dawned and along with it an expectation to be called to work any time during that day. I was not called. I surmised my junior position on the seventh crew of the Morrisville Pool meant I would be last out. When the telephone failed to ring on day two, I called the crew dispatcher, who told me things were a mess because computers had failed. It transpired CSX was in the same woeful position; their computers failed too. Perhaps Norfolk Southern and CSX placed too much faith in present-day technology.

I was eventually called to work in Harrisburg at 01:00 on Thursday 3rd June for what was TV2M under the old regime but 20Q under the new. We got only as far as CP-Plymouth at the beginning of the Morrisville Line, had to tie the train down and deadhead to the hotel. We brought back the 21Q (TV1) but took twelve hours to do it. Trains which used to sprint from Harrisburg towards the Atlantic were taking fifty per cent longer, or did not make it at all with one crew. I heard that hardly any trains ran on 1st June. Consequent upon that lack of movement, lines were choked with standing trains, which prevented the following day's trains from reaching their destinations. In the first few days some men in GI8 had been amused by the difficulty those from the south had in running trains, one or two even gloated. But before long, those who had initially scoffed at the outcome of a southern intrusion now joined all others, including me, in being genuinely distressed at the spectacle of a railroad struggling to railroad. I overheard an official in Harrisburg

GI8 say, "I've worked for Norfolk Southern for twenty years, and this is not Norfolk Southern."

Despite steady improvement in the second week, a persistent problem was getting crews that had run out of time off trains. Perhaps other difficulties were more pressing, those in charge were simply too busy to attend to outlawed crews. Or the taxi company could not cope with the huge increase in deadheading. When we brought back the 17G (MOPI) from Morrisville on 14th June, my regular engineer and I ran out of time at 02:00 at Millards on the Harrisburg Line. We came to a stand and informed the train dispatcher. The next thing we knew was a loud banging on the cab door at 05:30 as a crew arrived to relieve us. It is possible we were deliberately left there to avoid calling two separate jitneys.

However, by the third week of June traffic ran more freely.

Time solves most problems. Norfolk Southern hastened the healing process with two innovations. Some men agreed to temporarily transfer from train service to the office to help undo the tangle. And Norfolk Southern drafted in employees from other railroads, though they had to spend time learning territory before they were any use. I will say no more about a difficult period that was really just a hiccup when one considers the entire 185-year success story of American railroading. Though repair was uneven, by October 1999, normality for the most part had returned.

To return to my own position, changed circumstances under new ownership boosted seniority - making available even more opportunities. Competition from peers was non-existent, as almost all others hired in 1994 had gone through Engineers' School and were fully occupied in that grade. As a result of radically changed work patterns after 1st June, many conductors had fled what were once much sought-after jobs, the Jersey Pool being a case in point. Thus I was delighted to find doors wide open.

I continued in my appointed slot on the Morrisville Pool for eight weeks. But the pool turned faster than before owing to additional work in the form of slab trains that ran west from Morrisville, so it lost some of its appeal. On 25th July I exercised a thirty-day bump and moved to the now sparsely populated Jersey Pool. To hold the Jersey Pool I had to extend qualifications beyond Meadows Yard to the Northern Branch and to Croxton Yard, where intermodal trains now terminated. The Jersey grass must have seemed greener than it was, for thirty days later I bumped back to Morrisville. Happily taking advantage of new-found freedom to conduct almost any road job I wanted, on 30th September I returned to an old favourite, the Delaware job alias ML420, now the 46K. Troubles of a month or two ago now seemed far behind as I once more settled into contended predictability.

\* \* \*

Hence as October 1999 got under way the future looked promising. There had been rumblings of my being sent to Engineers' School, but I brushed them off. I was committed as I ever had been to life on a Class I railroad. But it should be noted the commitment had always fallen short of one hundred per cent for several reasons, chief of which was prospect of a long commute for the rest of working life. I made no secret of that standpoint, and when colleagues naturally suggested moving, I replied that uniqueness of our farmhouse-style stone cottage prohibited that. Moreover, the fact that most road jobs were night work did not encourage unbending loyalty. Above all, the original plan had always been a settled career with the Maryland & Pennsylvania; after all, that was why we bought our York County home. Having said all that, at the beginning of October 1999, sights were unreservedly fixed on employment with Norfolk Southern for the foreseeable future.

As the month progressed however, two developments placed me on a curved path to separate from that fealty. The first was news that the Maryland & Pennsylvania had urgent need of my services. The second was that previous rumblings about my going to Engineers' Training School became more persistent, culminating in a telephone call on Monday 25th October ordering me to attend the school in Conway Yard, Pittsburgh. In the Delaware job three-day cycle, I had been off duty at 05:20 hours that Monday morning, and would not have been back to work till Tuesday evening. Engineers' School had begun that Monday, but a last minute cancellation resulted in my being told to attend as substitute. Despite protestations, I had no choice but to pack bags for a lengthy stay, and make the five-hour journey by car on Monday evening to a hotel in the Pittsburgh area.

On Tuesday, after catching up with induction others had gone through the previous day, I attended classes that commenced on familiar ground with an introduction to the air brake, and on unfamiliar ground with tuition on workings of the diesel-electric locomotive. In the latter, the class were in turn asked questions. My question was particularly obscure, and may as well have been asked in Mandarin for all I understood. I cannot now remember it, but it was on a par with, "What is one of the advantages of the control air system with regard to manual operation of switchgear?" After the tutor had finished asking the question, the clock began to record the length of time a pupil sat in silent embarrassment not knowing the answer. Then a fellow classmate in the row behind whispered in my ear, "The magnet valve on the switchgear could be over-ridden and cause the switchgear to move," an answer that I repeated. Later, during a short break, I turned round to thank the man who had helped, and then told him in a voice loud enough for the tutor – whom I knew to be sitting just round the corner in the next room – to hear: "This stuff isn't difficult to understand, I just can't remember it." Ask me to compare different phyla of the animal kingdom or to list features of a glaciated valley and words pour forth. Ask me to compare relative merits of the General Electric four-stroke diesel engine and the Electro-Motive Diesel two-stroke engine and there is silence. In contrast with fellow classmates, who for all I knew stripped down marine engines as a hobby, the internal combustion engine held little fascination.

At the end of the day I did not congregate with others but slipped away to find a secluded spot. Steps leading up to the hump yard in a quiet corner of Conway provided a seat on which to ponder. After some thought, I said aloud, "This is not railroading." The pithy but false statement was as meaningless as a politician's catchy phrase, but was equally successful inasmuch as I persuaded myself that in more ways than one I was on the wrong course. The self-delusion succeeded because skills of an engineer were very different from railroading I had known so far, that of working the ground. Though knowledge of motive power was as important as correctly interpreting signals, it was irrelevant to conductors and brakemen. At Engineers' School I found myself being pushed in a direction I did not want to go, an extremely rare experience for me.

After the meditative interlude in Conway Yard I returned to the hotel room shared with another trainee, a mild-mannered, bearded young man. It was part of the union contract to put two men in a hotel room at Engineers' School. Though disagreeable as shared accommodation was, it was through a need for more time and space to think that I told my roommate I was going out. I strolled across a bridge over the Ohio River and back, around a nearby village, then headed for a trendy bar to consume a large amount of beer to assist decision making. A chance conversation with another patron uncovered the improbable coincidence that we had both at different times lived in rented accommodation in St. Paul's Road, Islington, London, possibly in adjacent addresses, or even more unbelievably in the same property. At the time I did not know what to make of the coincidence. Since then I have come to the conclusion such coincidences are a sign of being on the right track. The best example is the evening I met my wife: I was surprised to learn one of the friends accompanying her hailed from the same North Yorkshire market town in which I grew up!

I returned to class on Wednesday 27th October. Even though a tentative decision had been made overnight to make a U-turn on Norfolk Southern, I needed a sober mind to be absolutely sure a new plan was the right plan, so sat through the morning's tuition. It would be fair criticism to say that by turning my back on engineer training I was foolishly disregarding a vital part of railroading. Be that as it may, my mind was made up. At lunch break I found a pay telephone within Conway Yard and, armed with plenty of change, rang the supervisor in charge of engineer trainees. "Mr Patel, this is Mitchell Deaver at Engineers' Training School in Conway. I have to say something to you if you'll listen."

"Go on," said Mr Patel.

"Seven weeks ago you called me to Engineers' Training School and then cancelled it. One-and-a-half weeks ago I was told I was going to Engineers' School, and it was verbally cancelled a week ago. Half a week ago I had again verbal confirmation via my union man that I would not be going. I went to work on Saturday night to Delaware, took rest in the hotel and came back on the ML423 working till 5.20 on Monday morning. I did not expect to go to work again till Tuesday evening. You know what happened then. At 3 pm I got a phone call from you, then there was to-ing and fro-ing with the union rep. About 5.00 to 6.00 pm came final confirmation (from the union man) I had to go. So I did as you ordered me to, and I went to school. I had to drive to Conway that evening, didn't get much sleep, missed a day at school, and had to try and catch up. I'm not going to be able to complete the course. You've got me all messed up."

Mr Patel interrupted here, and said, "Hold on a minute, I've got another call." After a pause he said, "Now, carry on."

"I can't concentrate. I'm going to have to..."

"Hang on a minute," again interrupted Mr Patel, "you were told you were the first alternative. I put that in a letter."

"I never received any letter," I insisted.

"Now I understand you have a wedding you want to go to this weekend. Isn't that the issue? I've spoken to [so-and-so] and apparently it's up to the instructors whether they'll allow you off or not."

"It's partly the issue. I'm going to have to mark off sick."

"Well..." said Mr Patel, momentarily lost for words, "I'll just have to... er... take the appropriate action. I know you work part time on the M&P. You're going to have to make a decision whether you're gonna work full time for Norfolk Southern or part time on the M&P."

"You're gonna have to mark me off sick," I repeated.

"All right," said Mr. Patel. "I'm going to have to hold you off pending an investigation for subterfuge, using sickness as an excuse. I'll get you fixed up for a physical..."

I cut him off: "Mark me off sick. I'm going home." With that, I slammed down the telephone, returned to the hotel, picked up belongings, checked out and drove home.

By now, the Maryland & Pennsylvania had formally called me back to work the Extra Board. To take advantage of that call-back I had first to accept it and then submit to a medical examination. I had delayed a response because to sever links irreversibly with Norfolk Southern would be the most difficult employment decision I would have to make in my entire life. Doubts lingered about the wisdom of cutting away from a large scale operation and its elevated level of income for more modest activities and remuneration on a short line. Another reason for procrastination was that to hand in my notice immediately to Norfolk Southern would have gambled on absolute certainty of re-employment with the Maryland & Pennsylvania.

Adding to this imbroglio was a troubling thought that Norfolk Southern could fire me for playing truant. Exposed, vulnerable, when back in York a day or so later, I enrolled with a temporary employment agency to be sure of income whilst events played out.

On Monday 8th November Mr Patel, in changed voice, telephoned to apologize for the manner in which my secondment to Engineers' School had been handled, but to say that I would probably be sent to school early the following year. He continued, "Tell me, Mr Deaver, how do you feel about going to Engineers' School?"

"If I had free choice I wouldn't go."

"Well, the contract under Norfolk Southern is that all post-1985 men..."

"I know all about that. I understand that," I said testily. He was restating what all new entrants had been told at the initial Conrail interview: we would be engineers.

However, the conversation would prove redundant, because my position on the Maryland & Pennsylvania became secure. As soon as possible, I made a telephone call to Norfolk Southern saying I was resigning. On Saturday 13th November 1999 I drove to Lancaster to hand in to the Trainmaster my Conrail radio and keys, along with a curt, formal letter of resignation:

> Dear Sirs,
> I resign. My new employer will be:
> Maryland & Pennsylvania Railroad Company...

Untidily, the association with a Class 1 railroad came to an end. The Conrail adventure was over.

For the record, the very last shift on Norfolk Southern took place on Sunday 24th October, on duty at Edgemoor Yard at 20:00 hours. With locomotives C40-8W 8448 and SD50 6702 we hauled forty-three loads and sixteen empties totalling 3928 tons, shifted Chrysler Yard from 21:55 till 23:10, were held up at CP-Pilot on the Port Road from 12:20 till 12:35, were held up just outside Enola Yard from 02:50 till 03:15, and were finally off duty in Enola at 05:20 hours, a modest nine-hour-twenty-minute day.

# CHAPTER 28

# RETURN

Many cases of coincidence and of the preternatural have appeared in this book so far, and for that reason the remarkable and fortunate synchronism of Norfolk Southern's decision to send a reluctant trainee to Engineers' School and of the Maryland & Pennsylvania's need to call that same individual back to their fold will be passed over without comment, and the narrative moved on.

First day back on the Maryland & Pennsylvania was Friday 5th November when I worked from 08:00 till 15:00. A coal train shift followed on Sunday 7th November when we worked sixteen hours; it will be recalled small railroads may be given permission to work extended hours on a regular basis. For several weeks thereafter I worked at a steady pace. Though I was prepared to accept a level of income somewhat below that enjoyed on Norfolk Southern, there followed a series of fortuitous developments that soon boosted earnings.

The Maryland & Pennsylvania was owned by a company called Emons, who also owned another short line based in York called York Rail. On 1st December 1999 the two were merged into York Railway Company, a marvellous title given that I was born in York, England. Following the merger, men on the Maryland & Pennsylvania Extra Board such as myself trained on York Rail assignments, and in due course covered vacancies. Whilst the Maryland & Pennsylvania had only one regular job, York Rail had three: YS1 that worked from Lincoln Yard in West York to Thomasville about four miles away, RJ2 that interchanged with CSX near Hanover and serviced a grain distribution plant in the East Yard (not far from Poorhouse Yard) and

TL3 that shuttled lime from Thomasville to a cement works adjacent to Lincoln Yard. After training, York Rail posts, particularly TL3, provided plenty of work when Maryland & Pennsylvania was quiet.

The next leap forward at first did not appear to be so: the employer decided to train me as an engineer. Once I recovered from the initial jolt, financial advantages became apparent. There would first be an extensive training period lasting many months, followed by Extra Board work deputizing for regular engineers. The engineer training course, which began on 16th June 2000, was less intensive than Norfolk Southern's. And there would be no signals to memorize because York Railway was signal-less yard limits from end to end. A further vast improvement on the previous engineer course was that it was carried out in York, not two hundred miles away.

The experience confirmed however what I had long thought, that I was not best suited to be a train driver, engineer. The profession demands consistent and unbroken concentration. My brain is better at dealing with irregular and frequent packages of information. Although I did receive praise, some skills took longer to acquire than others.

Most practical tuition was given on York Rail's RJ2 train that ran to the outskirts of Hanover on tracks once belonging to Western Maryland, later CSX. The route was now officially designated the York Branch. After picking up interchanged cars from CSX, RJ2 faced a long descending gradient where cycle braking had to be used as no York Railway locomotives were equipped with a working dynamic brake. Thus the RJ2 provided plenty of practice at cycle braking. An experienced engineer, with the right length of train, by making a ten pound reduction in train line air pressure at just the right place could complete the incline without resorting to cycle braking, though brakes would be biting hard at the bottom of the hill.

Demanding special attention was the process of shifting over a summit, which could take place at two locations on RJ2's eastbound journey (heading back to York). At one summit near Smith Station Road it was sometimes necessary to re-arrange the interchange from CSX to ensure hazardous material cars were no closer to the engines than the sixth car. When setting off cars at the paper mill in Spring Grove, the train worked over a summit at the Codorus Creek bridge. In both cases it was quite a juggling match ensuring, when reversing, that the train was sufficiently braked to make a gentle coupling on the down side of the hill yet not braked so hard the train could not climb the up side of the hill. Even so, confidence in train handling techniques grew, and I was passed out as qualified engineer on 22nd February 2001.

The best news by far of an upswing in prospects came over the locomotive radio one day. We were shifting a canned goods warehouse in central York, when the dispatcher announced: "We've been taken over by Genesee & Wyoming." Genesee & Wyoming, Inc., an organization that owned a number of small and medium-sized railroads in America, plus some overseas properties, had bought out Emons. It became effective 22nd February 2002. After a few excited exchanges between crew members and the dispatcher, we resumed work, the first move being one initiated by me as brakeman. I said on the radio, "Okay, Genesee & Wyoming engine number 1500, take 'em ahead, set five cars out on the Main." In time, the new owners would lift the scale of York operations to an unprecedented level.

Concerning train handling techniques, Genesee & Wyoming introduced a new term to York Railway: coasting. The company encouraged running whenever possible with neither brake nor throttle in order to minimize draught and buff forces on the train, and to save fuel. Opportunities were few of course, but level ground and a gradient profile in the shape of a bowl were instances.

\* \* \*

During the period from 1989 when I first started till the Genesee & Wyoming takeover, little had changed on the Maryland & Pennsylvania side of York Railway. Coal trains to the paper mill remained reliably stable, running about thirty weekends a year. They were especially remunerative owing to long hours, to a small incentive bonus encouraging men to give up their weekends, and to extra shifts when the train was frozen and could not be emptied in one day.

The worst case of an iced-up train occurred one weekend when, through successive thawing and freezing, coal in the unloading pockets accreted into a solid lump. After extended application of the vibrating mechanism, a four-cubic foot chunk eventually eased out of the pocket to become wedged between the car and the unloading pit grid. It was dislodged by moving the whole twelve-car train backwards and forwards a few feet at a time - "rock and roll" as we used to call it. Each car took, maybe, forty minutes to empty as opposed to the usual eight minutes. We worked all week trying to unload the train, but did not finish. Remaining cars in this huge black iced lollipop had to be set aside because a new coal train arrived.

As for non-coal train work, only the A1 crew on the Maryland & Pennsylvania still regularly worked Monday to Friday. As before, men were called off the Extra Board for a train to Hanover two or three times a week. Unfortunately, even with my return and crews having been cut by union agreement to engineer and conductor only, the carrier still had trouble putting together a crew for Hanover. The traffic was in due course transferred to the York Rail RJ2 crew. In time, most of the Maryland & Pennsylvania line to Hanover fell out of use, a condition still prevailing in the 2010s.

However, the overall level of business on the Maryland & Pennsylvania side grew after purchase by Genesee & Wyoming. The canned goods warehouse mentioned above expanded into the East Yard, displacing the grain distribution facility there which relocated to Lincoln Yard. A plant receiving tank cars of liquified petroleum gas – propane – set up alongside the Maryland & Pennsylvania West Branch Main in West York. A rock-salt distribution facility became established alongside the Central Branch just south of York City. Source of the rock-salt was a mine located on a short line that was birthplace of our owning company: the Genesee & Wyoming. The product was thus shipped from one constituent company to another, much of it in Genesee & Wyoming's own thirty-foot covered hoppers, highly satisfactory from a financial point of view. The mine was unworkable in winter, so the salt pile in York grew in summer months. At peak period, the customer required two shifts of five cars each day. Such volume of work required a second crew on the Maryland & Pennsylvania, a crew which came to be known as the MPA2.

The busiest period I ever saw was in 2005 when the MPA2 ran regularly, at least Monday through Thursday. A typical week was that commencing 11th July: I worked twelve hours on Monday, eleven-and-a-half hours on Tuesday and Wednesday and nine-and-a-quarter hours on Thursday. Add to these long hours a coal train and earnings were back in the Class 1 railroad league! MPA2 was the only American railroad position held long enough to become thoroughly familiar with it. (Conrail's Delaware job came close.)

When the MPA2 ran, the A1 crew broke down the inbound set-in from Norfolk Southern, serviced the salt distributor and various other customers before finishing about 13:00 hours. The MPA2 could then use the same locomotives, usually CF7s 1500 and 1504. On duty at about 14:00, the MPA2 shifted the salt a second time, conveyed traffic back and forth between Poorhouse and Lincoln Yards, then made a set-out to Norfolk Southern. Making a set-out always seemed like a grand finale to the day!

At the peak of this extremely busy period, even though working twelve hours, the MPA2 often failed to complete its duties on Mondays, leaving the Norfolk Southern set-out for the A1 crew on Tuesday. When I first started fifteen years prior, the number of cars interchanged between Maryland & Pennsylvania and York Rail was typically a dozen. In the mid-2000s this figure was sometimes in the forties. The company had to reinstate the east end of Track 1 in Poorhouse Yard to permit running round such large numbers, the maximum that could then be run round became forty-seven.

Most traffic between Poorhouse and Lincoln Yards were cars originating on Norfolk Southern destined for customers on the York Rail side. But other traffic also made the journey, and dealing with it was a Gordian knot. A typical evening's work is described below.

One customer located between the two yards could only be shifted on the way back, as the switch faced east, so his lumber car was positioned on the hind end of the westbound trip. After running round in Lincoln Yard the car was plucked off the hind end and placed on the head end of the return consist. A scrap yard customer on the East Branch needed his gondola cars weighed on York Railway's scales at the east end of Lincoln Yard, both prior to and after loading. They were placed on the hind end too, handy for weighing and for the return journey. After weighing, loaded scrap cars for Norfolk Southern were positioned with other Lincoln Yard outbound traffic, whereas empty gondolas and any overweight loads were placed behind the lumber car. Another customer, one adjacent to Poorhouse Yard, also had an eastward facing switch. His box car was placed behind the scrap cars. Cars picked up in Lincoln Yard that came in from CSX and were destined to be shoved up the East Branch were placed on the hind end of the train leaving Lincoln Yard.

The procession then left Lincoln Yard, and after dropping off the lumber car, the whole train ran down Track 2 in Poorhouse Yard to execute a run round movement. Holding onto scrap metal gondolas and one box car that were next to the engines, we came back down Track 1 and straight into the customer's siding to spot the box car. Scrap cars were left on the lead to that siding, a lead referred to as The Hole. It will be recalled East Branch cars were on the rear of the train coming from Lincoln Yard. After running round in Poorhouse Yard, they became the head end, and remained in that position when a set-out was made to Norfolk Southern by shoving down to Windsor Yard. After setting out, the East Branch traffic was brought back up to Poorhouse Yard. We then coupled to scrap cars in The Hole, and proceeded up the East Branch with engines sandwiched between scrap cars on the hind end and other traffic on the head end. I of course rode the head end giving car counts by radio. Flares, called fusees on the railroad, were ignited and placed on the leading vehicle at night.

Arranging the eastbound train in Lincoln Yard was one of the most puzzling yet most enjoyable railroading tasks I had to perform. I was delighted at my own ingenuity. Until, that is, a new man started. When faced with having to spot a box car for the Poorhouse Yard customer at the wrong-way-round switch, he said, "I'm just going to leave this car on Track 1, then when we come back from Lincoln Yard and run round, we'll come down Track 1 and shove it straight in to spot." Year after year I had been taking the car all the way to Lincoln Yard and back just to get round it. It took a fresh mind to see an easier way, as so often happens.

I mentioned lumber cars above. At some point the curious system for dealing with such traffic originating in Canada came to light. Apparently brokers buy prepared lumber and dispatch it south across the border without a consignee. Whilst the wood is in transit, customers are found and the cars' routings established. Occasionally a buyer cannot be secured. One such car turned up in Poorhouse Yard, whereupon York Railway immediately sent it back to Norfolk Southern with the customary fee for wrong placement, about $180:00 I think.

Working as conductor on the MPA2 was like circuit training in school physical education classes. Climbing up and down ladders on the sides of cars, throwing switches, bending to fasten air hoses and the considerable amount of walking necessary on conductor-only crews all kept a man trim and fit. Tightening and releasing hand brake wheels built strength in the upper part of the body. A couple of colleagues were particularly muscular. One was so strong when a faulty brake wheel refused to turn, in attempting to overcome the resistance he broke the wheel completely off!

I was no starring athlete at school, and was always slight when a younger man, though a few 1980s visits to a London gymnasium improved the physique. Intensive, arduous work on the MPA2 was such that at age sixty I was as strong as I ever had been my whole life. This is borne out by an occasion, one warm summer's day, when I had to load planks into our Ford Ranger truck in a hardware store parking lot. When I took my shirt off to the task, two youngish women standing a couple of hundred yards away took keen interest. The distance between us concealed my age!

*  *  *

As the new millennium got into its stride the coal train routine changed. Early in the 2000s it was re-routed over the York Branch to Spring Grove, rather than taking the Maryland & Pennsylvania route. Commencing in 2004 it was moved from Sunday to Saturday. At some point, attrition and long-term absences effectively placed me third on the seniority roster. Since the two most senior men took the middle job, I could have taken any conductor or engineer position on the first and third jobs. I chose engineer on the third job. I had no fear of taking the loaded coal train from York to Spring Grove, I just did not like rising that early.

When the Maryland & Pennsylvania first began running Spring Grove coal trains in the 1970s they used run-through power, that is, they used Conrail's power. Then for most of my association they used their own power, a typical consist being CF7s 1500 and 1504, GP9 1754 and GP16s 1602 and 1604. Early in the 2000s York Railway reverted to run-through power whereby Norfolk Southern's engines remained with the train till return. At this point I need to digress on the matter of over-the-road power.

The General Electric C40-8Ws, first introduced in 1989, came to be widely known simply as Dash 8s. Bowing to common usage, official nomenclature of this type of locomotive was changed to D8-40CW. It will be recalled C signified a three-axle truck. W referred to wide cab, not that locomotive dimensions were increased, but cab re-arrangement created more space giving the illusion of greater width. Instead of controls being mounted on a stand at the engineer's elbow, where operating the throttle was by a tugging motion similar to steam engines, controls on Dash 8s were arranged in front of the engineer in desk-top fashion. Handles were operated by pulling and pushing actions, pulling towards the engineer to increase throttle and braking. Even though desk-top controls were commonplace on Amtrak locomotives, many Conrail engineers disliked them. Indeed, Dash 8s were tricky for York Railway staff to handle when spotting coal hoppers over the unloading pit. The general unsatisfactoriness must have been acknowledged, for in the 2010s Dash 8s were being converted to conventional design with a control stand to the left of the engineer.

The next generation of General Electric diesels, which would at one time have been referred to as C40-9W but now as D9-40CW, are commonly referred to as Dash 9s. Dash 9s became the predominant model for run-through power on York Railway coal trains.

Starting at 15:00 hours, the coal train's third crew's usual Saturday routine was to finish unloading - usually two strings of fifteen cars - conduct an initial terminal brake test before leaving Spring Grove and deliver the whole empty train back to Norfolk Southern. As engineer, I took delight in letting the mile-long train free-wheel like a roller coaster, whenever physical characteristics permitted – but keeping within speed limits of course. At one time the train was always put away in Windsor Yard, but more and more it was taken up to station sign Flour on the outskirts of York, involving about three mile's travel on Norfolk Southern's York Running Track which required the Main Line Dispatcher's permission. Accordingly, with Dash 9 power, it became my regular duty to run the empty coal train back onto Norfolk Southern about midnight on Saturday nights. Thus, ironically, I ended up engineer not only on Norfolk Southern's locomotives but on Norfolk Southern's rails after all!

Very occasionally a foreign locomotive appeared in the consist, an example being Union Pacific Class SD70M number 4535. All locomotive cabs vary slightly, but in this case it took some time to find the horn control! Incidentally, Union Pacific had so many locomotives they ran out of four-digit numbers, so added 1-999 to their numbering system.

About one coal train in three did not follow the prescribed pattern; it was messed up, we used to say. Either a break-down occurred or cold weather intervened causing an additional crew or crews to return on Sunday to finish. One Saturday the train was so late arriving in York it fell to me to be engineer and take the loaded train to Spring Grove. This was the only occasion I handled a train of great weight; it was about 14,000 tons. Conditions were perfect and the trip went splendidly!

Interchanging the coal train back at weekends and making a set-out on the MPA2 during weekdays required dialogue with Norfolk Southern. Contact frequently brought me face-to-face with former colleagues and prompted exchange of recollections. Cordial relations prevailed between York Railway and Norfolk Southern employees, because smooth operations depended on them. Cordiality led to innovative humour.

The most popular head wear amongst railroaders (and amongst American workers generally) was the baseball cap. I usually wore no head protection except in extreme weather. Eventually I found that a cowboy-style hat was ideal for keeping off both rain and hot sun. Reception was mixed amongst York Railway staff. Some found it laughable, others were displeased at use of a revered icon by an Englishman. A Norfolk Southern employee took a different view: he nicknamed the wearer The Limestone Cowboy, derived from the slang *limey* for a British person.

\* \* \*

A junior management position held in Liverpool during the 1970s was so taxing that Friday afternoons found me hardly capable of anything but the simplest tasks. Thank goodness for the weekend, I thought. Days leading up to annual vacation similarly brought on a capitulating attitude. And as retirement approached on York Railway, I could not wait for the final day. As the date grew nearer, it became clear that an identical mechanism was at play in each of these circumstances. It was *not* that I was incapable of work through fatigue, it was just that joyful anticipation of the upcoming break eroded natural industriousness. In other words, I just gave up.

In the final months, absences of several employees guaranteed plenty of work. Actual date of retirement was not chosen till June 2011. I had toyed with the idea of finishing in early 2011, taking a couple of vacation days and a sick day each week bringing working life to a leisurely end. But financial benefits of staying till full retirement age of sixty-six held sway, thus the final day would be Friday 30th September 2011.

The A1 job had to be covered every day of the last week. I conducted for the first three days, putting in a twelve and two nine-and-a-half hour days. On Wednesday, for complex operating reasons, I decided to *shove* the train, about twenty cars, all the way from Poorhouse Yard to Lincoln Yard. As far as I know it had never been done before. On Thursday I used up a last vacation day.

With neither regular man available on Friday 30th, I spent the very last shift on York Railway, the very last working day of my entire life, as engineer on the A1 crew. As we began, I said to the conductor, "You know, this is going to be the last time I drive a train!" We clocked up eleven hours, producing a fat final pay cheque (spelt check in America) for the week.

A retirement party followed on Friday evening. When my wife arrived to collect me at 21:00, the General Manager said to her, "It was always different working with Mitch. I learnt a whole new vocabulary! If paperwork was not right, other men would say 'The paperwork's all screwed up'. Mitch would say 'There appear to be some discrepancies in the paperwork'!"

York Railway and predecessor Maryland & Pennsylvania had looked after me well. A short commute and mostly day-time work contributed to an entirely satisfactory final phase of working life, a working life that had lasted fifty years. Many of my generation have been able to retire early. Most of those younger will not begin work until their twenties owing to college. To have begun work at sixteen and continued working almost uninterrupted till age sixty-six is uncommon, an achievement.

# CHAPTER 29

# RETIREMENT

The intention had been to spend the entire Saturday 1<sup>st</sup> October celebrating with beer, but the plan was abandoned in favour of chores. As I settled into a new, more relaxed way of life, thoughts returned to humorous notions I had had whilst still at work, but which I never acted upon.

After a year or two on Conrail I could have written to friends and relations in England telling them about taking trains to American destinations of York, Lancaster, Carlisle, Newark and Reading. I never got round to it. When working with Big John I had intended to scold him on a suitable occasion when he was misbehaving by saying, "I'm gonna climb up a ladder and punch you in the knee!" but never remembered to do so.

Another Conrail new entrant and I had observed how many fellow workers were preoccupied with the opposite sex. We had thought of one of us calling out to the other in Harrisburg GI8, "Hey pervert!" to see how many heads would turn, but never summoned courage. I should point out that the word pervert is used loosely amongst males to refer to overt sexual interest, not to violent, illegal or other unsavoury activity.

On York Railway, Lincoln Yard office was more conducive to light-hearted banter than the Maryland & Pennsylvania signing-on point, in part because at different times of day in Lincoln Yard a crew would often be joined by other employees. Colleagues occasionally took delight in reminding me I was the oldest on the railroad, so I dreamt up a rejoinder: "Yeh, but you're only saying that 'cause it's true! Now listen here Steve Smith, just because you're younger than me you think I'm older than you! Don't you now, admit it! Well let me tell you something about that. You see it's all to do with, no matter what you think, and that's how it is. So *there!*" Unfortunately in the final months an opportunity to recite the carefully rehearsed lines never arose.

Off and on I have practiced yoga - not meditation, just stretching exercises - and am still able to stand on my head for a few seconds. I had planned to amuse fellow York Railway workers with a demonstration before I left, but never did.

Certain aspirations never materialized. In the early 1990s, talk circulated on the Maryland & Pennsylvania of a possible commuter passenger service from York to Harrisburg. I genuinely looked forward to being conductor on that train in later years. Alas, it never came to be.

The appellation The Limestone Cowboy put a pre-retirement idea into my head. During the last year, I daubed initials TLC as a tag on a few box car sides. In the final week I was going to expand the monogram into the full name, then on the very last day write "The Limestone Cowboy rides off into the sunset 9/30/2011". But it never happened. It was a shame this slice of romantic silliness never came to pass.

\* \* \*

Amongst retirement resolutions was a trip to England. As I will no longer fly, I had not been able to return since emigrating in 1988. In 2013 my wife and I sailed to England on the Queen Mary 2 ocean liner. I had been warned of many changes in England, but was delighted to find much the same, particularly the unspoilt countryside. Most architecture, pleasingly, remained unchanged for twenty-five years. Two redevelopments I did see - Liverpool's city centre and London's Kings Cross and St. Pancras stations - were impressive.

It was good to ride the British railway network again. Many changes became evident, including the unexpected loss of a direct Liverpool to Newcastle passenger service. Those trains used to run through the Yorkshire village where I lived, and they were convenient when I lived in Liverpool. Numerous multi-coloured liveries of privatization companies were no surprise as I had been following the British railway press. It seemed twice as many trains ran than before, though they were shorter. The explosion in passenger figures reflected in a sense of urgency amongst railway staff.

The tour around England passed many extant mechanical signalling installations, notably between Crewe and Derby and on the line to Hull. Eastfield signal box, strictly speaking a ground frame, with its collection of semaphore signals remained defiant amongst Peterborough's modern signals. Whilst waiting for a train on one leg of the journey, the signal at the end of a platform displayed the normal British aspect for a diverging move, green with junction indicator of five white lights. For a split second I thought it was wrong and should be showing the American red-over-green MEDIUM CLEAR! This momentary confusion aside, to have had the good fortune of being immersed in both British directional signalling and American speed signalling is rare, if not unique. I have been able to pass on to fellow signalling enthusiasts benefit of the experience.

England had one surprise. Daylight seemed so much brighter! An American who vacationed in Britain observed the same. I noticed no diffusion when moving from Britain to the States in 1988, on the contrary was delighted with blue skies.

Back in the United States, principal leisure pastime during retirement is construction of an extensive "00" gauge model railway in the garage. Unlike most American dwellings, our house does not have a basement, which is where most model railroads are built. The layout is set in the 1960s, is exclusively steam, and features home-made block telegraph instruments and semaphore signals worked by thread from lever frames fully interlocked, just like the real thing!

Life is full, so I join the chorus of many retired people in complaining about having too much to do. At one stage, in order to get a break, I telephoned my former supervisor on York Railway and asked if I was entitled to vacation when in retirement!

But, looking back, there is so much to be grateful for: for a country signal box; for a ride home on a workmen's trolley; for the joy of watching steam engines at work; for an opportunity to try and bring them back; for the wonderful city of Liverpool; for a signalman's job; for the route to a lasting marriage; for a foothold in two continents; for being shielded from harm; for health; for the gift of a boyhood dream in England that foretold events in America.

Thank you.

# About the Author

Mitchell Deaver was born in York, England, and
acquired a passion for railways in youth.

The first half of a long working life was spent mainly in commerce,
followed by eight years as a British Railways employee. After
emigrating to the United States in 1988, a railway career continued
with employment on both a short line and a large railroad.

Mitchell Deaver is now retired and lives with his wife of
thirty years in Lower Windsor Township, Pennsylvania,
where together they enjoy gardening and walking.

Follow Mitchell Deaver on Facebook.